Oxford Shakespeare Topics

Shakespeare and Queer Studies

OXFORD SHAKESPEARE TOPICS
Published and Forthcoming Titles Include:

David Bevington, *Shakespeare and Biography*
Colin Burrow, *Shakespeare and Classical Antiquity*
Michael Caines, *Shakespeare and the Eighteenth Century*
Lawrence Danson, *Shakespeare's Dramatic Genres*
Janette Dillon, *Shakespeare and the Staging of English History*
Paul Edmondson and Stanley Wells, *Shakespeare's Sonnets*
Gabriel Egan, *Shakespeare and Marx*
Sonya Freeman Loftis, *Shakespeare and Disability Studies*
David Fuller, *Shakespeare and the Romantics*
John S. Garrison, *Shakespeare and the Afterlife*
Andrew Gurr and Mariko Ichikawa, *Staging in Shakespeare's Theatres*
Jonathan Gil Harris, *Shakespeare and Literary Theory*
Russell Jackson, *Shakespeare and the English-speaking Cinema*
Alexa Alice Joubin, *Shakespeare and East Asia*
John Jowett, *Shakespeare and Text: Revised Edition*
Douglas Lanier, *Shakespeare and Modern Popular Culture*
Hester Lees-Jeffries, *Shakespeare and Memory*
Ania Loomba, *Shakespeare, Race, and Colonialism*
Raphael Lyne, *Shakespeare's Late Work*
Russ McDonald, *Shakespeare and the Arts of Language*
Randall Martin, *Shakespeare and Ecology*
Steven Marx, *Shakespeare and the Bible*
Robert S. Miola, *Shakespeare's Reading*
Marianne Novy, *Shakespeare and Outsiders*
Lois Potter, *Shakespeare and the Actor*
Phyllis Rackin, *Shakespeare and Women*
Catherine Richardson, *Shakespeare and Material Culture*
Tom Rutter, *Shakespeare and Science*
Duncan Salkeld, *Shakespeare and London*
Will Sharpe, *Shakespeare and Collaborative Writing*
Stuart Sillars, *Shakespeare and the Victorians*
Bruce R. Smith, *Shakespeare and Masculinity*
Zdeněk Stříbrný, *Shakespeare and Eastern Europe*
Michael Taylor, *Shakespeare Criticism in the Twentieth Century*
Alden T. Vaughan and Virginia Mason Vaughan, *Shakespeare in America*
Gary Watt, *Shakespeare and the Law*
Stanley Wells, ed., *Shakespeare in the Theatre: An Anthology of Criticism*
Martin Wiggins, *Shakespeare and the Drama of his Time*

Oxford Shakespeare Topics

Shakespeare and Queer Studies

MARIO DIGANGI

OXFORD
UNIVERSITY PRESS

OXFORD
UNIVERSITY PRESS

Great Clarendon Street, Oxford, OX2 6DP,
United Kingdom

Oxford University Press is a department of the University of Oxford.
It furthers the University's objective of excellence in research, scholarship,
and education by publishing worldwide. Oxford is a registered trade mark of
Oxford University Press in the UK and in certain other countries.

Published in the United States of America by Oxford University Press
198 Madison Avenue, New York, NY 10016, United States of America

British Library Cataloguing in Publication Data
Data available

Library of Congress Control Number: 2025935491

ISBN 9780198888031 (hbk)
ISBN 9780198888048 (pbk)

DOI: 10.1093/9780191994951.001.0001

Printed and bound by
CPI Group (UK) Ltd., Croydon, CR0 4YY

The manufacturer's authorised representative in the EU for product safety is
Oxford University Press España S.A. of Parque Empresarial San Fernando de Henares,
Avenida de Castilla, 2 – 28830 Madrid (www.oup.es/en or product.safety@oup.com).
OUP España S.A. also acts as importer into Spain of products made by the manufacturer.

Links to third party websites are provided by Oxford in good faith and
for information only. Oxford disclaims any responsibility for the materials
contained in any third party website referenced in this work.

To Bruce R. Smith (1946–2024)

Acknowledgements

I am grateful to have had the opportunity to present material from this book at the Trans Philologies seminar (organized by Joey Gamble) at the 2024 Shakespeare Association of America, and as the 2023 Edwin Savage Lecture in the Renaissance at the University of Mississippi (with thanks to Karen Raber and Ari Friedlander). For inspiration and guidance, I have often relied on the generosity and brilliance of Julie Crawford, Will Fisher, Miles Grier, Nick Radel, and Melissa Sanchez. The Folger Shakespeare Library (especially Melanie Leung), the Rijksmuseum, and Alycia Sellie at the Graduate Center Library all gave essential assistance with images. Rob Yates and Andrew Stone helped with research. This book wouldn't exist without Ellie Collins at Oxford University Press. Also at OUP, Hannah Doyle, Jo Spillane, and the editorial board of Oxford Shakespeare Topics expertly shepherded this project to completion.

My ability to do this kind of work has been sustained by John Antosca, and by my family, Franco DiGangi, Jeffrey DiGangi, and the late Christine DiGangi.

This book is dedicated to Bruce R. Smith, a generous mentor and formidable scholar whose pathbreaking *Homosexual Desire in Shakespeare's England* taught us new ways of understanding love, desire, and friendship.

Contents

List of Figures   xi

Queer Theories, Queer Histories, and Shakespeare Studies   I

1. Queer(ing) Couples   20

2. (Queer) Desire and Disorder   54

3. Queer Gender Transformations   84

4. Queer Asexuality   115

5. Queer Heteroeroticism   144

Historical Perspectives, Present-Day Concerns   169

Endnotes   175
Further Reading   197
General Bibliography   203
Index   205

List of Figures

1.1 Nature 'desireth his lyke': homonormative male
friendship. Thomas Trevilian, *Trevelyon Miscellany*
(1608), folio 175 recto: 'Of Civil Friendship.' Call#:
V.b.232, image 5113. Folger Shakespeare Library.   21

1.2 'Is love a tender thing?': love as homonormative
likeness. Otto van Veen, *Amorum Emblemata*
(Antwerp: [Henrici Swingenij], 1608), page 17. Call#:
STC 24627a.5 copy 1, image 63430. Folger Shakespeare
Library.   27

1.3 'An equal yoke of love': spouses as yokefellows. 'The
Happy Marriage, the Unhappy Marriage' (London:
[John King], mid to late seventeenth century?). Call#:
ART File S528t1 no.64 parts 1–2, image 29337.
Folger Shakespeare Library.   37

1.4 'like Juno's swans / Still we went coupled': Venus'
coupled swans. Monogrammist IQV after Giulio
Romano, 'Venus op een strijdwagen door twee zwanen
voortgetrokken' [Venus on a chariot pulled by two
swans]. (Fontainebleau, c.1540). Rijksmuseum,
Amsterdam.   50

2.1 'Beastly and outrageous men': the destruction of
Sodom. Philips Galle after Maarten van Heemskerck,
'Loth en zijn familie verlaten de stad Sodom' [Lot and
his family leave the city Sodom]. (Haarlem: 1569).
Rijksmuseum, Amsterdam.   57

2.2 'This siren that will charm Rome's Saturnine':
monstrously seductive femininity. Aegidius
Sadeler (II), 'Fabel van de zeemeermin' [fable of the
mermaid]. (Prague: 1608). Rijksmuseum, Amsterdam.   78

3.1 'Pretty youth': Jupiter embracing Ganymede.
Cherubino Alberti after Polidoro da Caravaggio,
'Jupiter en Ganymedes' [Jupiter and Ganymede].
(Italy: 1590–1600). Rijksmuseum, Amsterdam.   91

3.2 'his hand with his': *As You Like It*, First Folio (1623).
William Shakespeare, *Mr. William Shakespeares
Comedies, Histories, and Tragedies* (London: [Isaac
Jaggard and Ed. Blount], 1623), folio 206, sig. S1 verso.
Call#: STC 22273 Fo.1 no.09. Folger Shakespeare
Library.   93

3.3 'A woman clad in armor': Joan la Pucelle. Peter Le
Moyne, *The Gallery of Heroick Women* (London:
[R. Norton], 1652), plate facing page 119. Call#:
131–611f, image 9287. Folger Shakespeare Library.   109

4.1 'Like a man, but of no woman bred': Adonis' birth
from a tree. Philips Galle after Anthonie Blocklandt,
'Geboorte van Adonis' [birth of Adonis]. (Antwerp:
c. 1577–c.1581). Rijksmuseum, Amsterdam.   120

4.2 'From love's weak childish bow she lives unharmed':
Chastity defeating Love. Pieter Jalhea Furnius,
'Kuisheid overwint Liefde' [Chastity conquers Love].
(1550–1625). Rijksmuseum, Amsterdam.   129

5.1 'Let no man mock me, / For I will kiss her':
Pygmalion and his statue. Crispijn van de Passe,
'Pygmalion die verliefd wordt op zijn beeld' [Pygmalion
falling in love with his statue]. (1602–1607).
Rijksmuseum, Amsterdam.   145

5.2 'inequality in years occasions of many mischiefs': sexual
incompatibility. Crispijn van de Passe, after Jacques
Bellange, 'Een jonge vrouw bedriegt haar oude
echtgenoot' [a young woman cheats on her old
husband]. (1574–1637). Rijksmuseum, Amsterdam.   161

Queer Theories, Queer Histories, and Shakespeare Studies

Queer

If 'queer' has become such a familiar term in contemporary Anglophone culture, it's arguably because of its appeal to multiple communities, as well as its ability to convey something edgy but also familiar, even banal.[1] Historically, 'queer' has been used since the sixteenth century to designate that which is 'strange, odd, peculiar, eccentric', or 'bad, contemptible, worthless', without a necessarily sexual meaning.[2] 'Queer' became firmly attached to the idea of 'strange' genders and sexualities only in the early twentieth century, when it was used to describe (primarily male) homosexual people, usually in a derogatory fashion.[3] Around 1990, 'queer' suddenly exploded into visibility in the United States and United Kingdom, as lesbians and gay men defiantly reappropriated the term to name themselves, their communities, and their intellectual and political engagements in opposition to cultural norms. The activist group Queer Nation—known for the slogan 'We're here! We're queer! Get used to it!'—formed in New York City in the spring of 1990 to promote the cultural visibility and contributions of lesbian and gay people. At the New York City Lesbian and Gay Pride Parade that summer, Queer Nation famously distributed a provocative polemic featuring an essay called 'I Hate Straights'. A collection of essays from 1991 is usually cited as the academic origin of 'queer theory'.[4] Neither were the creative arts left behind in the queer revolution. In a 1992 article published in New York City's *The Village Voice*, critic B. Ruby Rich heralded 'The New Queer Cinema': a flourishing of politically engaged and stylistically innovative films by independent lesbian and gay filmmakers.

We can thus confidently identify the early 1990s as the period when 'queer' took on new life as a confrontational, galvanizing, forward-looking banner under which lesbian and gay people might proudly and defiantly march, produce scholarship, and make art. Or not. Even as it was in ascendance, 'queer' was vigorously rejected by some gay men and lesbians who found the term a painful reminder of social stigmatization. Today, some people still reject 'queer' for various reasons, including the belief that its pejorative connotations have not diminished. From the moment of its spectacular appropriation by lesbians and gay men, 'queer' has continued to be both a unifying and a divisive term.

That simultaneously unifying and divisive quality is also evident in the academic fortunes of 'queer', which has been used to capture the broad range of possible non-normative gender and sexual identities, as well as to critique the very notion of identity. As Kadji Amin observes, in the early 1990s queer theory presented itself as 'a sophisticated critique of identitarian knowledges emphatically *not* defined by the study of gays and lesbians'; at the same time, paradoxically, it 'became one of the major sites for the study of (homo)sexuality and gender transgression in the US academy'.[5] Often considered the co-founding texts of queer theory, Judith Butler's *Gender Trouble: Feminism and the Subversion of Identity* (1990) and Eve Kosofsky Sedgwick's *Epistemology of the Closet* (1991) are accurately described by Amin as 'sophisticated critique[s] of identitarian knowledges'. Because Butler's and Sedgwick's highly influential books theorized gender and sexuality not as biological facts but as sites of ongoing cultural conflict and negotiation, they were, in Amin's words, 'emphatically *not* defined by the study of gays and lesbians', in contrast to the more sociologically oriented lesbian and gay scholarship of the 1970s.

In *Gender Trouble*, Butler undermines the very idea of gender identity. According to Butler, gender is not an inherent trait of bodies but a 'regulatory practice' intended to render people 'intelligible through becoming gendered in conformity with recognizable standards of gender intelligibility'.[6] Butler defines 'intelligible' genders as 'those which in some sense institute and maintain relations of coherence and continuity among sex, gender, sexual practice, and desire'.[7] For example, an 'intelligible' woman would be one who was born with 'female' genitalia, who behaved in a conventionally 'feminine' manner, and who acted on 'normal' heterosexual desire for men. But how do we recognize 'normal' gender behaviour when we see it? What is it that makes a body 'intelligible' according to a particular culture's gender norms?

In the essay 'Imitation and Gender Insubordination' (1991), Butler argues that gender is a daily 'performance', in an unconscious, habitual way, of what only seems to be a 'natural' set of behavioural norms. Butler uses drag—the theatrical practice of men performing an exaggerated version of female gender through clothing, cosmetics, gesture, voice, etc.—as a graphic illustration of the idea that everyday gender itself is not 'natural' or biologically embodied but artificial and performatively enacted:

> Drag constitutes the mundane way in which genders are appropriated, theatricalized, worn, and done; it implies that all gendering is a kind of impersonation and approximation. If this is true, it seems, there is no original or primary gender that drag imitates, but *gender is a kind of imitation for which there is no original*; in fact, it is a kind of imitation that produces the very notion of the original as an *effect* and consequence of the imitation itself. In other words, the natural effects of heterosexualized genders are produced through imitative strategies; what they imitate is a phantasmatic ideal of heterosexual identity, one that is produced by the imitation of its effect. In this sense, the 'reality' of heterosexual identities is performatively constituted through an imitation that sets itself up as the origin and the ground of all imitations. In other words, heterosexuality is always in the process of imitating and approximating its own phantasmatic idealizing of itself—*and failing*. Precisely because it is bound to fail, heterosexual identity is propelled into an endless repetition of itself.[8]

In other words, heterosexuality is not a natural norm or standard for measuring supposed deviations such as homosexuality; it is merely an approximate, imitative performance of a non-existent ideal. Because heterosexual identity is an ideal, it can never be fully or successfully embodied by any person, no matter how stringently they conform to norms of gender or sexual behaviour. Gender can thus be defined as an always imperfect or incomplete 'practice of improvisation' within a 'scene of constraint'—meaning that 'the terms that make up one's gender are, from the start, outside oneself, beyond oneself in a sociality that has no single author'.[9] Butler's theory of gender performance can be defined as queer because it radically undermines the putative naturalness of heterosexuality—and, indeed, of *any* gender or sexual identity—understanding it instead as a site of laborious, endlessly failed, cultural citation.

In *The Epistemology of the Closet*, Sedgwick destabilizes heterosexuality by demonstrating how inconsistent are the grounds of our knowledge ('epistemology') about it. According to Sedgwick, late nineteenth-century cultural developments produced a new

world mapping by which every given person, just as he or she was necessarily assignable to a male or female gender, was now considered necessarily assignable as well to a homo- or hetero-sexuality...New, institutionalized taxonomic discourses—medical, legal, literary, psychological—centering on homo/heterosexual definition proliferated and crystallized with exceptional rapidity in the decades around the turn of the century.[10]

These 'taxonomic discourses' articulated two contradictory 'paradigms' or models for defining sexuality: 'minoritizing' and 'universalizing'. The 'minoritizing' model holds that most people are heterosexual, and that homosexuality is a trait inherent to a small minority of people. The 'universalizing' model holds that everyone is capable of experiencing homosexual desire, because sexuality exists on a 'continuum' between the exclusively homosexual and the exclusively heterosexual. Sedgwick uses the presence of this unresolved contradiction to show how modern definitions of heterosexuality and homosexuality are inherently unstable, thus calling into question the supposed naturalness, priority, or superiority of heterosexuality.

Although Sedgwick and Butler challenged the epistemologies through which modern concepts of gender and sexual identity—including lesbian and gay identity—take root, their commitments to feminist and antihomophobic politics galvanized lesbian and gay thinkers, scholars, and activists. *The Epistemology of the Closet*, which Sedgwick describes as a work of 'antihomophobic inquiry', analysed the representation of male homosexuality in the work of Oscar Wilde, Henry James, and Marcel Proust, writers who had long been of interest to gay scholars. In her radical critique of identity politics, Butler cites 'gay and lesbian perspectives on gender' and the gay/lesbian gender-parodic practices of drag, cross-dressing, and butch/femme roles.[11] The fact that Sedgwick and Butler undermined the idea of stable gender and sexual identities did not prevent scholars who identified as lesbian and gay from finding their work affirming and inspiring.[12]

Lesbian/gay/queer Shakespeare studies emerged in this environment of intellectual and political ferment. Throughout this Introduction and book, I will refer to this field as 'queer Shakespeare studies' or 'Shakespeare and sexuality studies' instead of using the now familiar acronym 'LGBTQIA+', for several reasons. During the 1990s, queer Shakespeare scholarship focused on male and female homoeroticism and on the concept of sodomy, but paid little attention to other elements of the LGBTQIA+ spectrum such as bisexuality, transgender, intersexuality, asexuality, or the other genders and sexualities captured by the plus sign (or by the double duty of 'Q' as both 'queer' and 'questioning').[13] For this reason, to use the LGBTQIA+ acronym would mispresent this earlier scholarship as more capacious than it actually was. Moreover, although bisexuality, transgender, intersexuality, and asexuality have since been explored in Shakespeare scholarship, the equal standing of the identity-signifying letters in the acronym LGBTQIA+ might give the misleading impression that much more attention has been given to these issues than is actually the case.[14] Despite not using the LGBTQIA+ acronym, I will address issues of bisexuality, transgender, intersexuality, and asexuality throughout this book, in an effort both to acknowledge the work that has been done and to advance further research in these areas. Finally, when considering terminology, I have taken a cue from titles in Shakespeare studies published during the last decade, which show a marked preference for the terms 'queer', 'sex', and 'sexuality'. I have therefore found it reasonable simply to refer to this academic field as 'queer Shakespeare studies' or 'Shakespeare and sexuality studies'.

In Shakespeare scholarship, 'queer' tends to function as it does in the LGBTQIA+ acronym: as a general placeholder for any non-normative, marginalized, or dissident expression of gender or sexuality. In *Tendencies* (1993), Sedgwick proposes 'queer' as a more flexible alternative to the binary categories of homosexuality/heterosexuality:

'queer' can refer to: the open mesh of possibilities, gaps, overlaps, dissonances and resonances, lapses and excesses of meaning when the constituent elements of anyone's gender, of anyone's sexuality aren't made (or *can't be* made) to signify monolithically. The experimental linguistic, epistemological, representational, political adventures attaching to the very many of us who may at times be moved to describe ourselves as (among many other possibilities) pushy femmes, radical faeries, fantasists, drags, clones, leatherfolk, ladies in tuxedoes, feminist women or feminist men, masturbators, bulldaggers, divas, Snap! queens, butch bottoms, storytellers, transsexuals, aunties, wannabes, lesbian-identified men or lesbians who sleep with men, or…people able to relish, learn from, or identify with such.[15]

This much-cited passage contains two very powerful claims. First is the idea that gender and sexuality elude attempts to capture them in language. In early modern studies, Gregory Bredbeck, Jonathan Goldberg, and Madhavi Menon have emphasized what Sedgwick calls 'lapses and excesses of meaning' produced by textualizations of gender and sexuality.[16] Bredbeck argues that '[t]hroughout the Renaissance homoeroticism is figured and refigured as a slippery category that is at once both a type of sexual meaning and an effacement of sexual meaning'.[17] According to Goldberg, in early modern texts sodomy exists only as a product of the language used (or not used) to describe it, 'through slippages capable of being mobilized in more than one direction'.[18]

Menon has most fully elaborated an understanding of 'queer' as 'not a category but the confusion engendered by and despite categorization'.[19] Claiming that 'queerness is not a synonym for embodied homosexuality' or for 'specific bodily practices' such as homosexual sex, Menon argues that 'queer' concerns 'more wide-ranging issues of non-normativity and non-coincidence' that elude precise definition: '[i]f queerness can be defined, then it is no longer queer—it strays away from its anti-normative stance to become the institutionalized norm.'[20] To declare that queerness is 'no longer queer' once it is defined is of course, para-doxical, for Menon implicitly defines queerness, even if only nega-tively, as *non-normativity that cannot be defined*. Whereas for Sedgwick queer refers to the ways that *gender* or *sexuality* cannot be made to 'signify monolithically', for Menon queer describes '[a]ll things' that 'militate against the obvious, the settled, and the understood—in other words, nothing that may be fully or finally grasped'.[21] One productive effect of defining 'queer' so broadly is to produce uncertainty regarding the boundaries of our inquiries into sexuality. How can we know in advance that some form of non-normativity or category confusion that might not explicitly centre on human bodies isn't 'queer' (e.g., charged with desire or eroticism)? At the same time, as Elizabeth Freeman warns, whereas defining queer as a 'position of pure negativity' can prompt us to examine the non-normative wherever we might encounter it, it also 'risk[s] evacuating the messiest thing about being queer: the actual meeting of bodies with other bodies and with objects'.[22]

A second crucial idea in Sedgwick's definition of 'queer' is that gender and sexual identities are provisional and contingent: they are 'experimental', an exciting 'adventure' upon which we embark without a map or destination. It's telling that of the 'possible' gender and sexual identities Sedgwick catalogues in 1993, some are still pertinent—such as the drag queen—while others seemed dated, and new ones have emerged. Some of these identities are highly idiosyncratic: I'm not really sure what Sedgwick means by 'wannabees' (straight people who aspire to be queer?), 'ladies in tuxedos' (masculine women? lesbians at weddings? drag kings?), or 'fantasists' (people who prefer sexual fantasies to sexual acts?). But that failure or excess of meaning is precisely to Sedgwick's point about how queer embodiments can elude understanding. Although scholars haven't generally explored the possibility of finding such distinct figures as the 'butch bottom' or the 'pushy femme' in Shakespeare's texts, Sedgwick's open-ended definition of 'queer' encourages us to conceptualize a multitude of finely textured, ephemeral, improvisational gender and sexual identities that might get lost within the bagginess of broader categories such as 'same-sex'.

Although in the wake of work by Butler, Sedgwick, and others 'queer' has become a productive site for the exploration of non-normative genders and sexualities, others have cautioned that the very familiarity of the term can produce inadequate understandings of the contingency of gendered and sexual meanings. Several critics, for instance, have advocated for more nuanced understandings of the dynamics of normativity and transgression. Benjamin Kahan warns that reliance on the normal/queer binary can become another unthinking, even 'normative', way of reducing the complexity of gender and sexual politics.[23] Karma Lochrie urges premodern scholars to abandon altogether the terminology of norms and the normal, since those concepts were first articulated in the context of seventeenth-century empirical science and only came to fruition with the nineteenth-century advent of statistics. 'Before the advent of the normal, no sexuality or other cultural ideal was normal.'[24] But even premodern scholars who find normality an analytically useful concept point out that there are always 'ongoing negotiations among competing norms, ideals, and ideologies', and that in a period 'without a fixed sense of sexual normalcy, norms may be produced but they are only temporarily dominant and always contestatory'.[25] From an explicitly political angle, Judith Butler argues for the need to distinguish

among the norms and conventions that permit people to breathe, to desire, to love, and to live, and those norms and conventions that restrict or eviscerate the conditions of life itself. Sometimes norms function both ways at once, and sometimes they function one way for a given group, and another way for another group. What is most important is to cease legislating for all lives what is livable only for some, and similarly, to refrain from proscribing for all lives what is unlivable for some.[26]

Butler reminds us that gender and sexual norms can literally be legislated—such as the hundreds of recent US laws that seek to curb the rights of transgender people—and that the effect of such laws might be unevenly distributed among different communities, sometimes reinforcing already existing inequalities. Acknowledging that laws can make life unlivable for some queers but not for others means recognizing the inadequacy of an overly idealized and abstract understanding of queerness as a 'resistance to' or 'transgression of' gender and sexual norms.

The importance of distinguishing the material power dynamics of sexual relations we might label 'queer' also applies to our readings of early modern texts. Consider Ian Moulton's account of the paradoxically conservative obscenity of *Hermaphroditus*, a fifteenth-century Italian collection of poems by Antonio Beccadelli. Drawing on a classical tradition of pederasty in which it was socially acceptable for adult men to have sex with adolescent boys, Beccadelli's text 'openly praises anal sex with boys' and never suggests 'that sex with boys is any more to be condemned than sex with women'.[27] As might be expected, the *Hermaphroditus* was in its own time met with 'outrage and accusations', including the charge that Beccadelli was himself a pederast.[28] Although *Hermaphroditus* 'was clearly transgressive in the context of early modern Christian sexual morality', its depiction of male-male sex, Moulton argues, is 'deeply traditional', in that it defines 'masculinity as the physical penetration of social inferiors: women, boys and slaves'.[29] In other words, because it advocated 'non-normative' sex between males, *Hermaphroditus* was considered shockingly queer by contemporary moralists. But its *sexual* queerness was conveyed through an extremely conservative (non-queer) view of *gender* and *status* in which adult men were authorized to sexually dominate social inferiors of any gender. In such cases, we need to be precise about how we define norms, how we determine which practices transgress those norms, and how we acknowledge the impact of norms on different bodies and lives.

History, Sexuality, and Language

One form of precision to which this book aspires regards the concepts of heterosexuality and homosexuality. In his immensely influential *The History of Sexuality: An Introduction* (1976, English translation 1978), French philosopher Michel Foucault established that sexuality has a history. 'Sexuality', Foucault argued, is not an inherent human 'drive', but rather a 'technology' invented in a particular society—the nineteenth-century West—to surveil and control individuals. Nineteenth-century medical, psychiatric, and legal 'discourses' (the specialist languages used by particular disciplines or institutions) defined sexuality as being by nature 'a domain susceptible to pathological processes, and hence one calling for therapeutic or normalizing interventions'.[30] These professions relentlessly produced, described, and catalogued sexual perversions as a way to cure, control, or punish those people who came to be defined by the abnormal sexual subjectivities they supposedly embodied and exhibited. Examples of the 'manifold sexualities' or perversions that were newly identified in the nineteenth century include

those which appear with the different ages (sexualities of the infant or the child), those which become fixated on particular tastes or practices (the sexu- ality of the invert, the gerontophile, the fetishist), those which, in a diffuse manner, invest relationships (the sexuality of doctor and patient, teacher and student, psychiatrist and mental patient), [and] those which haunt spaces (the sexuality of the home, the school, the prison) . . .[31]

Although sexual identities were used by powerful institutions, such as the medical and psychiatric professions and the carceral state, to manage those people that they labelled as abnormal, they would also become available as sites of political self-identification and resistance. For instance, those who identified as homosexual could organize to resist police oppression, demand civil rights, and so on.

If the homosexual was one of the many abnormal kinds of person created by the modern invention of sexuality, it follows that there were no homosexuals before the modern era. To posit the absence of homosexuals in premodernity does not mean that same-sex desires or intimacies did not exist before the nineteenth century, only that they were not understood to constitute a distinct, identifiable type of *person* who could be subjected to medical or legal discipline on the basis of an inherent sexual orientation or inclination. As Peter Coviello writes, 'What does sex even look like if it is somehow removed from the idea of sexuality as a thing within us, a thing that somehow sweepingly binds together...scattered attributes' of 'being, of experience and affect, sensuality and selfhood', and 'fuses them into a definitive sense of who we are'?[32] Early modern laws against sodomy (non-reproductive sexual acts, particularly anal intercourse between men), provide evidence of what Coviello calls the historically earlier 'disaggregat[ion]' of disparate sexual attributes that would be violently yoked together by the modern idea of a comprehensive 'sexuality'.[33] Sodomy laws identified not kinds of *persons* but kinds of *acts* deemed unnatural or socially disruptive. In a much debated passage from *The History of Sexuality*, Foucault draws a distinction between the premodern sodomite *who is punished by the law* for committing sodomy and the modern homosexual *who is given an inherent sexuality by the medical/psychiatric establishment*:

As defined by the ancient civil or canonical codes, sodomy was a category of forbidden acts; their perpetrator was nothing more than the juridical subject of them. The nineteenth-century homosexual became a personage, a past, a case history, and a childhood, in addition to being a type of life, a life form, and a morphology, with an indiscreet anatomy and possibly a mysterious physiology. Nothing that went into his total composition was unaffected by his sexuality. It was everywhere present in him: at the root of all his actions because it was their insidious and indefinitely active principle; written immodestly on his face and body because it was a secret that always gave itself away. It was consubstantial with him, less as a habitual sin than as a singular nature. We must not forget that the psychological, psychiatric, medical category of homosexuality was constituted...less by a type of sexual relations than by a certain quality of sexual sensibility, a certain way of inverting the masculine and feminine in oneself. Homosexuality appeared as one of the forms of sexuality when it was transposed from the practice of sodomy onto a kind of interior androgyny, a hermaphroditism of the soul. The sodomite had been a temporary aberration; the homosexual was now a species.[34]

This passage has sometimes been used to justify the claim that whereas we moderns have sexual 'identities' (a word Foucault does not use in the original French), early moderns had only sexual 'acts'.[35] If that is true, some have argued, then early modern people did not connect their sexual acts with their subjectivity or sense of self.

Yet what gets overlooked in the positing of a strict binary between early modern sexual acts and modern sexual identities, explains historian David Halperin, is that Foucault is not addressing in this passage how the thoughts, values, or subjectivities of early modern people might have been shaped by their sexual desires, acts, or habits.[36] Foucault is merely drawing a historical distinction between the dominant *social discourses* that defined and regulated male-male sexual expression in the early modern and modern eras. In the early modern era, sex was regulated primarily by laws, which defined sodomy as non-reproductive acts that could theoretically be committed by anyone. In the modern era, sex is regulated primarily by psychiatry, which attributes to persons an inherent, 'consubstantial' sexuality that defines their 'singular nature' and is expressed in their faces, bodies, thoughts, habits, and sensibilities.[37] Just because early modern people did not have a concept of what Foucault calls a 'sexuality'—a totalizing sexual nature that informed everything that one thought and did—it does not necessarily follow that they had no awareness of their own or others' erotic proclivities, preferences, or subjectivities.

As several scholars have argued, in fact, premodern cultures attributed something like a sexual 'identity' to particular kinds of men and women, although these identities 'do not neatly correspond to modern formulations and may not be involved in the same cultural work'.[38] For instance, Sarah Salih posits that the holy virgin constitutes an early modern 'sexual identity category' because she 'is a coherent figure, with a particular personal history and a particular kind of body'.[39] Melissa Sanchez concurs that Jean Calvin's and Martin Luther's 'very precise definition of virginity as the miraculous *lack* of desire, rather than the willed *suppression* of desires, situates the lifelong virgin as a distinct sexual type', or recognizable identity.[40] Ruth Mazo Karras argues that medieval culture applied the identity of whore to women who had sex outside of marriage.[41] Certain kinds of men were also recognized as constituting distinct sexual types.[42] As Jennifer Panek demonstrates, manual labourers were often represented as possessing exceptional sexual stamina.[43] Ari Friedlander argues that sixteenth-century pamphlets about rogues (poor vagabonds) consistently associate them with promiscuous sex in a way that comes to constitute a 'socio-sexual identity': a 'durable, reproducible discursive category of personhood'.[44]

As the above discussion indicates, an important implication of Foucault's *The History of Sexuality* is that we cannot casually speak of 'sexuality', 'homosexuality', or 'heterosexuality' in the early modern period without misleading anachronism, since 'sexuality' in the precise sense of a psychologized sexual personhood is a modern idea. Because heterosexuality is a concept so taken for granted in our own time and so easily conflated with marriage—the dominant institution for defining both men's and women's social identities in early modernity—it is particularly important to defamiliarize it.[45] The modern concept of heterosexuality expresses a belief in the '"oppositeness" of the sexes' as 'the basis for a universal, normal erotic attraction between males and females', in sharp distinction to an abnormal homosexuality.[46] Even though they might have desired each other romantically or sexually, early modern men and women would not have thought of themselves as possessing a normal sexuality that bestowed a particular identity upon them and that distinguished them from the 'abnormal' sexuality of a (homosexual) minority.[47] Moreover, sexual reproduction within marriage 'does not require that either partner...be motivated by heterosexual desire'.[48] Below, I reproduce a number of scholarly accounts of early modern *heteroerotic* (male-female erotic) relations not because I find all of them equally convincing, but to suggest the many ways in which pre-modern views of male-female love, sexual desire, and conjugal intimacy differ from the modern norm of *heterosexuality*.

• The idea of 'opposite' sexes on which contemporary heterosexuality rests was not assumed in the early modern period, which had inherited from ancient Greek thinkers the belief that male and female sex organs were structurally homologous, not opposed. Whereas male genitalia (penis, scrotum, and testes) were *outside* the body, female genitalia (vagina, uterus, and 'female testes'—organs later identified as egg-producing ovaries) were *inside* the body. Temperature, not genitalia, constituted the essential difference between men and women: because male bodies were generally hotter than female bodies, that greater heat pushed their genitalia outside of their bodies. Moreover, since heat could fluctuate, some held it possible that women could 'transform into' men if, through physical exertion, their bodies heated up to the point that their genitalia would extrude. Although the details of human anatomical structure and function were debated, in general it was believed that male and female bodies were not different in kind but in degree, as colder and hotter variations on a *single* sex.[49]

- For the medieval theologian Thomas Aquinas, the 'paramount distinction' of sexual morality was between 'abstinence and activity'. Whereas sexual abstinence was the ideal, the best kind of sex was 'the union of husband and wife desiring children', because it respected both 'reason'—social convention or morality—and 'nature'—procreation as the biological purpose of sex. Some sexual acts (fornication, seduction, adultery, rape) violated reason but not nature, because reproduction was still possible; other sexual acts (masturbation, sodomy, bestiality) violated both reason and nature, because reproduction was impossible. A world in which 'rape is a *less* serious offense than masturbation or oral sex between husband and wife because rape can lead to conception' is a very different world than one that regards 'heterosexuality' as natural.[50]

- In seventeenth-century New England, the 'operative contrast' used to evaluate sexual morality was 'between fruitfulness and barrenness, not between different-sex and same-sex eroticism'.[51] Because 'sexual sin was founded in universal corruption, the temptation to engage in "uncleanness" afflicted everyone'.[52]

- Likewise, the 'extraordinary proliferation of discourses on the regulation of sexual behavior' in early modern Europe 'was governed not by concepts of heterosexuality but by the regulation of sex between men and women in order to assure the production of legitimate children and to prevent bastardy'.[53]

- The orthodox Christian notion that marriage turns husband and wife into 'one flesh' and 'members of [Christ's] body', articulated in Paul's influential Letter to the Ephesians (5:30–31), makes the 'dyad' of the married couple intelligible as a 'plurality', in that the conjugal pair becomes 'married to all in Christendom'.[54]

- The notion of marriage as a companionate, monogamous fellowship derives 'to a surprising extent, from a classical ideal of dyadic friendship' between men.[55] In *Of Domestical Duties* (1622), Protestant minister William Gouge advises husband and wives to model their 'loving mutual affection' after the Biblical Jonathan, who 'loved David as his own soul'.[56] Admonishing husbands to remain constant in their conjugal love, Gouge again recommends David and Jonathan, who enjoyed 'the soundest love that ever was' between two people (418).

- Early moderns commonly believed that '[w]omen are dangerous to men' because desire for women could render men 'effeminate' in two ways: first, by vitiating the rational self-control that was an essential quality of manhood; second, because desiring a woman might cause a man to neglect typically manly pursuits in favour of more feminine habits.[57] This belief is diametrically opposed to the contemporary assumption that a man can prove his virility through sex with women.

- Relatedly, early modern writers advised bridegrooms to be gentle on their wedding nights, when they would presumably be having sex with their wives for the first time. Such texts address 'women's fears about crossing a threshold from one state of repression known as virginity to another known as marriage', and at the same time 'grapple with men's fears about sexual performance and the exercise of authority'.[58] A husband's superior power as 'king' of the household was commonly acknowledged as imbuing marital sex with anxiety and fear for both partners, as well as raising difficult questions about the degree to which husbands should restrain, temper, or even defer their sexual desires for their wives. In short, orthodox gender ideologies, which required wives' submission to their husbands, necessarily affected the most legitimate expression of male-female eroticism: conjugal intercourse.[59]

- Early modern England was governed by a rank-stratified ideology of 'homosociality' (a social system that prioritized male-male bonds) according to which women of all ranks 'naturally desire sexual variety' and 'men of different ranks think and behave differently in relation to sex with women'. Contemporary culture is instead governed by an ideology of heterosexuality that 'values heterosexual intercourse for pleasure, values men's sexual desire for women, and sees women as naturally less desirous than men'.[60]

- It was generally considered 'scandalous that spouses could treat another as lovers would'; for instance, English minister Richard Capel condemned the '"immoderate desires" of married couples along with sodomy, adultery, and masturbation'.[61] Similarly, minister William Whately cautioned that God ordained matrimony 'not to enkindle lustful desires, but to quench them'.[62] Attitudes that look more like modern heterosexuality appear only in the later seventeenth century, when the increasing value attributed to private intimacy apart from a public sphere of commerce and politics emphasized the importance of mutual sexual desire between spouses.[63] This new 'emphasis on erotic desire placed individual wishes above those of the community', such as the spouses' kin, and 'muted the interdependence of marriage and economics'.[64]

- In the early modern period, sexual availability and economic dependence rendered boys and women equally attractive and legitimate objects of erotic desire to adult men. Early modern eroticism was therefore 'not gender-specific' or 'grounded in the sex of the possibly "submissive" partner', but was 'an expectation of that very submissiveness'.[65] In other words, *status* difference (mastery/submission) was at the basis of early modern sexuality—regardless of whether it was homoerotic or heteroerotic—just as *gender* difference (male/female) is at the basis of modern (hetero)sexuality.

The above list aims to 'disaggregate' and historicize 'those now-coordinated vectors of selfhood' encompassed by the modern notion of heterosexuality: the anatomical difference of partners ('opposite sexes'), the ideal of mutual erotic desire, the valorization of non-reproductive sexual acts, the distinction of a 'normal' sexuality from homosexuality, the association between sexual and gender normality, and the expectation of sexual privacy.[66]

Although I have been endorsing Foucault's theory that 'sexuality'—as a totalizing sexual nature that informed one's entire selfhood—is a late nineteenth-century concept, I join other Shakespeareans in finding 'sexuality' useful as a *general term* for naming the embeddedness of sexual desires and acts within collective ideals of propriety, legality, and morality. This usage of the term approximates Foucault's broad account of sexuality as 'an especially dense transfer point for relations of power'—an apt description of how early modern authorities and institutions (i.e., parents, teachers, local officials, the church, the state) took an interest in regulating and disciplining who had sex, with whom, how, when, and where.[67] Similarly, when Shakespeareans use phrases like 'heterosexual marriage', it is usually not to imply that early modern people identified as heterosexual, but to stress how marriage, which was available only to male-female couples and provided social and legal validation of their reproductive sexual activities, might also be understood as a 'dense transfer point for relations of power'. Still, Karma Lochrie convincingly argues that using 'heterosexuality' or even 'heteronormativity' when discussing premodern societies perpetuates the misconception that a binary concept of normal sexual orientation existed before the modern era.[68] For this reason, I avoid 'homosexual' and 'heterosexual' in this book. Moreover, despite the value of the scholarship mentioned above that describes certain kinds of persons, such as the lifelong celibate, in terms of sexual identity, I will not speak of Shakespeare's characters as having sexual identities. I do so to avoid the implication that characters in a play or poem are real people instead of rhetorical constructs. More importantly, I fear that in granting sexual identity to Shakespeare's characters we might minimize or discount the crucial ways, detailed above, in which early modern sexual beliefs and experiences differ from those of the twenty-first century.

Another strategy for avoiding the projection of anachronistic concepts onto the early modern past that I employ throughout this book is close attention to the language that Shakespeare uses to represent sexual desires, inclinations, and acts. Jeffrey Masten has coined the phrase 'queer philology' to describe a method of reading early modern texts that meticulously analyses how language conveys (and sometimes confounds) sexual meaning. I employ queer philological methods in three primary ways. First and foremost, I frequently consult the *Oxford English Dictionary* [*OED*] to access the multiple sexual denotations and connotations of particular words in Shakespeare's time. Second, I occasionally demonstrate how modern editors of Shakespeare's plays alter words found in the original seventeenth-century printings of his texts based on mistaken assumptions about which gender or sexual meanings were or were not possible at the time. Finally, each chapter develops a series of careful readings of Shakespeare's texts that are attentive to linguistic and rhetorical patterns, associations, and provocations to thought. I believe that any understanding of the queerness of Shakespeare's texts has to begin with an appreciation of how his extraordinarily rich language creates the imaginative conditions for exploring the multifarious possibilities of gendered and erotic experience.

Chapter Breakdown

Chapter 1, 'Queer(ing) Couples', analyses Shakespeare's representations of same-sex desire both within and beyond the couple form. The chapter introduces the concept of 'homonormativity', or the valorization of similarity within same-sex couples, as one of the key factors shaping same-sex relationships in Shakespeare's plays. Both *Romeo and Juliet* and *The Merchant of Venice* demonstrate how homonormativity might define the special intimacy of male friends, at the same time that it connects those friends to larger male communities. Although in *Romeo and Juliet* and *The Merchant of Venice* male friendship can accommodate one friend's desire to marry, albeit with some degree of tension and conflict, in *The Two Noble Kinsmen* the frail friendship of the protagonists is destroyed by their emulous compulsion to marry the same woman. I conclude with an analysis of female homonormative friendship in *As You Like It* that addresses how the advent of male-female courtship leading to marriage might both confirm and displace the centrality of same-sex bonds.

Chapter 2, '(Queer) Desire and Disruption', examines the relationship between sexual transgression and political disorder in several of Shakespeare's history plays and tragedies. In *Henry V*, King Harry's condemnation of his bedfellow, Lord Scrope, for treason intimates that he has abused their physical intimacy. Whereas Harry's exposure of Scrope's sodomitical betrayal preserves England from French treachery, in *Troilus and Cressida*, the Trojan Paris' rape of the Greek Helen is ultimately responsible for the destruction of Troy. At the same time, the Greek hero Achilles' love for both his friend Patroclus and the Trojan princess Polyxena unmans him, keeping him idle and dilating a brutal war of attrition. In the three *Henry VI* plays, sexual disorder within England ravages the court and the nation. Internal political dissent is exacerbated by King Henry's amorous doting on Queen Margaret, who is committing adultery with the ambitious Duke of Suffolk. In her desire to become queen, another unruly woman, Lady Macbeth in *Macbeth*, goads her husband to regicide, thus fulfilling the prophecy of the 'weird sisters', a queer trio living on the margins of Scotland's patriarchal society. The chapter ends with an analysis of two tragedies, *Titus Andronicus* and *Anthony and Cleopatra*, in which an adulterous interracial affair destabilizes the Roman Empire from within.

Chapter 3, 'Queer Gender Transformations', reads the gender-crossing found in several Shakespeare plays through a transgender lens. Although transgender scholarship has not always found a comfortable home within queer studies, I concur that the two fields 'are linked through shared histories, methods, and commitments to transforming the situation of gender and sexual outsiders'.[69] I argue that in the comedies *As You Like It*, *The Two Gentlemen of Verona*, and *Twelfth Night*, Shakespeare explores the emotional and social consequences of temporarily adopting a different gender identity. I then turn to a different kind of non-binary female protagonist, Joan la Pucelle (Joan of Arc) in *1 Henry VI*, who wears male armour and engages in battle without trying to pass as a man. Although Joan claims that the Virgin Mary has authorized her military interventions, her queer gender transformation makes her vulnerable to the constant suspicion of sexual promiscuity.

Chapter 4, 'Queer Asexuality', explores the causes and consequences of refusing sex or marriage in the narrative poem *Venus and Adonis* and in five plays: *A Midsummer Night's Dream*, *Romeo and Juliet*, *Measure for Measure*, *Love's Labors Lost*, and *All's Well that Ends Well*. Although characters sometimes offer reasons for their temporary or permanent states of celibacy, at other times one character will invidiously attribute an innate coldness or hardness to another in an attempt to understand the refusal of sexual intimacy. Particularly at these moments, asexuality can appear as a queer disruption of dominant social and physiological expectations—a subject of wonder, consternation, scorn, and sceptical analysis.

Chapter 5, 'Queer Heteroeroticism', considers how certain male-female sexual desires and intimacies represented as unnatural, illicit, or socially inappropriate subject women to male control and censure. *A Midsummer's Night Dream*, *All's Well that Ends Well* and *Measure for Measure* each features a woman who masochistically seeks the affection of a man who humiliates her. In both *Henry V* and *The Taming of the Shrew*, a husband-to-be's indecorous joke about anal sex conveys an intention to subject his wife to his authority; Oberon in *A Midsummer Night's Dream* successfully tames his disobedient wife by magically compelling her to dote on the ass-headed Bottom. Antiochus in *Pericles* perverts the father-child bond to incite his daughter to incest. Finally, male-female relationships characterized by highly visible bodily differences—of size (*Venus and Adonis*, *The Comedy of Errors*), ability (*Richard III*), and race (*Othello*)—provoke reactions of disgust, ridicule, or fear based on conventional social beliefs about beauty, gendered hierarchy, and sexual compatibility.

A brief Conclusion outlines the six methodological premises that have guided my queer readings of Shakespeare's plays and poems throughout this study.

Shakespeare and Queer Studies. Mario DiGangi, Oxford University Press. © Mario DiGangi 2025.
DOI: 10.1093/9780191994951.003.0001

Queer(ing) Couples

Romeo and Juliet and *The Two Noble Kinsmen* are among a handful of Shakespeare plays whose titles focus on a single couple. Because the couple, then as now, is the most culturally privileged form for intimate relationships, such titles can mislead us into underestimating the entanglement of dyadic relations in other amorous, erotic, affective, or sexual bonds. Romeo initially fantasizes not about Juliet but Rosaline, and he shares his amorous woes with his friends Mercutio and Benvolio. In *Anthony and Cleopatra*, when Anthony departs from Cleopatra she finds solace in two female servants, who will loyally accompany her even to her death. The long-standing same-sex bonds between Antonio and Bassanio in *The Merchant of Venice* and Rosalind and Celia in *As You Like It* are able to accommodate a different-gender partner when Bassanio courts Portia and Rosalind courts Orlando.[1] We can 'queer' or expand the erotic purview of Shakespeare's male-female and same-sex couples, this chapter will argue, by paying attention to the various social, affective, and erotic relations in which intimate partners participate.

To be sure, Renaissance thinkers celebrated the ideal of a perfectly matched couple. Shakespeare's same-sex couples often exemplify what Laurie Shannon calls 'Renaissance homonormativity': the cultural valuation of compatibility manifested through similarities of age, religion, nation, education, and/or status.[2] Similitude [the *homo*] within a couple was considered more conducive to true intimacy than difference [the *hetero*]. For instance, Sir Thomas Elyot describes the famous friends Titus and Gisippus as 'equal' in age, 'stature, proportion of body, favor, and color of visage, countenance, and speech'.[3] The friends'

of ciuill frind——fhipe:

Figure 1.1 Nature 'desireth his lyke': homonormative male friendship. Thomas Trevilian, *Trevelyon Miscellany* (1608), folio 175 recto: 'Of Civil Friendship.' Call#: V.b.232, image 5113. Folger Shakespeare Library.

similarity of build, skin colour, and facial features suggests that Renaissance homonormativity might take a physiological or even racial form (see Figure 1.1). Early modern philosophy held that it was natural for like to seek out like. According to John Tiptoft's English translation of Cicero's *De Amicitia*, the best known classical text on friendship among Shakespeare's contemporaries, it is in the 'nature of thynges' that something 'desireth his lyke & fleeth his contrarye'.[4] Because all things desire what is most like them, nature is homonormative and homonormativity is natural.

Contemporary readers might find it odd to attribute 'an erotics of similitude' to friendship.[5] The term 'friend zone' suggests that we regard friendship as a bond of limited emotional and physical intimacy. In contrast, early modern writers regarded male same-sex friendship as the richest and most elevated bond. In Misha Teramura's summary,

Influenced by foundational classical accounts in such works as Aristotle's *Nicomachean Ethics* and Cicero's *De amicitia*, early modern writers advanced a model of perfect friendship as the consummate human relationship, found in the reciprocal love of two virtuous men, harmonious in their tastes and opinions, whose company stimulates both toward greater virtue and wisdom, and who consider each other, in the Erasmian adage, an *alter ipse*, "another self."[6]

The familiar idea of the friend as another self sometimes involves strikingly embodied imagery of shared desires, habits, and intimacies. The philosopher Michel de Montaigne defines his own same-sex friendship as a 'commixture' of two souls and bodies. Montaigne extols friendship as a force 'which having seized all my will, induced the same to plunge and loose it self in his [friend's], which likewise having seized all his will, brought it to loose and plunge itself in mine, with a mutuall greediness'.[7] The homoerotic 'mutuality' of this passage, observes Jeffrey Masten, manifests in its 'mirroring syntactic structure' and in the sexual connotations of words like 'will', 'plunge', and 'loose'.[8] Will Tosh's analysis of letters written by Nicholas Faunt to Anthony Bacon corroborates the importance of bodily intimacy to Elizabethan figurations of male friendship. Assuring Bacon that a man can give affection 'in the highest measure but to one only' friend, Faunt wonders, in an allusion to the marriage ceremony, 'why I shold not close my hand with yours, in witness of our perfecte and sincere union and band'.[9]

Renaissance homonormativity—the celebrated compatibility between men of equal gender, age, status, education, etc.—must be kept distinct from homonormativity as a contemporary term used to decry the conservatism of gay men and lesbians. Lisa Duggan defines homonormativity as 'a politics that does not contest dominant heteronormative assumptions and institutions, but upholds and sustains them, while promising the possibility of a demobilized gay constituency and a privatized, depoliticized gay culture anchored in domesticity and consumption'.[10] Through the term 'demobilized', which refers to the disbanding of military troops, Duggan describes the desire of some gay people to assimilate into the dominant heterosexual culture instead of resisting its imposition of normative values. Such assimilation typically manifests as the agenda of a gay 'moneyed elite' who value and pursue legal equality, traditional family structures (marriage, monogamy, procreation), a free market economy, and a centrist rejection of progressive social transformation.[11] Regardless of what they do in bed, such a couple could hardly be considered 'queer' in the sense of anti-normative, marginalized, or dissident, although they wouldn't necessarily be immune from anti-gay discrimination.

Although Shannon's 'Renaissance homonormativity' does not describe the same phenomenon as Duggan's contemporary 'homonormativity', the shared vocabulary does suggest that early modern same-sex relations could also be aligned with the dominant social, economic, and political values of the time. If we unthinkingly assume that all same-sex relationships in Shakespeare are 'queer' in the sense of socially or politically transgressive, we risk overlooking the racial, gender, religious, or status hierarchies that lend certain same-sex relationships considerable prestige and power, including the ability to oppress others. For instance, in *The Merchant of Venice*, Antonio both devotedly supports his friend Bassanio and ardently attacks his enemy Shylock, a Jewish moneylender and resident alien. If Antonio's love for Bassanio is facilitated by their commonalities (as white, Christian, Venetian, high-status men), his hatred for Shylock is equally grounded in their racial, religious, national, and economic differences. Because those who participate in same-sex relationships are not necessarily immune from racism, misogyny, or other forms of cultural prejudice, when reading Shakespeare it is important to remain attuned to the ways that Renaissance homonormativity—the cultural valuation of likeness over difference—might resonate with contemporary homonormativity— the social, economic, and ideological conservatism of assimilationist same-sex couples.

In what follows, I begin with an analysis of homonormative friendships in *Romeo and Juliet* and *The Merchant of Venice*. Both plays demonstrate how Renaissance homonormativity might define the special intimacy of a pair of friends while also connecting them to wider male communities. In both plays, homonormative male friendship can accommodate one friend's courtship of women, even though the subsequent tensions between male-male and male-female loyalties must be carefully negotiated. In *The Two Noble Kinsmen*, however, negotiation cannot save the friendship of Palamon and Arcite, cousins who enter into a deadly rivalry to marry the same woman. That these men claim sexual possession over a woman whose romantic feelings seem oriented exclusively toward other women exposes marriage as a dominant social institution that can disrupt and distort the affective bonds between men and between women alike. I conclude the chapter with an analysis of female homonormative friendship in the context of courtship and marriage in *As You Like It*. Although Rosalind's burgeoning desire for Orlando, whom she will eventually marry, might seem to displace her homonormative affection for Celia, Celia's participation in their courtship, as well as Rosalind's homoerotic flirtation with Orlando while disguised as the young man Ganymede, provides further demonstration of the porous boundaries of romantic coupledom.

Romeo and Juliet

When scholars discuss same-sex friendship in *Romeo and Juliet*, they tend to focus on the bond between Romeo and Mercutio, an exuberant wit with a graphic sexual imagination and an evident need for Romeo's affection. Nonetheless, it would be more accurate to see Romeo and Mercutio as part of a friendship 'throuple' with Benvolio. Not only are Romeo and Benvolio cousins—biological kinship, as we shall see, significantly contributes to homonormativity—but we first encounter Romeo as the object of Benvolio's affectionate concern. Benvolio recounts how a 'troubled mind' drew him to walk alone in a sycamore grove, where he spied Romeo, also alone (1.1.113). The sycamore tree, via a pun on 'sick-amour', was associated with melancholy lovers. Melancholy Benvolio appreciates his melancholy cousin's desire for solitude:

> I, measuring his affections by my own—
> Which then most sought where most might not be found,
> Being one too many by my weary self—
> Pursued my humour not pursuing his,
> And gladly shunned who gladly fled from me. (1.1.119–123)

Through rhetorical parallelisms and repetitions—'his affections'/'my own' [affections]; 'pursued my humour'/'not pursuing his' [humour]; 'gladly shunned'/'gladly fled'—Benvolio's language evinces the same kind of 'mirroring syntactic structure' that Masten cites as evidence of homoerotic 'mutuality' in Montaigne's essay on friendship.[12] Although they both seek solitude, Benvolio and Romeo are affectively and spiritually united.

Adopting the role of 'affection's counsellor' to Romeo, Benvolio aims to discover what his friend has been hiding (1.1.140). Romeo's confession of his unrequited love for Rosaline only confirms the cousins' bond:

ROMEO
　Dost thou not laugh?
BENVOLIO　　　　　No, coz, I rather weep.
ROMEO
　Good heart, at what?
BENVOLIO　　　　　At thy good heart's oppression.
ROMEO Why, such is love's transgression.
　Griefs of mine own lie heavy in my breast,
　Which thou wilt propagate to have it pressed
　With more of thine. This love that thou hast shown
　Doth add more grief to too much of mine own.　(1.1.176–182)

Twice, Benvolio completes Romeo's verse lines, a rhetorical device that can convey emotional or intellectual harmony between two speakers. Moreover, when lamenting the suffering of Romeo's 'good heart', Benvolio echoes Romeo's affectionate moniker '[g]ood heart'. For his part, Romeo acknowledges that 'love' can describe the bond between two men as well as between a man and a woman. Benvolio's expression of 'love' and 'grief' only compounds Romeo's own love-fuelled grief. Throughout this scene, Romeo and Benvolio frequently refer to each other as 'cousin', 'coz', or 'my coz', 'coz' being a particularly charged expression of same-sex affiliation (1.1.153, 176, 188).[13] Because Mercutio's garrulous exuberance and witty mockery of Romeo's love-melancholy are so entertaining, it is easy to underestimate the importance of Benvolio's friendship with Romeo.[14] Yet it is Benvolio who first attempts to cure Romeo of melancholy and bring him back into the fold of cheerful male companionship. Urging Romeo to '[e]xamine other beauties' who might be more receptive than Rosaline to his advances, Benvolio advocates against not heteroerotic desire but anti-social melancholy (1.1.221). Benvolio convinces Romeo to attend the Capulet feast, at which he will fatefully meet Juliet, in the hope that he will meet other 'beauties of Verona' who will cure his melancholy (1.2.84).

Like Benvolio, Mercutio counsels Romeo, but where Benvolio gently cajoles, Mercutio boisterously provokes. And whereas Benvolio attributes Romeo's heteroerotic desire to the yearning of his 'heart' and 'eyes', Malvolio relentlessly localizes Romeo's desire in his penis (1.1.176, 1.1.220, 1.2.47). For instance, when Romeo complains that he sinks under the heavy burden of love, Mercutio, personifying love as the boy god Cupid, advises Romeo to transform his emotional passivity into sexual activity:

> And to sink in it should you burden love—
> Too great oppression for a tender thing.
> ROMEO Is love a tender thing? It is too rough,
> Too rude, too boist'rous, and it pricks like thorn.
> MERCUTIO If love be rough with you, be rough with love.
> Prick love for pricking, and you beat love down.   (1.4.23–28)

Because Cupid is sinking Romeo *down* with grief, Mercutio urges him to turn the tables: Romeo should sink his body *into* Cupid's body, roughly burdening or pressing it down. In the explicitly sexual context of this conversation, Mercutio possibly imagines Romeo mounting a 'tender', younger man from behind. When Romeo objects that love is not tender but 'rough', Mercutio urges Romeo to treat love just as roughly, by 'prick[ing]' him in return—that is, by using his own prick to prick or pierce Cupid, possibly through anal sex. Roughly penetrating Cupid would at once satiate Romeo's frustrated sexual desire (for Rosaline) and 'beat down' or punish Cupid for having pricked him with love in the first place. Having an orgasm would also make Romeo's 'prick' come 'down' (deflate). Pragmatically, Mercutio might be advising Romeo to masturbate (beat his erect prick down) in order to relieve his sexual frustration and reestablish a state of emotional and physiological equilibrium. Even this brief exchange indicates Mercutio's investment in Romeo's sex life. Still, that their sexual banter is heard by Benvolio and symbolically mediated by the figure of Cupid places Mercutio and Romeo in a larger network of both real and imagined male intimacies (Figure 1.2).

If Benvolio's strategy for curing Romeo's love-sickness is to encourage him to pursue more receptive women, Mercutio's is to ridicule his idealization of women. For Mercutio, women are to be enjoyed

Figure 1.2 'Is love a tender thing?': love as homonormative likeness. Otto van Veen, *Amorum Emblemata* (Antwerp: [Henrici Swingenij], 1608), page 17. Call#: STC 24627a.5 copy 1, image 63430. Folger Shakespeare Library.

physically, not worshiped as distant goddesses through stale poetic conventions such as the blazon: a catalogue of attractive bodily features, such as starry eyes, golden hair, and cherry lips. Parodying the blazon by indecorously sexualizing it, Mercutio implies that when a male lover praises a woman's upper body, he is actually thinking about her lower body. Mercutio jokes to Benvolio that Romeo, having died from love-sickness, has become a spirit who must be magically 'conjure[d]' (2.1.19). To conjure spirits, a magician would stand inside a protective circle and intone a spell. Mercutio conjures Romeo by naming those parts of Rosaline's body that would attract his interest: her 'bright eyes', 'high forehead', 'scarlet lip', 'fine foot', 'straight leg', 'quivering thigh' and the territories 'that there adjacent lie' (2.1.17–20). When Benvolio warns

Mercutio that his irreverence will anger Romeo, Mercutio defends the
unobjectionable implications of his sexual humour:

> 'Twould anger him
> To raise a spirit in his mistress' circle
> Of some strange nature, letting it there stand
> Till she had laid it and conjured it down.
> That were some spite. My invocation
> Is fair and honest. In his mistress' name,
> I conjure only but to raise up him.   (2.1.23–29)

Mercutio explains that he hasn't 'raise[d]' a 'strange' spirit in Rosaline's
'circle'—that is, made an unknown man erect in Rosaline's hole—until
she 'had laid it' (made him orgasm) and 'conjured it down' (deflated his
erection). Instead, by conjuring Rosaline's body parts, Mercutio intends
only to 'raise up' Romeo—make him appear and make him erect.
Mercutio seems to imagine his role in Romeo's sexual encounter with
Rosaline as a kind of 'fluffer': in the pornography industry, a person
who is responsible for getting a male actor ready for a scene by making
him erect. Whatever the exact nature of his fantasy, Mercutio displays
'a personal investment' in Romeo's erection.[15]

Though most readings of Mercutio's conjuration analogy assume
that he is referring to penile-vaginal intercourse between Romeo
and Rosaline, when speaking of Mercutio it is unwise to limit sexual
possibilities to standard reproductive acts. Mercutio's references to
Rosaline's 'circle' and to the regions 'adjacent' to her thigh might well
encompass the anus as well as the vagina. Mercutio in fact goes on to
make a joke about Romeo's supposed desire for anal sex with Rosaline:

> Now he will sit under a medlar tree
> And wish his mistress were that kind of fruit
> As maids call medlars when they laugh alone.
> O Romeo, that she were, O that she were
> An open-arse, and thou a popp'rin' pear.   (2.1.34–38)

Benvolio, we will recall, first encounters Romeo nursing his love-
melancholy in a sycamore grove. Mercutio instead imagines Romeo
sitting under a medlar tree fantasizing about penetrating Rosaline:
'popp'rin'' pears are from Poperinge, a town in Flanders, with a pun on

'pop-her-in' or 'pop it in her'. The round shape and large hole of the medlar fruit (echoed in Mercutio's two 'O' interjections) made it a common slang term both for the vagina and the anus, as the term 'open-arse' indicates.[16] Mercutio shares this fantasy of male-female penetrative sex with Benvolio, making him part of this queer tangle of male and female bodies. In a further entanglement of bodies and desires, Mercutio attributes the slang term 'open arse' to 'maids' who 'laugh alone' with each other when sharing titillating sexual knowledge, suggesting young women's erotic pleasure with both men and each other. Finally, the typical lover's sigh—'O Romeo'—that Mercutio mockingly associates with Rosaline's presumed refusal of anal sex is repeated by Juliet when she laments that her beloved comes from an enemy clan: 'O Romeo, Romeo, wherefore art thou Romeo?' (2.1.75).

Through jokes about anal sex, Mercutio reveals a preoccupation with male-male intimacies. Returning to the subject of Cupid from his earlier conversation with Romeo, Mercutio complains to Benvolio that Romeo's heart has been cleft 'with the blind bow-boy's butt-shaft' (2.3.14–15). A 'butt-shaft' is a blunted arrow used for target practice; however, 'butt' could also refer to an animal's buttock used for meat.[17] Although the *OED* doesn't record the usage of 'butt' for a human buttock until 1675, it seems reasonable that, given Mercutio's penchant for anal humour, Shakespeare's audiences could have imagined Cupid's 'butt-shaft' as a shaft that pierced Romeo's behind as well as his heart.[18] Shortly thereafter, Romeo and Mercutio engage in an extended battle of wits that generates sexual innuendoes from words such as 'business' (sex), 'case' (vagina, but also possibly anus), 'flower' (vulva), to 'pink' (to prick), and 'pump' (penis). Mercutio's portrait of love as a fool who seeks to 'hide his bauble in a hole' might also allude to anal sex (2.3.79–80). Court fools sometimes carried a 'bauble': a staff capped with a small fool's head or stuffed pouch. When Benvolio urges Mercutio to desist from bawdy talk, he objects, 'Thou desirest me to stop in my tale against the hair' (2.3.82–83). It's easy to visualize a 'tail' (or penis, in the sense of an appendage hanging near the anus) lying against the 'hair' of a 'hole'—a vagina or possibly an anus, since 'against the hair' means 'contrary to the natural set of a thing'.[19]

I have avoided using the word 'sodomy' to describe Mercutio's evident interest in anal eroticism. As the next chapter will detail, sodomy was a term used to demonize non-reproductive sex—especially male-male anal intercourse—as the source and symptom of social, moral, theological, and political disorder. Despite the recognition that men and women could have anal sex, it was typically seen as an 'unnatural' or 'preposterous' accommodation to the lack of a vagina in a sexual encounter between two men. As we have seen, Mercutio evokes both male-female and male-male anal sex as a way to ridicule and disrupt poetic conventions for idealizing women and for personifying love as Cupid, but he clearly regards anal sex as a source of wit and pleasure. He does not use the condemnatory rhetoric of sodomy for anal sex because he does not seem to consider it an unnatural or unholy practice—the closest he comes to this dominant cultural perspective is to joke about his tale (story)/tail (penis) lying 'against the hair', or contrary to nature.

Romeo's enemy Tybalt does, however, associate Mercutio with the social disorder of sodomy. When Tybalt accuses Mercutio of 'consort[ing]' with Romeo, Mercutio takes the term as an insulting reference to 'minstrels', since a consort can mean a group of musicians (3.1.40). A nobleman, Mercutio objects to being associated with common wage-earning musicians. To consort, however, also meant 'to be a consort or spouse to, to espouse; to have sexual commerce with'.[20] As Nicholas Radel argues, Tybalt seemingly evokes this sense of the word 'to turn the normally erotic discourse of friendship into a discourse of sodomy'.[21] Although Tybalt's jibe seems a strategic denigration of the friendship of his enemy, it also suggests that the same-sex intimacy between Mercutio and Romeo is public knowledge: they are a recognizable 'couple' in Verona. Ironically, Mercutio's tragic decision to duel Tybalt on Romeo's behalf derives from the fact that whereas the intimacy between Romeo and Mercutio is common knowledge, the marriage between Romeo and Juliet—which makes Romeo and Tybalt cousins—is still a secret.

The Merchant of Venice

Whereas Mercutio, Romeo, and Benvolio form a kind of friendship thruple, in *The Merchant of Venice* Bassanio and Antonio form a distinct dyad within a larger network of friends. The special status of their bond establishes Antonio, Bassanio's longtime friend, and Portia, Bassanio's new wife, as structurally equivalent partners in relation to him. Hence the 'conjunction of marriage and friendship' in *The Merchant of Venice* 'belies either union's restriction to a dyad'.[22] If *Romeo and Juliet* features an all-male thruple, *The Merchant of Venice* features a more fraught male-male-female thruple.

The opening conversation among Antonio and the often paired (and similarly named) Salerio and Solanio, another distinct couple, establishes the dynamics of male friendship in Venice. Antonio's mysterious sadness distances him from the Venetian friendship group's 'affective ethos', which prioritizes good cheer and wit.[23] Whereas Benvolio draws on a heartfelt bond to console and advise Romeo, Salerio and Solanio seem more interested in 'verbal games of male comradery' than in genuinely engaging with Antonio's emotions.[24] Consider Salerio's baroque account of Antonio's anxiety:

> Your mind is tossing on the ocean,
> There where your argosies with portly sail,
> Like signors and rich burghers on the flood—
> Or as it were the pageants of the sea—
> Do overpeer the petty traffickers
> That curtsy to them, do them reverence,
> As they fly by them with their woven wings.   (1.1.8–14)

Tossing his mind on an imaginary ocean, Salerio crafts an ornate tableau in which ships enact Venetian social rituals: elite argosies 'overpeer' (meaning both 'peer over' and 'outrank') petty merchant boats, who reverently 'curtsy' to them. This fantastic 'pageant' has little to do with Antonio's particular worries. Even as they show concern over Antonio's sadness, Salerio and Solanio seem motivated mainly by the pleasure of rhetorical performance, as Salerio's clever wordplay suggests: 'Shall I have the thought / To think on this, and shall I lack the thought / That such a thing bechanced would make me sad?' (1.1.36–38). The highly patterned forms and sounds of 'thought'/'think'/'thing' and '[s]hall I have / shall I lack' point to language play more than emotional empathy.

This opening conversation establishes both the affordances and the limitations of homonormative friendship in *The Merchant of Venice*. The social and emotional alignment of friends—'It wearies me, you say it wearies you', Antonio remarks of his sadness (1.1.2)—facilitates identifications, but these might go no deeper than a superficial and public performance of intimacy. We observe a carefully negotiated performance of this intimacy when Salerio and Solanio ceremoniously leave Antonio to the care of his 'worthier friends' Bassanio, Gratiano, and Lorenzo (1.1.61):

> SALERIO I would have stayed till I had made you merry
> If worthier friends had not prevented me.
> ANTONIO Your worth is very dear in my regard.
> I take it your own business calls on you,
> And you embrace th'occasion to depart.
> SALERIO Good morrow, my good lords.
> BASSANIO Good signiors both, when shall we laugh? Say, when?
> You grow exceeding strange. Must it be so? (1.1.60–67)

This short exchange is bookended by the Venetians' frequently reiterated expectation that friends should be 'merry' and 'laugh'. Solanio judges the constitutionally sad Antonio to be one of Nature's 'strange fellows', and Graziano warns Antonio not to use sadness to earn a reputation as a serious man, stiff and still 'like his grandsire cut in alabaster' on a funeral monument (1.1.51, 84). Complaining that Salerio and Solanio have grown 'strange', or unsociable, Bassanio asks when they will again 'laugh' together. Later, Bassanio encourages Graziano to 'put on / Your boldest suit of mirth, for we have friends / That purpose merriment' (2.3.182–184). According to the dominant ethos of Venetian sociability, then, to absent oneself from amicable mirth is to be 'strange' or queer.[25]

Salerio's inclination to judge friends according to their relative 'worth' recognizes the status and financial differentials that inform male-male intimacies in Venice. Bassanio's relationship with his 'dearest friend' Antonio is characterized by heightened emotional and financial obligations (3.2.291). 'To you, Antonio, / I owe the most in money and in love', Bassanio admits, right before deepening this double indebtedness by requesting a loan that will allow him to travel to Belmont, where he hopes successfully to court and marry the heiress Portia (1.1.130–131). Adopting a comparable language of heightened intimacy, Antonio responds, 'My purse, my person, my extremest means / Lie all unlocked to your occasions' (1.1.138–139). It is far easier to understand the offer of an unlocked purse than the offer of an unlocked 'person'. Antonio's image of an open body, or of a body with open orifices, suggests either a history of or a yearning for sexual intimacy, particularly since 'purse' was a common metaphor for the scrotum. Antonio's repeated 'my' stresses the exclusivity of his offer of money and body to Bassanio alone.

At the same time, Antonio's loan not only enables Bassanio's access to Portia as a potential spouse, it also entangles the friends in an emotional and financial bond with a 'stranger': the Jewish moneylender Shylock (3.3.27). Although homonormative Venetian friendship can tolerate a degree of affective strangeness, to be 'strange' in the early modern sense of 'foreign' fully disqualifies Shylock, a Jew and resident 'alien' of Venice, from local friendship networks (3.3.27, 4.1.344). We might recall Thomas Elyot's description of the friends Titus and Gisippus as identical in 'color of visage'. As Geraldine Heng has argued, premodern European Christians treated Jews not only as a religious minority but also as a distinct race.[26] Despite being incapable of homonormative friendship with Venetian Christians, Shylock claims that his refusal to charge Antonio interest on the loan or to take a financial penalty should Antonio default attests to his desire to 'be friends' and have his 'love' (1.3.133). In the spirit of what Venetians might appreciate as 'merry sport', Shylock offers to take a pound of Antonio's 'fair flesh' from 'what part of [his] body pleaseth [him]' in the event of a default (1.3.141, 146–147). As we later discover, the bond stipulates that the pound of flesh is to be cut from Antonio's breast. If Antonio demonstrates friendship by unlocking his body to Bassanio's needs, Shylock demonstrates friendship through a written instrument that would literally 'unlock' Antonio's body and 'procure its heart'.[27]

Here and elsewhere, *The Merchant of Venice* draws upon an invidious distinction between a supposed Jewish literalism and Christian spiritualism. In Romans 2:29, St. Paul writes that 'circumcision *is that* of the heart, in the spirit, *and* not in the letter': Christian faith in God depends not on literal circumcision of the penis as in Jewish custom, which is 'outward in the flesh', but on inner, spiritual belief (*KJV* Romans 2:28–29). Through the language of the bond, Shylock treacherously inscribes himself into the networks of Venetian friendship from which he is racially excluded. Antonio interprets Shylock's duplicitous offer to 'extend…friendship' to him as a sincere desire to become more like him: 'The Hebrew will turn Christian; he grows kind' (1.3.164, 174). To 'turn Christian' is to convert from Judaism; to 'grow kind' is to become 'akin' to, as if Shylock were able to erase the racial distinction of Jewishness and achieve a 'natural' homonormative likeness with Christian men.

In the event, Shylock's bond signifies a turn not from Judaism to Christianity, however, but from a fantasized to an actual, legal, domination of Antonio's body. Having been subjected to Antonio's habitual abuse, Shylock fantasizes about immobilizing and consuming Antonio's body: 'If I can catch him once upon the hip / I will feed fat the ancient grudge I bear him' (1.3.41–42). To 'catch on the hip' is a wrestling term for throwing down an opponent; to 'feed fat' a grudge represents revenge as devouring, as if Shylock were fattening up Antonio in order to make his death more palatable. Through the possible meaning of 'flesh' as 'penis', the bond's claim to a pound of flesh alludes to the Jewish practice of circumcision, here conflated with castration.[28] In *Romeo and Juliet*, as we have seen, Mercutio displays an interest in what Romeo has been doing (or wants to do) with his penis; Shylock's interest in Antonio's penis takes the racialized form of either a conversion fantasy—circumcising Antonio to turn him into a Jew—or a castration fantasy—turning him into a eunuch. Shylock's desire to 'feed fat' his grudge echoes in his insistence that he could not literally sell Antonio's pound of flesh for human consumption, since human flesh is not as 'estimable' for food as that of 'muttons, beeves, or goats' (1.3.162–163). By comparing Antonio's value to that of edible animals, Shylock debases the competitive measures of worth that the Venetians use to evaluate male intimacies: judgments about which friends are 'worthier' than others, which behaviours are normative or 'strange', or which debts one owes to whom.

Just as Shylock's new intimacy with Antonio alters the equilibrium of Antonio's and Bassanio's homonormative friendship, so too does Portia's new intimacy with Bassanio. Portia's generic description of friendship is usually taken as an accurate, unbiased account of the relationship between Bassanio and Antonio. For instance, Ian Smith describes Portia's reference to the 'proportion / Of lineaments' between friends as an 'emphatic attention' to Bassanio's and Antonio's 'similarity in physical build and appearance', which 'reifies the physical bonds of whiteness that are manifest in the beauty of the men's sinuous muscularity'.[29] Yet even if Portia rightly assumes that her husband's close friend is white, how could she comment on the similarity between Bassanio's physique and that of a man she has never seen? A production of the play might even emphasize the physical disparities between the men by modelling them after another famous pair of Shakespearean friends: the fat, older, John Falstaff and the lean, younger, Prince Hal from *1 Henry IV*.[30]

It might be more productive to understand Portia as citing a familiar *theory* of friendship in the hopes of capturing the dynamics of her new husband's bond to a 'bosom lover' whose existence has just come to her notice:

> For in companions
> That do converse and waste the time together,
> Whose souls do bear an equal yoke of love,
> There must be needs a like proportion
> Of lineaments, of manners, and of spirit,
> Which makes me think that this Antonio,
> Being the bosom lover of my lord,
> Must needs be like my lord. If it be so,
> How little is the cost I have bestowed
> In purchasing the semblance of my soul
> From out the state of hellish cruelty.   (3.4.11–21)

Portia yearns to know what 'this Antonio', whom she has never met, '[m]ust needs be like', because she has an interest in comprehending the nature of her husband's involvement with his dearest friend and financial backer. Laurie Shannon argues that Portia's 'female "gaze" at male friendship discourse' represents her attempt to elevate her status from Bassanio's wife (theoretically his inferior) to his friend (theoretically his equal)—in other words, to establish herself as like Bassanio in gender.[31] Shannon stresses Portia's self-serving calculation in identifying Antonio as the 'semblance of [her] soul', which makes him the image of both her soulmate (Bassanio) and of her own soul (herself). In short, Portia 'inserts herself into the very "likeness" that she concludes pertains between Bassanio and Antonio', fashioning the three of them into a kind of homonormative thruple of soulmates.[32]

Nonetheless, the 'likeness' that Portia projects onto Bassanio and Antonio through her citation of male friendship discourse is more speculative than descriptive. As the articulation of an ideal, it maps unevenly onto what the play shows us of this central friendship. To the degree that Bassanio and Antonio 'converse and waste the time together', they have not indulged the kind of leisurely pleasure in each other's company that Portia seems to imagine as typical of friends. Rather, they have had a single weighty conversation about Bassanio's financial indebtedness to Antonio. Whereas Portia might be correct (or not—who really knows?) in positing that their 'souls' are bound in an 'equal yoke of love'—a phrase that appropriates the familiar early modern Protestant language of spouses as 'yokefellows' (Figure 1.3)—she does not acknowledge the more certain truth that they are connected unequally and materially through Antonio's generosity and Bassanio's neediness (*OED*, yoke *n.*, 12). Likewise, although Portia implies that Bassanio and Antonio are equally 'bosom lover[s]', Antonio has literally staked his bosom—the pound of flesh nearest his heart—as collateral to finance Bassanio's voyage to win Portia. Finally, Portia's claim that the 'spirits' ('character, disposition, or outlook') of Antonio and Bassanio are in 'like proportion' seems mistaken, since Antonio's melancholy starkly contrasts with Bassanio's mirthfulness.[33]

During the trial scene, in which Portia is disguised as the lawyer Balthazar, she confronts Bassanio's resistance to her plan to appropriate the 'likeness' of friends in order to achieve greater intimacy and equality with her husband. Believing that he is about to die, Antonio eulogizes himself as Bassanio's only true lover:

> Commend me to your honourable wife.
> Tell her the process of Antonio's end.
> Say how I loved you. Speak me fair in death,
> And when the tale is told, bid her be judge
> Whether Bassanio had not once a love.   (4.1.268–272)

To speak Antonio 'fair in death' is both to speak fairly or impartially of the dead, but also, in line with the play's racial discourse, to praise his appearance and behaviour at the moment of death as 'fair' in the sense of 'admirable', 'desirable', or 'noble'.[34] Ultimately, Bassanio's 'tale' would convey to Portia that Antonio loved Bassanio more than she did or perhaps ever could. Far from challenging Antonio's invidious distinction between friend and wife, Bassanio endorses it:

Figure 1.3 'An equal yoke of love': spouses as yokefellows. 'The Happy Marriage, the Unhappy Marriage' (London: [John King], mid to late seventeenth century century?). Call#: ART File S528t1 no.64 parts 1–2, image 29337. Folger Shakespeare Library.

> Antonio, I am married to a wife
> Which is as dear to me as life itself,
> But life itself, my wife, and all the world
> Are not with me esteemed above thy life.
> I would lose all, ay, sacrifice them all
> Here to this devil, to deliver you.   (4.1.277–282)

In another example of the comparative valuation that characterizes Venetian love and finance, Bassanio 'esteems' Portia as his life, but esteems his life (and the world) less than Antonio's life. Bassanio's double rhyme of 'my wife' and 'thy life' pits Portia against Antonio as the lesser partner. Acknowledging that she has not achieved equal friendship with her husband, Portia ironically complains in an aside that Bassanio's wife would be unhappy to hear him offer to sacrifice her for Antonio. Graziano's eagerness to sacrifice *his* new wife, Nerissa, to save Antonio reasserts the proclivity of Venetian men to esteem friends above wives—and once more positions Antonio and Bassanio not as a unique dyad but as two closely connected nodes in a larger friendship network. John Garrison argues that, in Belmont, Graziano serves as Bassanio's closest friend; Bassanio must henceforth 'divide his loyalties between Graziano and Antonio'.[35]

   In the end, Portia resourcefully turns Bassanio's valuation of friendship over marriage to her advantage. Bassanio does not have to sacrifice his wife to save his friend because Portia (as Balthazar) saves Antonio through her rhetorical skill. When Bassanio urges Balthazar to accept a gift as a token of gratitude, Portia requests the ring that she had given Bassanio upon their betrothal, and which he faithfully wears on his finger. At that time, Portia had stipulated that if Bassanio ever lost the ring, it would signify the demise of his love, with the implication that Portia would then be freed from the expectation of wifely obedience. Although Bassanio initially refuses Balthazar's request, Antonio convinces him to relent: 'Let his deservings and my love withal / Be valued 'gainst your wife's commandëment' (4.1.446–447). Once again, Antonio asserts the greater 'value' of male-male bonds over the marital bond; once again, Bassanio endorses his friend's perspective. And once again, Graziano, who has also received a betrothal ring from Nerissa, imitates his friend by giving his ring to the 'lawyer's clerk', played by Nerissa. Back in Belmont, when Portia pretends to discover Bassanio's loss of the ring, she vows to withhold sex until the ring is recovered. Through its travels among various male and female characters, the ring, as Karen Newman argues, accumulates several meanings, including as a visual reference to the 'female genitalia' and anus.[36] Portia threatens that since Bassanio has given his ring to a man—with the implication of male-male sex via the association of ring with anus—she will give her 'ring' (vagina? anus?) to the same man.[37] Portia turns to her advantage Bassanio's valuation of other men (Antonio, Balthazar) over his wife by claiming an equivalent right to have sex with another man (Balthazar) instead of her husband.

Portia's seizure of extraordinary freedom from the expectation of marital chastity unleashes queer sexual possibilities, revealing how marriages 'are not truly dyadic'.[38] Newman observes that Portia 'imaginatively express[es] her own sexuality by cuckolding her husband with Balthazar'.[39] Imagining a sexual encounter with her male alter ego, Portia turns auto-eroticism into a transgressive act of adultery and revenge. Portia's strategy for returning the ring (which she had received from Bassanio as Balthazar) to Bassanio queerly reiterates and re-genders the contract by which Antonio had served as Bassanio's 'surety' for Shylock (5.1.253).[40] Portia hands the ring to Antonio, who hands it to Bassanio as the sign of a three-way contract among them. Whereas Antonio had once bound his 'body' to (Jewish) Shylock for Bassanio's material benefit, he now binds his 'soul' to (Christian) Portia to guarantee Bassanio's spiritual fidelity to her (5.1.258, 251). Hence, if Bassanio ever 'break[s] faith' with Portia, he will damn his Christian friend's soul (5.1.252). Because in Shakespeare's time Portia would have been played by a young male actor, a multitude of possible sexual configurations—Portia with Bassanio, Bassanio with Balthazar, Portia with Balthazar, Portia with Bassanio and Antonio—would have been presented to an audience through the staged bodies of men and boys. As Will Stockton remarks, the circulation of the ring 'confounds rather than clarifies the differences between the bodies of Portia, Balthasar, and the boy actor playing them'. The result produces 'a conjunction of marriage and friendship that belies either union's restriction to a dyad'.[41]

The conclusion of *The Merchant of Venice* thus appears to incorporate homoerotic friendship into harmonious martial relations, despite some interpretations that hold that Antonio loses Bassanio to Portia or is excluded from the happy ending. As Julie Crawford argues, marriage in Shakespearean comedy can be a mechanism for ensuring the continuation of same-sex bonds, not (just) for foreclosing such bonds.[42] It is possible to imagine Antonio and Bassanio retaining their intimate friendship, with Antonio joining his friend's new household in Belmont or returning with him to Venice for business or pleasure. In the play's final moments, moreover, the husbands imagine their first night of conjugal sex as same-sex encounters. Newly informed of their wives' male alter-egos, Bassanio and Graziano rejoice that the women had not received their rings through a sexual encounter with the lawyer and his clerk (the imagined path of the rings before this revelation was from wife to husband to lawyer/clerk to adulterous wife). When Bassanio teases Portia, 'Sweet doctor, you shall be my bedfellow. / When I am absent, then lie with my wife' (5.1.283–284), he imagines conjugal intimacy as sex between two men (Bassanio and Balthazar), or perhaps, via kinky role play, between a conventionally gendered man (Bassanio) and a woman pretending to be a man (Portia as Balthazar). Bassanio also hints at a benevolent cuckold fantasy when he invites Balthazar to lie with his wife during his absence. Graziano concludes the play with a similarly queer fantasy:

> But were the day come, I should wish it dark
> Till I were couching with the doctor's clerk.
> Well, while I live I'll fear no other thing
> So sore as keeping safe Nerissa's ring. (5.1.303–306)

In declaring the need to 'keep safe' Nerissa's 'ring', Graziano acknowledges the persistent threat of cuckoldry, since Nerissa might one day give her 'ring' to another man. Like Bassanio, moreover, Graziano jokes about having sex with his wife's male alter ego, thus evoking the 'ring' as anus, which might become 'sore' from sexual penetration.[43] Whether he is imagining the ring as a material or bodily property of the clerk, his wife, or himself, Graziano appears to recognize that marital sexuality might queerly extend beyond the couple and beyond reproductive sex.

The Two Noble Kinsmen

Like *Romeo and Juliet* and *The Merchant of Venice*, *The Two Noble Kinsmen* situates male friendship in an urban environment, the ancient Greek city of Thebes; unlike those plays, it centres on two friends and cousins, Palamon and Arcite, who find the debaucheries of city life inimical to their cultivation of honour. Arcite's initial description of Palamon and himself as 'unhardened in / The crimes of nature' vaguely glances at Sodom, the city that God destroyed because its citizens practiced 'unnatural' sex, among other sins (1.2.2–3).[44] Palamon defines Theben debauchery as a kind of perverted homonormativity: a contagious mirroring of unmanly behaviours. Bound exclusively to each other by 'love', 'blood', and 'faith', the cousins are not 'bound' to 'follow' the ridiculous gestures, speech, fashions, or hairstyles of the urban fops who surround them (1.2.1,46, 49–50). By refusing to imitate prominent men, however, Palamon and Arcite become queer 'strangers' in Thebes—unassimilated and alienated outsiders, like Shylock in Venice—despite their elevated status as the king's nephews (1.2.55, 41).

Captured and imprisoned in Athens by Duke Theseus following an attack on Thebes, Palamon and Arcite escape the dilemma of being queer strangers at home only to find themselves subjected to queer time in a strange land. J. Jack Halberstam defines queer time as 'the potentiality of a life unscripted by the conventions of family, inheritance, and child rearing'.[45] Queer time makes possible futures that 'can be imagined according to logics that lie outside of those paradigmatic markers of life experience—namely, birth, marriage, reproduction, and death'.[46] Pushing against conventional 'lifecycle narratives' such as the belief that an experimental adolescent homoeroticism naturally gives way to mature heterosexual love, marriage, and sexual reproduction, queer temporality also evades the restrictive heteronormative options for 'growing up' that can leave queer children feeling that there is 'simply nowhere to grow, feeling a frightening, heightened sense of growing toward a question mark'.[47] Lee Edelman argues influentially in *No Future: Queer Theory and the Death Drive* that 'reproductive futurism'— the social imperative to marry and reproduce children, so as to ensure the future of the species—imparts to heterosexuality a temporal dimension as a social norm. Although heterosexuality was unavailable to early moderns as a concept or norm, the high valuation placed on having children as a means of reproducing the social and religious order corresponds to the ideology of 'reproductive futurism'. God instituted marriage, according to the Church of England's Book of Common Prayer, for the raising of legitimately born Christian children. Thus we can speak of queer temporality in Shakespeare as the imagining of futures that might not involve marriage or children.

Palamon and Arcite anticipate precisely this kind of queer future, in which perpetual imprisonment will ruin their youthful 'graces' (physical 'attractiveness' or 'charm') before they can secure wives[48]:

> Here we are,
> And here the graces of our youths must wither,
> Like a too-timely spring. Here age must find us
> And, which is heaviest, Palamon, unmarried—
> The sweet embraces of a loving wife
> Loaden with kisses, armed with thousand Cupids,
> Shall never clasp our necks; no issue know us.
> No figures of ourselves shall we e'er see
> To glad our age... (2.2.26–33)

In Thebes, Palamon and Arcite refused to mirror inauthentic fops; in Athens, they will never have children who would offer them authentically mirrored 'figures of [them]selves' to cheer their old age. The queer temporality of a foreclosed future is particularly pronounced in the image of the 'too-timely' or prematurely early spring that treacherously encourages flowers to bloom, only to 'wither' them with frost. Reiterating the word 'here' several times in his complaint, Arcite pits unnaturally static place against naturally fluid time, as the cousins' constriction within prison will freeze time in a perpetual, barren winter: 'The vine shall grow, but we shall never see it; / Summer shall come, and with her all delights, / But dead-cold winter must inhabit here still' (2.2.43–45). 'We shall know nothing here but one another', Arcite concludes, lamenting the queer sterility of a friendship reduced to the bare presence of two people—an impossibility in the vibrant male communities of *Romeo and Juliet* and *The Merchant of Venice* (2.2.40).

Nonetheless, Palamon and Arcite believe that homonormative love has the power to redeem the social death of perpetual imprisonment. Knowing 'nothing' but 'one another', they will avoid 'liberty and common conversation', which 'like women', might '[w]oo' them from 'the ways of honour' (2.2.40, 73–76). 'Conversation' often meant sexual intimacy in this period.[49] For the cousins, women are either chaste wives who would reproduce their mirror images or sexual temptresses who would corrupt their honour. Although without wives Palamon and Arcite cannot biologically reproduce, they can still 'endless[ly]' reproduce their mutual love through homonormative 'conversation':

> ARCITE
>   And being here thus together,
>   We are an endless mine to one another,
>   We are one another's wife, ever begetting
>   New births of love; we are father, friends, acquaintance;
>   We are in one another, families—
>   I am your heir, and you are mine; this place
>   Is our inheritance.   (2.2.78–84)

In this vision of perfectly reciprocal love, each friend serves as husband and as wife to the other, as well as in all other familial roles.[50] Although their 'births of love' will be purely spiritual, each friend will alternate as impregnating husband and impregnated wife. They themselves will be the 'heirs' generated by these queerly metaphorical male pregnancies. As such, 'I am your heir, and you are mine' slides into the implied 'I am yours, and you are mine', and 'I am you, and you are me'.

In a pointed irony, the very homonormativity that Palamon and Arcite celebrate also tears them apart. Spying Emilia in the garden beneath their prison window, first Palamon and then Arcite declares his love for her and claims her as his wife. Justifying his desire for Emilia on the basis of their shared identity, Arcite asks Palamon, 'Am I not liable to those affections / …my friend shall suffer?' (2.2.191–192). The bitter division that ensues suggests that despite their familiarity with the rhetoric of virtuous friendship, Palamon and Arcite have not achieved a 'maturely seasoned' and temperate love for each other (1.3.56). Robert Stretter's claim that their fragile friendship 'disintegrates in the face of an inexorable drive toward marriage and procreation' problematically implies that homoerotic and heteroerotic desires are mutually exclusive or inimical.[51] Yet the cousins' later reminiscences about the 'wenches [they] have known' in Thebes reveal that they have already had casual sexual experiences with women (3.3.29). Palamon even teases Arcite for having gotten a young woman pregnant. In other words, the cousins' homonormative affection for each other had once comfortably existed alongside—and might have even been fostered by—sexual desires for women. What divides the cousins is not the advent of an 'inexorable' heteroerotic 'drive', but a 'familiar Renaissance view of love as subordination to dangerous passion, a weak succumbing to a form of madness', which their precarious friendship cannot endure.[52]

In addition to Arcite and Palamon, *The Two Noble Kinsmen* features a pair of life-long male friends, Theseus and Pirithous, who belie any assumption that 'mature' adulthood requires the abandonment of same-sex bonds. Theseus' and Pirithous' friendship 'coexists with the obligations of marriage and family by taking precedence over them'.[53] In *The Merchant of Venice*, as we saw, Portia can only speculate about the likeness between Bassanio and his friend, whom she has never met. By contrast, Hippolyta is aware that her new husband Theseus has long slept, traveled, and warred with Pirithous, yoked by a 'knot of love, / Tied, weaved, entangled with so true, so long, / And with a finger of so deep a cunning' that it can never be 'undone' (1.3.41–44). Because 'knot' might allude to the wedding bond, the 'virgin knot' of maidenhead, or the sexual intertwining of bodies, Jeffrey Masten describes this friendship—at least from Hippolyta's perspective—as paradoxically 'sexualized and virginal, consummated and impenetrable'.[54] What seems clear, however, is the sincerity and permanency of the friends' 'knot of love', which prompts Hippolyta to wonder if Theseus could determine whom 'he loves best', Pirithous or herself (1.3.47). Nonetheless, she simply assures herself that she 'more than his Pirithous possess / The high throne in his heart' (1.3.96–97). Unlike *The Merchant of Venice*, *The Two Noble Kinsmen* centres not on the rivalry between a friend and a wife, but on the animosity between two friends who claim the right to marry the same woman.

The breakdown of the cousins' friendship is especially disquieting because the woman they desire to marry appears to be emotionally and erotically oriented exclusively toward other women. Emilia and her sister Hippolyta are both Amazons, a legendary race of exotic (non-European) warrior women who lived without men—in 'some accounts crippling, castrat[ing]', and murder[ing]' men as well—and who had reproductive sex only to replenish their numbers.[55] Although Valerie Traub explains that early moderns did not generally interpret Amazons as 'erotic separatists', she cites a courtly masque of 1618 in which 'Brave Amazonian dames' reject men: 'Alas, would it might be, / women could live & lie with one another!'[56] Whereas Douglas Bruster describes this passage as a 'rare positive fantasy of female homoerotic practice', Traub stresses its lament for the 'impossibility of such a world'.[57] In *The Two Noble Kinsmen*, however, what renders

Amazonian independence 'impossible' is a specific political event: Theseus has conquered Hippolyta and Emilia, rendering them 'captives, prisoners of war, lives to be disposed of by decrees'.[58] Laurie Shannon rightly insists that under such circumstances—in which Theseus marries Hippolyta, an enemy combatant, and forces Emilia to marry against her inclination—'love and sexuality' are deeply political concerns.[59]

In Shannon's apt description, Emilia 'provides a fully developed articulation of an Amazonian position' by relating to Hippolyta her exclusive devotion to her 'playfellow' Flavina, who died at age eleven.[60] Their love was in harmony with nature, free from calculation or justification: 'Love for we did, and like the elements, / That know not what, nor why, yet do effect / Rare issues by their operance' (1.3.61). Despite its cosmic resonance, the girls' affection manifested in simple acts of homonormative imitation:

> What she liked
> Was then of me approved; what not, condemned—
> No more arraignment. The flower that I would pluck
> And put between my breasts—O then but beginning
> To swell about the blossom—she would long
> Till she had such another, and commit it
> To the like innocent cradle ... (1.3.64–70)

The homoeroticism of this passage is conveyed in part by its cascading mirroring: 'Not only are the two girls alike, but their breasts, each one like its counterpart and each pair of breasts like the other girl's, are likened to the flowers that they pluck.'[61] 'Bosom' is comprised within the word 'blossom' as analogously 'swell[ing]' manifestations of natural fertility. As Douglas Bruster observes, Emilia's imagery is 'remarkably sensual, despite—or perhaps because of—her insistence on the word "innocent"...'[62]

Innocence and female same-sex intimacy were not necessarily incompatible in a culture that defined female sexuality primarily in terms of reproductive sex with men. Because touching and kissing could not lead to pregnancy, they might be considered harmless 'play'. Thomas Heywood's mythological play *The Golden Age* represents such chaste same-sex play in the story of Callisto, a young woman who rejects 'all love with men' and joins the all-female community of Diana, the Roman goddess of virginity.[63] When Diana asks one of her nymphs to assign Callisto a 'Cabin-fellow' to 'sleep by her', she responds that all the nymphs are already 'coupled / And twin'd in love, and hardly is there any / That will be won to change her bed-fellow' (D4v). 'Twin'd in love' suggests two homonormatively *twinned* bodies that are *twined* (intertwined) in bed. However, when Jupiter arrives disguised as a virgin in order to seduce Callisto, Diana's admiration of the 'largeness' of this 'manly lass' implies that not all female-female bonds need be homonormative, since one woman might be more aggressive, experienced, or powerful than another (E1r).[64] Once alone with Callisto, the disguised Jupiter takes advantage of his greater knowledge and size, even as he attempts to assuage Callisto's fears through the rhetoric of homonormative similarity. Fondling and kissing Callisto, he assures her that it is harmless for two women to 'kiss and play': 'So a woman with a woman may'; 'My sweet, lie still, for we are far from men'; 'You need not blush to let a woman see' (E2v). Particularly significant is Jupiter's claim that sex between women is inconsequential because it cannot lead to shameful pregnancy: 'We maids may wish much, but can nothing do' (E3r). Frustrated by Callisto's resistance to his same-sex 'play', Jupiter finally reveals his true male self and rapes her.

Unlike Jupiter's violently masculinist appropriation of same-sex innocence, Emilia recalls a reciprocal and consensual same-sex love that proves the value of female friendship. According to Emilia, the 'end'—meaning both conclusion and rhetorical purpose—of her tale is the acknowledgment that 'true love 'tween maid and maid may be / More than in sex dividual' (1.3.81–82). Love between two women, in other words, may be 'more'—passionate? true? equal? enduring?— than love between the 'dividual' sexes, men and women:

> HIPPOLYTA   You're out of breath,
>   And this high-speeded pace is but to say
>   That you shall never—like the maid Flavina—
>   Love any that's called man.
> EMILIA   I am sure I shall not.
> HIPPOLYTA   Now, alack, weak sister,
>   I must no more believe thee in this point—
>   Though in't I know thou dost believe thyself—
>   Than I will trust a sickly appetite,
>   That loathes even as it longs. But sure, my sister,

> If I were ripe for your persuasion, you
> Have said enough to shake me from the arm
> Of the all-noble Theseus.... (1.3.82–94)

Hippolyta claims that, mislead by a 'sickly appetite' that loathes the food it craves, the 'weak' Emilia has deluded herself into believing that she could not love a man. Although this judgment might sound like a twentieth-century pathologizing of homosexuality, Hippolyta is not opposing homosexuality to heterosexuality but rather asserting the compatibility of same-sex and male-female love. Having loved a woman should not make Emilia incapable of loving a man. In fact, if Hippolyta were 'ripe for...persuasion', Emilia's idyllic portrait of female-female love would 'shake' her from Theseus' arm. Through the metaphor of ripe fruit shaken loose from a tree, Hippolyta concedes the possibility that were she not so attached to Theseus—whether by love, sexual desire, wedding vows, or political necessity—she could be persuaded to leave him for a woman. In her rejoinder—'I am not / Against your faith, yet I continue mine' (1.3.97–98)—Emilia uses 'faith', the same word that Palamon had used to describe his unique bond with Arcite in Thebes, to reiterate her exclusive devotion to women.

As Emilia becomes hopelessly entangled in the cousins' rivalry, which will finally force her into an unsought marriage with one of them, her inclinations continuously pull against Hippolyta's belief that she should be able to love men as well as women. While the Athenians praise Arcite's manly stature following his victory in an athletic competition, Emilia infers the beauty of his mother: 'His mother was a wondrous handsome woman— / His face methinks goes that way' (2.5.20–21). Hippolyta corrects Emilia's emphasis on maternal inheritance by asserting Arcite's paternal inheritance: 'But his body / And fiery mind illustrate a brave father' (2.5.21–22). Appointing Arcite as Emilia's servant, Theseus winkingly predicts that she will yield to his sexual charms: 'Sister, beshrew my heart, you have a servant / That, if I were a woman, would be master. / But you are wise' (2.5.62–64). Responding, 'I hope too wise for that, sir', Emilia avers that she is not so foolish as to make a servant her master, but also implies that she will not or cannot love any man, even one so irresistible as Arcite (2.5.64). When Theseus subsequently swears to execute both cousins for pursuing Emilia, her thoughts turn to the women who will blame her for their deaths:

> The goodly mothers that have groaned for these,
> And all the longing maids that ever loved,
> If your vow stand, shall curse me and my beauty,
> And in their funeral songs for these two cousins
> Despise my cruelty and cry woe worth me,
> Till I am nothing but the scorn of women.   (3.6.245–250)

Of all those relatives or friends who might mourn the cousins' death, Emilia acknowledges only their mothers. If the cousins die for her sake, '[a]ll the longing maids that ever loved' will find her beauty worthy of scorn rather than admiration. Denied the affection of maids like herself, Emilia will become 'nothing'. The cousins' rivalry, and the play, concludes with Arcite's death, leaving Palamon to marry Emilia. Although Emilia might have escaped women's general curse for the death of two noble kinsmen, Emilia's forced marriage to one of them might strike us as tantamount to the very negation of self that she had feared.

As You Like It

The female protagonists of *As You Like It*, a play that also explores the impact of marriage upon female friendship, enjoy much more agency than Emilia over their sexual futures. Like Palamon and Arcite, Rosalind and Celia share an intimate connection as both cousins and friends. Rosalind and Celia continually refer to each other as 'cousin' or 'coz', the latter of which 'often functions in early modern comedies' as a kind of erotically charged 'condensation' of the wider familial and familiar intimacies implied by 'cousin'.[65] Significantly, 'coz' appears in Celia's first line of the play, in which she tries to alleviate Rosalind's sadness over the banishment of her father by her uncle (Celia's father), Duke Frederick: 'I pray thee, Rosalind, sweet my coz, be merry' (1.2.1). When Rosalind refuses comfort, Celia complains that Rosalind's (sad) feelings for her father seem to outweigh her (affectionate) feelings for Celia, thus calling into question the reciprocity of their love:

Herein I see thou lov'st me not with the full weight that I love thee. If my uncle, thy banished father, had banished thy uncle, the Duke my father, so thou hadst been still with me I could have taught my love to take thy father for mine. So wouldst thou, if the truth of thy love to me were so righteously tempered as mine is to thee.   (1.2.6–11)

Like the balanced phrases in Montaigne's account of mutual friendship, Celia's speech is replete with imitative figures: 'thou lov'st me'/ 'I love thee'; 'my uncle'/'thy uncle'; 'thy...father'/'my father'; 'thy love to me'/'mine...to thee'. Had the political situation been reversed, Celia argues, she would have 'taught her love' for Rosalind to accept Rosalind's father as her own, as if their 'righteously tempered' homonormativity should perfectly align not only their likes and dislikes, but also their 'natural' affection for kin.[66]

When attesting to the 'truth' of her love for Rosalind, Celia uses 'truth' in the sense of 'faithfulness, fidelity, [or] loyalty', but also with a possible allusion to 'plighting one's truth' or 'troth' in a marriage ceremony.[67] Celia's 'truth' is thus analogous to the advocation of same-sex 'faith' in *The Two Noble Kinsmen*, both in Palamon's affirmation of the 'faith' that binds him to Arcite and in Emilia's declaration of her 'faith' in the superiority of female-female love. Emilia's claim that her homonormative love with Flavina manifested in similar value judgments—'[w]hat she liked / Was then of me approved; what not, condemned— / No more arraignment' (*TNK* 1.3.64–66)—is echoed by Celia's recommendation that Rosalind not arraign Duke Frederick's worthiness but simply love him as Celia does. Rosalind's response, 'Well, I will forget the condition of *my* estate to rejoice in *yours*', highlights the differences between the cousins instead of their seamless alignment, suggesting that, for Rosalind, their unequal economic and political situations introduce an imbalance into their homonormative bond (1.2.12, emphasis added).

When Duke Frederick banishes Rosalind as her 'father's daughter' and therefore potentially treacherous, Celia continues to insist on her unity with Rosalind (1.3.61). Averring that if Rosalind 'be a traitor, / Why, so am I', Celia offers evidence of their connection, much as Hippolyta rehearses the shared life experiences of Theseus and Pirithous (1.3.66–67):

> We still have slept together,
> Rose at an instant, learned, played, eat together,
> And wheresoe'er we went, like Juno's swans
> Still we went coupled and inseparable. (1.3.67–70)

Celia's account corroborates a courtier's description of their love as 'dearer than the natural bond of sisters'—sisters being a 'natural' kin model for a homonormative female couple (1.2.243). Along with the allusion to Juno, the goddess of marriage, Celia's claim to have always eaten and slept with Rosalind foreshadows the play's concluding wedding song: 'Wedding is great Juno's crown, / O blessèd bond of board and bed!' (5.4.130–131). Because swans were associated not with Juno but with Venus, the goddess of love, the image of Juno's swans conjoins 'erotic love and marriage in the service of female amity' (Figure 1.4).[68] 'Coupled' swans, moreover, are an aestheticized, fanciful version of the agricultural yoking of oxen to pull a cart or plow. The identification of husbands and wives as 'yoke-fellows' was one of the period's most common idioms for the shared bond of marriage (see Figure 1.3).

Figure 1.4 'like Juno's swans / Still we went coupled': Venus' coupled swans. Monogrammist IQV after Giulio Romano, 'Venus op een strijdwagen door twee zwanen voortgetrokken' [Venus on a chariot pulled by two swans]. (Fontainebleau, c.1540). Rijksmuseum, Amsterdam.

Oxen, however, were typically same-sex couples, as two males would be yoked together for their combined strength. Through these classical and agricultural allusions, Celia insists that she and Rosalind are essentially a married couple.

Because Celia appears to regard herself as already married to Rosalind, some readers have interpreted Rosalind's desire to marry Orlando as a rejection or replacement of her same-sex commitment to Celia. After all, marriage is a dyadic arrangement. In an earlier study, I refer to a 'shift in Rosalind's affections' from her girlhood companion to her future husband.[69] Valerie Traub similarly argues that Shakespeare typically represents female homoeroticism as 'the always already lost', as in Emilia's elegy for Flavina, or the 'always about to be *betrayed*', as in Rosalind's pursuit of Orlando.[70] This betrayal of a girlhood companion is sometimes founded on an 'implicit power asymmetry' in which one partner silently denies her friend's 'emotional claims' about the importance of their bond.[71] As we have seen, when Celia posits that Rosalind's love for her is not as 'righteously tempered' as hers for Rosalind, Rosalind says nothing to reassure Celia of her equal devotion to their friendship.

Nonetheless, consistent with the shared blood and affection that binds her to Celia, Rosalind understands her desire for Orlando as an affirmation of, not as a breaking of, her kinship bonds. When Celia asks Rosalind how she came to love 'Sir Rowland's youngest son', Rosalind responds, 'The Duke my father loved his father dearly' (1.3.23–24):

> CELIA Doth it therefore ensue that you should love his son dearly? By this kind of chase I should hate him, for my father hated his father dearly; yet I hate not Orlando.
> ROSALIND No, faith, hate him not, for my sake.
> CELIA Why should I not? Doth he not deserve well?
> ROSALIND Let me love him for that, and do you love him because I do.
>
> (1.3.25–31)

Hatred, according to Celia, is not passed from father to child genetically, temperamentally, or politically. Yet, according to Rosalind, love, if not earned simply by 'deserv[ing] well', can be transmitted through a father or cousin. However fanciful, Rosalind's claim demonstrates another way in which early modern notions of desire do not correspond to modern heterosexuality. Rosalind's 'love' for Orlando mimics her father's same-sex 'love' for Orlando's father and is ratified through her cousin's same-sex 'love' for her. Having already encountered the use of 'faith' to signify devoted same-sex love in *The Two Noble Kinsmen*, we might also hear in Rosalind's interjection 'faith'—meaning 'in faith' (i.e., 'in truth')—a plea that Celia love Orlando for the 'sake' of their mutual, faithful, same-sex bond.

If Rosalind's love for Orlando is consonant, in both its origins and effects, with same-sex love, the deepening of her affection for her future husband is also facilitated by same-sex love. To protect themselves while wandering through the forest, Rosalind disguises herself as a young man named Ganymede and Celia disguises herself as Ganymede's sister Aliena. Celia's name signifies that by following Rosalind into exile she has alienated herself from her father's love (and inheritance), but her choice might also signal an identification with the queer strangeness of those who don't fully conform to a dominant social ethos, such as Antonio in *The Merchant of Venice* or the cousins in *The Two Noble Kinsmen*. There is nothing ambiguous about Rosalind's alias, which alludes to a famous myth of same-sex desire. In Ovid's *Metamorphoses*, Ganymede is a beautiful young shepherd. Enflamed with desire, Jove, the king of the gods, carries the youth up to the heavens to serve as his lover and cupbearer. A poem of 1596 describes Ganymede as the boy '[w]hom Jupiter fetcht to be his page, / And ravisht all his beating vaines with joy, / Sucking the sweet taste of his tender age'.[72] When Rosalind as 'Ganymede' encounters Orlando in the forest, Ganymede offers to playact the role of Rosalind so that Orlando can practice his courtship. During their courtship, then, Rosalind and Orlando are never fully intelligible as (simply) a male-female couple: their desire is expressed and even nurtured through the performance of a same-sex courtship—a performance that was enacted on the early modern London stage through the bodies of a man (playing Orlando) and a youth (playing Rosalind). Moreover, 'ganymede' and its derivative form 'catamite' were early modern slang terms for a young man desired by or taken as a sexual partner by an older man.[73]

As Ganymede's sister Aliena, Celia also participates in this same-sex courtship, even if she is no longer the sole focus of Rosalind's affections and attentions. The complexity of this triangulated relationship is evident when Ganymede asks Aliena to officiate a wedding ceremony between him (in his 'pretend' role as Rosalind) and Orlando. Some scholars have read this episode as evidence of Rosalind's transfer of affection from Celia to Orlando, her new 'marriage' partner. When Celia protests that she 'cannot say the words' of the ceremony, she might be displaying a reluctance to facilitate Rosalind's growing intimacy with Orlando; nonetheless, she still accepts the important role of wedding officiant (4.1.109). Julie Crawford compares this wedding to the concluding 'triangulated wedding' of *The Merchant of Venice*, in which Portia asks Antonio to place her ring on Bassanio's finger.[74] Shortly after the wedding, moreover, Celia meets and immediately falls in love with Orlando's brother Oliver, a development that we can understand not as a refutation but as a consequence of homonormativity. Because Celia and Rosalind are alike, they are equally attracted to the sons of Sir Rowland de Boys. By marrying brothers, moreover, Rosalind and Celia become sisters-in-law, thus reinforcing and 'ensur[ing] their continued kinship' and intimacy.[75]

This chapter has argued that neither friendship nor marriage in Shakespeare is ever a purely dyadic affair. While both same-sex and male-female couples are central to the romantic plots of comedies (*The Merchant of Venice*, *As You Like It*), tragedies (*Romeo and Juliet*), and mixed-genre plays (*The Two Noble Kinsmen*), these couples might be more accurately understood as same-gender or mixed-gender thruples, or as nodes within larger affective and erotic networks of friends and kin. To argue for the porous boundaries of same-sex couples in particular is not to diminish the significance of homoerotic bonds in Shakespeare's texts or culture, but rather to acknowledge how same-sex relations were central to the formation of the marriages, families, and communities that comprised the dominant social fabric.

Shakespeare and Queer Studies. Mario DiGangi, Oxford University Press. © Mario DiGangi 2025.
DOI: 10.1093/9780191994951.003.0002

(Queer) Desire and Disorder

In the previous chapter we saw how, in *The Two Noble Kinsmen*, Palamon and Arcite consider themselves 'unhardened in / The crimes of nature' despite the temptations on offer in Thebes (1.2.3). For Shakespeare's audience, a city prolific in the crimes of nature would have evoked the Biblical Sodom, destroyed by God because its citizens indulged the 'daily wickedness' of same-sex fornication.[1] Taking its name from Sodom, sodomy was often identified with the specific act of anal intercourse between males; however, sodomy's association with the 'unnatural' gave it a much broader purchase in the realms of religion, morality, and politics. A pervasive early modern rhetoric portrayed sodomy as a sin so heinous that it was not to be named. Precisely because of this rhetoric's hyperbole, historian Alan Bray argues, it was difficult for English people to identify their friends, neighbours, or family members—who might have been committing physical acts of sodomy in a nearby room or field—with the demonic figure of the 'sodomite'. Moreover, male-male intimacies were a part of daily life in schools, the court, and households, where people of the same sex often shared the few available beds. For these reasons, Bray posits, a kind of cognitive dissonance rendered unrecognizable as the nefarious crime of sodomy the everyday practices of male-male intimacy and eroticism.[2]

Bray illustrates the hyperbolic linking of same-sex sodomy to cosmic disorder through Michael Drayton's satirical poem *The Mooncalf* (1627). In Drayton's bizarre narrative, the devil has impregnated the world, which subsequently gives birth in England to a mooncalf: a 'stupid or foolish person', or, more dramatically, 'a deformed animal; a monster'.[3] Drayton's monster takes the form of androgynous conjoined twins:

The man is partly woman, likewise she
Is partly man, and yet in face they be
Full as prodigious as in parts; the twin
That is most man, yet in the face and skin
Is all mere woman: that which most doth take
From weaker woman, Nature seems to make
A man in show, thereby as to define,
A feminine man, a woman masculine,
Before bred nor begot; a more strange thing
Than ever Nile yet into light could bring,
Made as creation merely to despite,
Nor man, nor woman, scarce hermaphrodite.[4]

According to the narrator, nothing this 'strange' has ever been born, not even from the fertile waters of the Nile River in Egypt or the wilds of Africa, the 'mother of monsters' (171). The mooncalf's existence blurs the supposed distinctions between civilized Europe and savage Africa as well as between male and female. 'Hermaphrodite', an early modern term for a person with both male and female genitalia, here names an even rarer creature who is only 'scarce[ly]' hermaphroditic: a double figure that is distinctly gendered (one twin is a 'man', the other a 'woman'), even as it confounds gender boundaries (the male twin is 'partly woman' and feminine, the female twin is 'partly man' and masculine). Whatever that description might suggest about the mooncalf's precise physiognomy or genitalia, this 'strange thing' evidently violates the putatively 'natural' categories of gender.

In *The Mooncalf*, the unnatural gender of the male twin manifests in unnatural same-sex appetites. It is important to note that there was no necessary correlation in early modern thinking between male same-sex desire and effeminacy. Effeminacy in men was generally attributed to sensual indulgence and loss of reasonable self-control, which might manifest through excessive sexual desire for either a woman or another male. In *The Mooncalf*, a midwife who assists with the creature's birth predicts that the 'feminine man' will become a debauched London gallant: a figure frequently ridiculed in seventeenth-century English satire as an indulger of sensual pleasures, including women and pretty boys. The mooncalf delights in 'his smooth-chin'd, plump-thigh'd catamite': a familiar term for an adolescent boy who provided sexual services to men (172). The catamite's beardless face and plump thighs—which might be a euphemism for the nearby fleshy buttocks—indicate that he has not (yet) attained a masculine physique and can therefore aptly 'bottom' for the mooncalf. At the same time, the effeminate mooncalf himself resembles a 'pathick' (another term for a male 'bottom') employed in a Jewish-owned male brothel:

> He looks like one for the preposterous sin,
> Put by the wicked and rebellious Jews
> To be a pathick in their male-kind stews.   (172)

In this astonishing image, Drayton conflates gender transgression (a feminine male body), racial/religious transgression (Jews who 'rebel' against Christian belief), and sexual transgression (the 'preposterous sin'). As Patricia Parker has shown, 'preposterous', from the Latin *pre* [before] + *posterior* [behind], means 'inverted' and often alludes to anal intercourse, understood as sex from 'behind': an inversion of 'natural' penile-vaginal intercourse.[5] In case we miss that implication, Drayton's speaker laments that the mooncalf's birth has caused Sodom to newly arise from hell 'and her sin agen / Imbrac'd by beastly and outragious men' (172) (Figure 2.1).

Drayton's *Mooncalf* nicely illustrates the pervasive early modern idea that transgressive sexual desires and acts can have devastating civic consequences. Shakespeare's contemporaries would have understood the Biblical tale of Sodom as a monitory lesson about God's terrible justice upon an entire community of the sexually debauched. Sodom's destruction was a 'graphic reminder that such behavior had forbidding communal, as well as individual, repercussions', namely, the 'threat of social breakdown, the utter destruction of the state, and the ultimate obliteration of the world at the end of time'.[6] Ministers warned parishioners that divine wrath at sin, including sexual sin, produced monstrous births, prodigious creatures, plagues, and other afflictions.

Although Shakespeare never uses the word 'sodomy', the tragedies and history plays analysed in this chapter represent sexual desire as a cause of social disorder, communal suffering, and political upheaval; for this reason, we might consider such desires 'queer', whether or not they involve same-sex partners. In *Henry V*, King Harry accuses his companion and bedfellow, Lord Scrope, of treasonously betraying him to the French in a plot that would have devastated England.

Figure 2.1 'Beastly and outrageous men': the destruction of Sodom. Philips Galle after Maarten van Heemskerck, 'Loth en zijn familie verlaten de stad Sodom' [Lot and his family leave the city Sodom]. (Haarlem: 1569). Rijksmuseum, Amsterdam.

Drawing on their habitual physical intimacy, Harry describes Scrope's treachery as a sodomitical violation of the royal body. Whereas Harry saves England by rooting out sodomy, Paris' rape of the Greek queen Helen in *Troilus and Cressida* sparks an interminable war that finally ruins Troy. The Greek camp faces its own sexual crisis when Achilles' enervating love for (male) Patroclus and (female) Polyxena keeps him from combat. Shakespeare also explores the political consequences of women's sexual transgressions in the three *Henry VI* plays and *Macbeth*. *Henry VI*'s Queen Margaret exploits King Henry's intemperate desires and weak rulership to advance her own sexual and political self-interests. *Macbeth* opens with three queerly gendered figures, the witches, whose political prophecies enflame Macbeth to commit regicide. Ironically, Lady Macbeth, who 'unsexes' herself in order to achieve her political ambitions, cites traditional ideologies of masculine bravery to goad Macbeth into the ultimate anti-patriarchal act: murdering the nation's political father. The chapter concludes with a discussion of two tragedies,

Titus Andronicus and *Anthony and Cleopatra*, in which rulers' interracial romances cause turmoil within the ancient Roman empire.

Henry V

Henry V links political treachery with same-sex intimacy. Before he departs England to invade France, King Harry discovers that three English lords have colluded with the French to assassinate him. Although all three men are identified as 'traitors' and 'monsters', King Harry describes the treachery of Lord Scrope, his 'bedfellow', as particularly egregious (2.2.1, 8, 82). It was not uncommon in early modern England for two men or women to share a bed, which were sometimes in short supply. The high valuation of same-sex intimacy we explored in the previous chapter also contributed to the familiar practice of sharing beds in schools, courts, military camps, and households. That Scrope was Harry's bedfellow indicates his extraordinary privilege, since, aside from personal servants, only an extremely narrow circle of friends, kin, and counsellors could enjoy intimate proximity to the monarch's body. Lord Exeter confirms this privilege in recounting how Harry 'hath dulled and cloyed' Scrope 'with gracious favours' (2.2.8–9). The nature of these 'favours' remains unclear—they might be noble titles, administrative positions, or financial endowments—but Exeter's point is that the king has loaded Scrope with enough honours and advantages to fully satisfy all of his desires. To 'cloy' means '[t]o satiate, surfeit, gratify beyond desire; to disgust, weary (with excess of anything)'.[7] That Scrope has benefitted so greatly from the king's generosity makes his treachery particularly shocking.

However, the hint of excessive affection in Exeter's account of Harry's 'dull[ing] and cloy[ing]' the appetite of his unfaithful bedfellow points to the possibility of sexual disorder. Elsewhere, Shakespeare uses the idea of dulled appetite in specifically sexual contexts. In Sonnet 95, for instance, the speaker warns the youth to refrain from 'lascivious' faults, since the 'hardest knife ill used doth lose his edge' (6, 14). At some point, the youth's sexual indiscretions will catch up with him and he will lose the 'privilege' of transgressing with impunity (13). Because the speaker is specifically describing the youth's sexual faults, the dulled knife seems to represent an exhausted penis that has lost the 'edge' of pleasurable sensation. Harry's having 'dulled' his bedfellow with favours carries a similar implication of sexual exhaustion.

A monarch's showering a bedfellow with 'favours', moreover, inevitably evokes the figure of the 'favourite': a courtier who is especially beloved by a monarch, often in overtly erotic or sexual ways.[8] Christopher Marlowe's tragedy *Edward II* concerns an irresponsible king who passionately dotes on and excessively rewards his male favourite, and Shakespeare's own *Richard II* hints that the king's indulgence of his male favourites has alienated his wife. A 'favor', moreover, could also be an item 'given to a lover' as a 'token of affection'.[9] Although the practice of royal favouritism would not rule out the possibility of a sexual relationship between Harry and Scrope, the play leaves room for interpretation either way. Describing Harry's favours to Scrope as 'gracious', for instance, Exeter does give them an air of legitimacy and even, considering the religious connotations of 'grace', of sanctity. Nonetheless, his account of Harry's excessive generosity does intimate a possible intemperance on the king's part. In the 1631 trial of the Earl of Castlehaven for sodomy and rape, it emerged that the Earl considered his servant Henry Skipwith 'more a "companion" than a servant and lavished him with gifts'.[10] The granting of excessive favours could be a sign of, and even an inducement to, sexual intemperance that could destabilize an entire household—or kingdom.

If Exeter only obliquely glances at the intemperance of Harry's love for Scrope, Harry himself flatly accuses Scrope of an unnatural wickedness drawn from the cultural mythology of sodomy:

> But O
> What shall I say to thee, Lord Scrope, thou cruel,
> Ingrateful, savage, and inhuman creature?
> Thou that didst bear the key of all my counsels,
> That knew'st the very bottom of my soul,
> That almost mightst ha' coined me into gold
> Wouldst thou ha' practised on me for thy use . . .
> . . . thou, 'gainst all proportion, didst bring in
> Wonder to wait on treason and on murder.
> And whatsoever cunning fiend it was
> That wrought on thee so preposterously
> Hath got the voice in hell for excellence. (2.2.90–96, 106–110)

Harry evokes some of the key signifiers of sodomitical disorder we saw in Drayton's *Mooncalf*, including the infernal, inhuman, disproportionate, marvellous or 'wonder[ful]', and 'preposterous'. Whereas in Drayton's poem the devil impregnates the world, here Harry imagines that a 'cunning fiend' has 'wrought on' Scrope, perverting not only his mind but also his body, as if impregnating him with the desire to commit 'treason' and 'murder'. The possibility of a devil's 'preposterous' (inverted, unnatural) assault on Scrope's body suggests Scrope's own sodomitical betrayal of Harry's body. This reading is corroborated by the racial language that associates both devils and sodomites with blackness. In premodern Europe, the devil was typically represented as black, and sodomy was often attributed to darker-skinned, non-Christian peoples such as Turks, Muslims, Africans, or Native Americans.

Scrope's sodomitical violation of the royal body is further evinced by Harry's reference to coining. Scrope enjoys special access not only to the king's political 'counsels' and secret thoughts, but also to his body, which he might have 'coined...into gold'. In premodern England, gold coins were often stamped with the image of the monarch's face. Harry suggests that because of their physical intimacy Scrope could have stolen his image to stamp counterfeit gold coins and invest them at 'use', meaning usury or interest. In making his claim, Harry draws upon a familiar early modern association of sodomy and usury. Just as sodomy was an 'unnatural' perversion of the 'proper' use of the genitals (for reproduction), usury was an 'unnatural' perversion of the 'proper' use of money as a medium of equal exchange. Both practices, moreover, were considered 'unnatural' because they 'violated communal values associated with friendship'.[11] In sum, Harry charges Scrope with perverting a loving and legitimate friendship between monarch and favourite into something queerly mercenary and monstrously threatening to the commonwealth.

Troilus and Cressida

Whereas King Harry's discovery of sodomitical treason facilitates England's successful expansion of its territories in France, *Troilus and Cressida* explores the sexual violation at the heart of a great civilization's collapse. Paris, a Trojan prince, has abducted Helen, wife of the Greek king Menelaus. When the play opens, the Greek army that has sailed to Troy to recover Helen has been besieging the city for seven years. Paris had abducted Helen in retaliation for the Greeks' prior abduction of his aunt, yet this act of vengeance is complicated by Paris' taking the incomparably beautiful Helen as a lover. Even Paris describes what he has done as a 'rape'—which could mean both 'abduction' and 'sexual violation'.[12] During a heated debate about whether the Trojans should end the war by surrendering Helen, Paris's father exposes the self-interest behind Paris' insistence on retaining his prize: '[Y]ou speak / Like one besotted on your sweet delights. / You have the honey still, but these the gall' (2.2.141–143). Drunk on the 'sweet delights' of Helen's body, Paris enjoys her 'honey': a word associated with the sexual violation of women elsewhere in Shakespeare. For instance, in *Titus Andronicus*, rape is described as the act of forcibly taking a woman's 'honey' (2.3.131); in *The Rape of Lucrece*, Lucrece accuses her rapist of having 'sucked the honey' which she had chastely preserved for her husband (840).

Paris' brother Hector elaborates Priam's argument about the dire social and political consequences of rape, which he describes as the 'hot passion of distempered blood' (2.2.168). Lecturing his brother on the sanctity of marriage, Hector claims that Paris has corrupted the 'law / Of nature' that grants husbands exclusive ownership of their wives (2.2.175–176). Every nation has laws that punish such violations of natural law:

> There is a law in each well-ordered nation
> To curb those raging appetites that are
> Most disobedient and refractory.
> If Helen then be wife to Sparta's king,
> As it is known she is, these moral laws
> Of nature and of nations speak aloud
> To have her back returned.   (2.2.179–185)

Hector's belief in the inherent stubbornness and wildness of 'raging appetites' or sexual desires, and of the need for a 'well-ordered' polity to restrain them, is remarkably orthodox. His patriarchal logic is brutally clear: wives belong to their husbands; Helen is Menelaus' wife; Helen must therefore be 'returned' to him. For Hector, the interests of 'nature' and of 'nations' are perfectly aligned, as these words' aural similarity suggests. Cynthia Herrup explains that early modern retellings

of the story of Helen and other raped women from classical mythology 'encouraged the belief that violence against women was a public
issue, that the disorder of rape disturbed more than even the family of
the assaulted'.[13] Although the Trojans decide to retain Helen, their
debate reveals an understanding that disorderly sexuality can destroy
not only a family but a 'well-ordered' nation.

Some of the Greek warriors are no less disgusted than their Trojan
rivals at having to fight a war over the sexual possession of a woman.
Whereas Hector lectures Paris about his violation of conjugal rights,
the satirical fool Thersites blames the war on 'a whore and a cuckold'
(2.3.65). Even the more temperate Diomedes refers to Menelaus
as 'a puling cuckold' who seeks to drink the 'lees and dregs of a
flat tamèd piece' (4.1.63–64). In other words, Helen is no longer
wholesome wine but the nasty refuse that settles at the bottom of a
'flat' or stale cask. Helen has been spoiled by her sexual relationship
with Paris, the 'lecher' who will breed bastards out of her 'whorish
loins' (4.1.65–66). Lamenting that Helen is 'bitter to her country',
Diomedes spells out the disastrous effects of a single person's sexual
intemperance (4.1.70):

> For every false drop in her bawdy veins
> A Grecian's life hath sunk; for every scruple
> Of her contaminated carrion weight
> A Trojan hath been slain.   (4.1.71–74)

Each drop of blood in Helen's whorish veins, Diomedes laments,
represents a dead Greek, and each ounce of her putrefying flesh represents a dead Trojan. Even as Helen is frequently praised as exceptionally fair, Diomedes portrays her as an infected carcass responsible
for countless deaths.

The Greeks are also grappling with another kind of sexual disorder:
their greatest warrior, Achilles, spends his time lounging in a tent with
his friend Patroclus instead of fighting. Just as Drayton's mooncalf
enjoys the smooth body of his young 'catamite', so Achilles, claims
Thersites, uses the 'boy' Patroclus as a 'male varlet' or 'masculine whore'
(5.1.13–14, 16). Thersites also calls Patroclus 'Achilles' brach' (bitch) as
well as a 'gilt counterfeit', recalling King Harry's charge that Lord
Scrope might have 'coined [him] into gold' (2.1.109, 2.3.2; *Henry V*

2.1.109). Using one of Shakespeare's favourite terms for sexual disorder, Thersites refers to his knowledge of the warriors' sexual relationship as a 'preposterous discovery'—in other words, a discovery of 'inverted' or sodomitical sex (5.1.19). Focusing on social rather than sexual transgression, Ulysses instead argues that Patroclus' indolent mockery of his superiors violates the natural order that organizes everything in the universe into a transparent hierarchy of value. To entertain Achilles, Patroclus

> Upon a lazy bed the livelong day
> Breaks scurrile jests
> And, with ridiculous and awkward action
> Which, slanderer, he 'imitation' calls,
> He pageants us.   (1.3.146–151)

The 'lazy bed' signifies sensual indolence in stark contrast to manly combat. Even though Ulysses does not accuse Achilles and Patroclus of having sex in that bed, the emphasis on ridiculous theatrical spectacle intended only 'to produce erotic pleasure' undermines any claim to a warrior identity grounded in masculine integrity and discipline.[14] Because the Greeks describe Patroclus as theatrical, boyish, and submissive to Achilles, the animus of sodomitical disorder falls mainly on him.

At the same time, Achilles' manhood is compromised by his enervating love not only for Patroclus but also, as we belatedly discover, for Polyxena, a Trojan princess. 'Effeminacy is a trait of excessive male desire' regardless of male or female object choice.[15] Significantly, it is Patroclus who urges Achilles to restore their manly reputations by channelling his lovesickness into a predatory appetite for violence:

> A woman impudent and mannish grown
> Is not more loathed than an effeminate man
> In time of action. I stand condemned for this.
> They think my little stomach to the war
> And your great love to me restrains you thus.
> Sweet, rouse yourself, and the weak wanton Cupid
> Shall from your neck unloose his amorous fold
> And like a dew-drop from the lion's mane
> Be shook to air.   (3.3.210–218)

The Greeks condemn Patroclus not only for his own cowardice, but also for his influence on Achilles, whose 'great love' for his friend supposedly 'restrains' him from fighting. Although Patroclus objects specifically to being reputed 'effeminate', his rhetorical pairing of the effeminate man with the mannish woman conveys a larger point about how gender inversion is generally 'loathed'. The real cause of Achilles' indolence, Patroclus observes, is Achilles' submission to Cupid, who has ominously wound himself around the great warrior's neck. What the Greeks consider queer, in other words, is not the 'great love' of one manly warrior for another, but a warrior's 'effeminate' indulgence of his 'wanton' or undisciplined desires at the expense of his public duty to his male peers. In a dialogue on love, the ancient philosopher Plutarch condemns the

delicate and effeminate love that keeps home and stirs not out of doors, but keeps continually in women's laps, under canopies, or within curtains in women's beds and soft pallets, seeking always after dainty delights, and pampered up with unmanly pleasures.[16]

Thus, far from renouncing Achilles' love for him, Patroclus is drawing on that love to 'rouse' his '[s]weet' friend from 'unmanly pleasures' to the manly 'action' that will restore their honour. Inspired by his 'sweet' friend, Achilles expresses his 'woman's longing', an 'appetite' that sickens him, to fight his Trojan rival, Hector (3.3.230–231). When it spurs a man to violent physical action, turning him from a fool to a lion, same-sex desire aligns with the aims of socially validated masculinity. As Ulysses advises, 'Better would it fit Achilles much / To throw down Hector than Polyxena' (3.3.200–201).

The *Henry VI* Plays

The First Part of Henry the Sixth [*1 Henry VI*] ends with an allusion to the Trojan War. The Duke of Suffolk has been sent to France to negotiate a political marriage between King Henry VI and the daughter of the powerful Earl of Armagnac. When he happens to capture the princess Margaret, however, Suffolk is immediately smitten by her extraordinary beauty. To keep Margaret close as his own lover, Suffolk entices his king to marry her instead of the Earl's daughter. In the closing lines of the play, Suffolk gloats over his success:

> Thus Suffolk hath prevailed, and thus he goes
> As did the youthful Paris once to Greece,
> With hope to find the like event in love,
> But prosper better than the Trojan did.
> Margaret shall now be queen and rule the King;
> But I will rule both her, the king, and realm.   (5.7.103–108)

Despite Suffolk's confidence, his allusion to the fall of Troy bodes ill for England. To begin with, Margaret comes at a high cost: her father will not consent to her marriage unless the English relinquish certain French provinces that the previous king, Henry V, had won. Having convinced Henry VI, through a tempting account of Margaret's beauty, to accept these disadvantageous and humiliating terms, Suffolk maintains a long-standing affair with Margaret in England that undermines the king's authority and contributes to the destructive internal dissention among England's ruling families. Although Suffolk does not in fact manage to rule Margaret, Henry, or England as absolutely as he imagines here, his plan to usurp political power through access to Margaret's body reveals how disruptive erotic desire can be to national stability.

When the English peers protest the economic and political losses that England will suffer to achieve Margaret, Suffolk justifies his choice in terms of Henry's affections. Whereas the peers rightly understand a royal marriage as a precious opportunity to consolidate international alliances and accumulate new territories, Suffolk debases such motives as vulgarly pragmatic, especially when counterposed to the supposedly more noble aims of love:

> So worthless peasants bargain for their wives,
> As market men for oxen, sheep, or horse.
> Marriage is a matter of more worth
> Than to be dealt in by attorneyship.
> Not whom we will but whom his grace affects
> Must be companion of his nuptial bed.
> And therefore, lords, since he affects her most,
> That most of all these reasons bindeth us:
> In our opinions she should be preferred.
> For what is wedlock forced but a hell,
> An age of discord and continual strife,
> Whereas the contrary bringeth bliss,
> And is a pattern of celestial peace.   (5.7.53–65)

To choose a queen based on financial considerations, argues Suffolk, is to descend to the level of 'worthless peasants' who 'bargain' for their wives as if buying livestock. The 'worth' of marriage, he claims, derives not from the economic benefits that it might bring, but from the loving bond between husband and wife. Suffolk's definition of marriage closely hews to orthodox Protestant theology, which held that God established marriage so that Christian men and women could live together in loving companionship and raise children in the faith. The effects of his argument, however, are quite unorthodox, in that considerations of wealth, alliance, and property were always paramount in the arrangement of royal marriages, regardless of whether or not the partners even knew (let alone loved) each other. Suffolk deflects a proper discussion of arranged royal marriage by scorning what he calls marriage by 'attorneyship' and by evoking the domestic misery of what he calls 'wedlock forced'.

Drawing a contrast between the 'discord' of 'forced' marriage and the 'bliss' of marriage between loving partners, Suffolk stresses the importance of satisfying Henry's sexual desires. Since Henry 'affects' Margaret the most, she is the only fitting 'companion of his nuptial bed'. Moreover, their sexual compatibility will produce valiant heirs to a pure racial lineage[17]:

> Whom should we match Henry, being a king,
> But Margaret, that is daughter to a king.
> Her valiant courage and undaunted spirit,
> More than in women commonly is seen,
> Will answer our hope in issue of a king.
> For Henry, son unto a conqueror,
> Is likely to beget more conquerors
> If with a lady of so high resolve
> As is fair Margaret he be linked in love.   (5.7.66–76)

Exceptionally for a woman, Margaret has the 'valiant courage and undaunted spirit' associated with manly 'conquerors' or warriors. Suffolk represents Margaret's manly qualities not as an 'impuden[ce]' to be derided as Patroclus does, but as evidence of an admirable royal 'resolve' or steadfastness (*TC* 3.3.210). Suffolk concludes with a striking image of reproductive futurism via the proliferating 'issue' of the royal couple. Though more interested in praying than in fighting, Henry is still the son of a conqueror, and once 'linked in love' with the resolute Margaret, he will doubtless 'beget more conquerors'.

Even as he attempts to reassure the lords that England will benefit from Margaret's presence as queen, Suffolk unwittingly reveals something dangerously queer about Margaret as a foreign-born woman with the ability to seduce and dominate the king. Suffolk's report of Margaret's beauty has made Henry desperate to possess her: 'I feel such sharp dissention in my breast, / Such fierce alarums both of hope and fear, / As I am sick with working of my thoughts' (5.7.84–86). Henry's internal 'dissention' over Margaret foreshadows the dissention among the English nobility that breaks out in *The First Part of the Contention of the Two Famous Houses of York and Lancaster*, also known as *The Second Part of King Henry the Sixth* [*2 Henry VI*]. Henry is no less shaken when he first meets Margaret upon her arrival in England: 'Her sight did ravish', he announces, but her graceful words move him from 'wond'ring' to 'weeping joys' (1.1.30, 32). Although weeping was not always considered a sign of weakness in men, that Henry is first 'ravish[ed]'—meaning both 'delighted' and 'raped'—by Margaret and subsequently reduced to tears suggests a dangerous loss of masculine self-control.[18] As Jean Howard and Phyllis Rackin observe in their feminist analysis of the play, 'The young king's excessive passion for Margaret marks him instantly as an effeminate or womanish man'.[19] Even worse, ambitious courtiers plan to exploit his weakness for their own gain. The Duke of York, who plots to seize the crown for himself, will 'pry into the secrets of the state' while Henry suffers 'surfeit', or a sickening excess, 'in the joys of love' (1.1.249–250). The Duchess of Gloucester warns Henry that Margaret will 'pamper' and 'dandle' him like a baby while appropriating his sovereign authority (1.3.149).

Unfolding the threat of Henry's marriage to England's honour, security, and territorial claims, the Duke of Gloucester describes a link between sexual disorder and political disorder that resonates with the early modern understanding of sodomy:

> O peers of England, shameful is this league,
> Fatal this marriage, cancelling your fame,
> Blotting your names from books of memory,
> Razing the characters of your renown,
> Defacing monuments of conquered France,
> Undoing all, as all had never been!   (1.1.94–99)

Gloucester here articulates the 'heroic values associated with history as the preserver of masculine fame and glory'.[20] Through the recording capabilities of paper and stone, historical chronicles and monuments materially carry into the future the heroic 'names' and 'characters' of the past—just as the page you are reading now serves to remind you that an actual Duke of Gloucester existed in fifteenth-century England. So inimical is Henry's marriage to English honour and prosperity, however, that it ushers in a queer temporality with the power to erase history—as if 'all' of England's accomplishments 'had never been' in the first place. Gloucester's fear of a sexual relationship that could radically 'cancel', 'blot', 'raze', 'deface', and 'undo' English glory evokes the early modern mythology of sodomy as a kind of apocalyptic solvent of natural and divine order.

As Margaret's influence grows throughout *2 Henry VI* and *3 Henry VI*, her gender inverting domination of Henry becomes increasingly extreme. Shakespeare follows his historical source Edward Hall in portraying Margaret as 'a manly woman, usyng to rule not to be ruled'.[21] For instance, in Henry's absence, Margaret conspires with her lover Suffolk and Cardinal Beaufort to murder Gloucester, the king's staunchest protector. When a grief-stricken Henry insinuates Suffolk's role in Gloucester's death, Margaret deflects suspicion by describing her suffering as a neglected wife. Accusing Henry of 'unkindness' (3.2.96)—both cruelty and unnaturalness—Margaret denounces Henry's love for Gloucester as excessive and misplaced:

> Is all thy comfort shut in Gloucester's tomb?
> Why, then Queen Margaret was ne'er thy joy.
> Erect his statue and worship it,
> And make my image but an alehouse sign.   (3.2.78–81)

Margaret's memorial imagery ironically recalls Gloucester's fears that the royal marriage will raze or deface the written and stone monuments of English fame. For Margaret, Gloucester's tomb, along with a hypothetical statue that might be raised in his honour, serve not to memorialize his heroism but to represent his usurpation of her rightful place as Henry's 'comfort' and 'joy'. Whereas Henry would erect a durable statue to 'worship' Gloucester, he would reproduce Margaret's image only as a cheaply painted, ephemeral, alehouse sign.

In the same melodramatic speech, Margaret evokes the fall of Troy to represent herself as a victim of Henry's deception; nonetheless, the allusion foreshadows an ominous fate for England under the king's and queen's unruly leadership. Margaret recounts that during the long sea voyage from France to England she would ask Suffolk to tell her tales of Henry's manliness to inflame her desire for him. This mode of seduction reminds Margaret of an episode from Virgil's epic poem *The Aeneid*, which celebrates the founding of Rome by the Trojan hero Aeneas. Having escaped the destruction of Troy, Aeneas travels to Carthage, where he is harboured by Queen Dido. Aeneas' mother, the goddess Venus, ensures Dido's hospitality to Aeneas by sending Cupid to seduce Dido with stories of Aeneas' heroic acts, 'commenced in burning Troy' (3.2.118). Enchanted by these tales of heroism, Dido takes Aeneas as a lover, but he finally abandons her to fulfil his imperial destiny in Italy. Margaret accuses Henry, 'Am I not witched like her? Or thou not false like him?' (3.2.119). In this layered analogy, Henry, having falsely seduced Margaret, cruelly neglects her to fulfil his more pressing political duties. But in casting herself as the African queen who tries to prevent Aeneas from founding a great European empire, Margaret also casts herself as a foreigner whose self-serving sexual desires threaten to curtail England's glorious future.

In *3 Henry VI*, the disorder at the heart of the royal marriage destabilizes the kingdom beyond repair, as Gloucester had predicted. Taking advantage of Henry's weak leadership, the Duke of York asserts a rival claim to the throne. In exchange for being allowed to remain king, Henry desperately agrees to entail the crown to York and his heirs, thus alienating his son from future sovereignty. Previously loyal peers bitterly denounce Henry as 'base', 'fearful', 'faint-hearted', 'degenerate', and 'unmanly'; even Henry admits to having behaved 'unnatural[ly]', a judgement that Margaret angrily confirms (1.1.179, 184, 187, 194). In the language of queer temporality, Margaret complains that Henry has not only 'undone' his family, but has foreclosed his own future: 'To entail him [York] and his heirs unto the crown— / What is it, but to make thy sepulchre / And creep into it far before thy time?' (1.1.233, 236–238). Shockingly, rather than share this curtailed future with her husband, Margaret 'divorce[s]' herself from his 'table' and 'bed' (1.1.248–249). Although divorce was not legal in early modern England, church law sometimes allowed separation of spouses 'from bed and board' in cases of adultery, heresy, or abuse. Paradoxically, Margaret endorses the traditional law of primogeniture for her son by abandoning her husband and subsequently marshalling an army against the king's enemies like an 'Amazonian trull' (1.4.115): an allusion to the mythical race of warrior women who 'systematically killed and maimed men—even their own children, begotten without benefit of husband or marriage'.[22] As Kathryn Schwarz observes, Margaret strategically performs both femininity and masculinity, making 'efficient and disruptive use of heterosocial norms'.[23]

Ironically, in the wake of Henry's defeat the newly crowned king, Edward IV of York, seems destined to repeat his predecessor's mistakes. In *1 Henry VI*, as we saw, Henry breaks his engagement to the Earl of Armagnac's daughter, after Suffolk convinces him to marry Margaret. In *3 Henry VI*, the Earl of Warwick travels to France to propose to King Louis a marriage between his sister-in-law, Lady Bona, and King Edward, thus cementing an alliance between the two nations. While Warwick is negotiating with Louis, Edward remains in England negotiating with the Lady Gray for her sexual consent. Lady Gray has come to ask the king for the restoration of her slain husband's lands, which were seized during the recent war, thus depriving her children of their rightful inheritance. Edward agrees to grant this legitimate request only if Lady Gray will consent to sex, an outrageous demand that clearly 'wrongs' her and her children (3.2.75). When Lady Gray refuses to yield to Edward's coercion, he peremptorily offers to marry her, thus betraying and humiliating Warwick, making an enemy out of King Louis, and disparaging his royal blood through marriage to a commoner. When Warwick hears the news, he furiously renounces his allegiance to Edward, devoting himself to helping Margaret's forces restore Henry to the throne.

Despite having alienated several powerful allies, Edward refuses to acknowledge or repent for his bad judgment, instead declaring that his 'will'—meaning both 'wishes' and 'sexual desires'—shall 'stand for law', a dangerous assertion of tyrannical rule (4.1.49). English monarchs were expected to rule according to the laws ratified by Parliament, not to give free reign to their own desires and appetites, which could wreak havoc on the commonwealth. Warwick articulates to Edward the unfitness of a monarch who rules according to his caprices and pleasures—including sexual pleasures—instead of prioritizing policies that serve the national interest:

> Alas, how should you govern any kingdom
> That know not how to use ambassadors,
> Nor how to be contented with one wife,
> Nor how to use your brothers brotherly,
> Nor how to study for the people's welfare,
> Nor how to shroud yourself from enemies.   (4.4.8–13)

Although Edward ends the play securely installed as king and triumphant over his enemies, Warwick's unheeded warning continues to resonate. In the closing lines of the play, Edward's concern with 'mirthful comic shows' and the 'pleasure of the court' seems to justify his reputation as '[l]ascivious Edward' (5.7.43–44, 5.5.34). Under such a king, the gender inversions and sexual transgressions that have shaken England since Henry's marriage to Margaret seem destined to shape the nation's future.

Macbeth

If Henry's queer rejection of primogeniture violates sovereign temporality, the desire of Macbeth and Lady Macbeth to achieve sovereignty through violent treachery queerly dislocates time. As Heather Love observes, the Macbeths' ambition 'does not respect temporal sequence', causing a collapse of the present, past, and future.[24] Ushering the play into queer temporality, the three witches exist outside the familiar boundaries of gender and sexuality: they look like women albeit with 'beards', and they refer to each other as 'sisters', although it is unclear if they are biologically related or form a kind of perverted religious community (1.3.44, 1–2):

> FIRST WITCH   When shall we three meet again?
>   In thunder, lightning, or in rain?
> SECOND WITCH   When the hurly-burly's done,
>   When the battle's lost and won.
> THIRD WITCH   That will be ere the set of sun.   (1.1.1–5)

The triple repetition of 'when' at the beginning of these lines not only corresponds to the number of speakers, but imparts to them a queer relationship to time. How does the Third Witch know that the battle will end before sunset? Do the witches really have the prophetic ability to predict the end of a battle, or, as they soon will do, to identify Macbeth as the future king? Even when planning their next gathering, the witches estrange natural expectations of time. The First Witch's suggestion that they reconvene in 'thunder', 'lightning', *or* in 'rain' presents those three meteorological conditions as temporally distinct, as if one could choose to meet only during thunder, without the presence of lightning or rain.[25] The Second Witch's anticipation of a time when 'the battle's lost and won' might simply mean that a battle usually ends with a winner and a loser, but her elliptical phrasing sounds paradoxical, a version of the witches' confounding of antithetical meanings: 'Fair is foul, and foul is fair' (1.1.10).

That both queer temporality and political subversion appear to originate with the witches is particularly important because of their symbolic relationship to Lady Macbeth. Provoked by the witches' prediction, Lady Macbeth determines to materialize as a present reality a potential future in which her husband reigns. The mere promise of sovereignty turns Lady Macbeth into a kind of time-traveller, '[t]ransport[ing]' her in imagination and sensation 'beyond / This ignorant present', and into a future in which she and Macbeth are already enthroned (1.5.54–56). And that future feels like absolute power: the 'solely sovereign sway and masterdom' of all their 'nights and days to come' (1.5.67–68). The relentless alliteration of 'solely sovereign sway' emphasizes Lady Macbeth's determination queerly to control time by undertaking the violent deeds that will fulfil the witches' prophecy.

What makes Lady Macbeth's disruption of time so queer is the transgressive embodiment of gender and eroticism that she also shares with the witches. The witches' manly beards are a gender anomalous physical trait, and although the play makes no allusion to this idea, witches were commonly believed to engage in sexual acts with devils. Although presumably unremarkable in her outward gender presentation, Lady Macbeth enacts a strange ritual to purge the softer feminine traits that might interfere with her deadly resolve to murder the king. Famously, she calls for demonic 'spirits' to 'unsex' her: to fill her body with cruelty, thicken her blood, and exchange her breast milk for bitter gall (1.5.38–39). To carry out an unnatural regicide, Lady Macbeth must rid herself of the 'compunctious visitings of nature' typical of her sex, such as compassion, gentleness, and even the ability to give and sustain life (1.5.43). To be unsexed, then, is to be denatured, to turn herself from a woman into something else that is difficult to name, but that draws strength from the masculine and demonic realms.

Equally queer, when Macbeth's own scruples weaken his resolve to go through with the murder, Lady Macbeth offers a parable of perverted motherhood to provoke him into action:

> I have given suck, and know
> How tender 'tis to love the babe that milks me.
> I would, while it was smiling in my face,
> Have plucked my nipple from his boneless gums
> And dashed the brains out, had I so sworn
> As you have done to this.   (1.7.54–59)

Lady Macbeth's point is not that she would feel no remorse about murdering her infant while it was tenderly nursing at her breast. Rather, she is arguing that she would perform the cruellest and most horrifying act of violence imaginable had she sworn to do it. Her lesson is about the importance of keeping one's word, despite how agonizing it might feel to do so. Shaken by her resolve, Macbeth advises his wife, 'Bring forth men-children only, / For thy undaunted mettle should compose / Nothing but males' (1.7.72–74). In other words, Lady Macbeth is made out of such fearless stuff that she should give birth only to male children, who would inherit her tough character. But Macbeth's queer insinuation that his wife might give untimely birth to 'men-children'—completely grown men—is highly unsettling, and a seeming admission of her power over him.

Lady Macbeth's transgressive wish to be un-sexed, to be physically unable to give birth to or nurse a child, reflects the Macbeths' inability to produce children, in contrast to the fertility of Macbeth's rival, Banquo. Critics have sometimes wondered how Lady Macbeth could claim that she has nursed an infant if the Macbeths have no children, as the play makes clear is the case. Although Shakespeare sometimes sacrifices consistency for dramatic effect, he might simply have been following his historical sources, which reported that Lady Macbeth had children with a former husband, but not with Macbeth. What is important for our purposes is the correlation between what I have called the queer temporality of the Macbeths and their inability to participate in or benefit from reproductive futurism. The witches predict a balance of good fortune and ill fortune for Macbeth, who will be a king but evidently will not father kings, and for Banquo, who will not be a king but will 'get kings' (1.3.65). Here as elsewhere, the witches' language is equivocal. Banquo will not literally beget kings: the play ends with the crowning of Duncan's son Malcolm, not Banquo's son Fleance, who historically never became king of Scotland. Since the first Stuart king of Scotland was a distant descendant of Banquo, however, Banquo might figuratively be considered 'the root and father' of the Stuart royal dynasty (3.1.5)—so, for that matter, could Fleance. The distinction between a literal and a figurative understanding of the prophecy is important because it means that Banquo's 'hope' for this glorious future is entirely theoretical; even had he survived Macbeth's assassination plot, he would presumably have died long before a descendent of his ever ruled Scotland (3.1.10). But by creating a stark contrast between the fertile Banquo and the infertile Macbeth, the play suggests that it is enough for Banquo to know that the crown will one day revert to his bloodline, and never to Macbeth's. In this regard Banquo is '[l]esser than Macbeth, and greater', '[n]ot so happy' in life yet 'much happier' in his future prospects (1.3.63–64).

Macbeth's decision to murder Banquo is based on both political and psychological considerations: he fears Banquo as a rival but also bitterly resents Banquo's fortune as the father of future kings. Macbeth rehearses the implication of the witches' prophecies:

> They hailed him father to a line of kings.
> Upon my head they placed a fruitless crown,
> And put a barren sceptre in my grip,
> Thence to be wrenched with an unlineal hand,
> No son of mine succeeding. If't be so,
> For Banquo's issue have I filed my mind,
> For them the gracious Duncan have I murdered,
> Put rancours in the vessel of my peace
> Only for them, and mine eternal jewel
> Given to the common enemy of man
> To make them kings, the seeds of Banquo kings. (3.1.61–71)

If, in killing Duncan, Macbeth hoped only to achieve the future that his wife imagined—days and nights filled with sovereignty—it is difficult to understand his disappointment. He has gotten exactly what he wanted. Still, he is tormented by the knowledge of a future without a son to carry on his royal legacy. This future colours everything in Macbeth's present, making him regard the crown he so ardently desired as 'fruitless', and forcing him to acknowledge that his 'barren' sceptre will be wielded by an 'unlineal hand' belonging to some other man's 'issue'. Macbeth speaks as if he regrets having tainted his mind, destroyed his peace, and given up his soul to become king only because not his own 'seeds' but Banquo's will benefit from his sacrifice. The implication that it would be worth spending eternity in hell as long as you were remembered as the father of 'a line of kings'—the cultural work that *Macbeth* itself performs in memorializing Banquo as the distant ancestor of King James of Scotland and England—is quite extraordinary. There is perhaps in all of Shakespeare no stronger illustration of the political implications of the ideology of reproductive futurism than this.[26]

Tragedies of Interracial Desire

In the final section of this chapter, I examine the interracial relationships in *Titus Andronicus* and *Anthony and Cleopatra* as a source of social and political disorder. Like the *Henry VI* plays, *Titus Andronicus* explores how a crisis of leadership, exacerbated by a disorderly marriage, can undo a great nation from within; like *Macbeth*, it also explores a crisis of royal succession. Unlike Macbeth, who has no sons to inherit his title, the former Emperor of Rome, who has evidently died shortly before the play begins, has two sons who claim the right to inherit his title. The eldest son, Saturninus, attempts to persuade the Roman patricians that they should honour the principle of primogeniture by bestowing the 'successive title' of Emperor on him (1.1.4):

> I am his first-born son that was the last
> That ware the imperial diadem of Rome.
> Then let my father's honours live in me,
> Nor wrong mine age with this indignity. (1.1.5–8)

Saturninus advocates lineal succession by claiming that the 'first-born' son should inherit the crown from the 'last' ruler: the dead father's honours would thus continue to 'live in' the son of greatest 'age'.

Bassianus, Saturninus' younger brother, makes an alternative claim for his own sovereignty based on the paternal inheritance not of blood but of character; he argues that his brother will 'dishonour' the throne by violating 'justice, continence, and nobility' (1.1.13, 15). In this debate, one political system's method of reproducing political honour (through primogeniture) is challenged by another political system's method of reproducing political honour (through election of the worthiest candidate). Bassianus' concern for 'continence' introduces into the debate the idea of masculine self-control as essential for just rule. We might recall here that in *3 Henry VI*, the sexually incontinent King Edward justifies marrying Lady Gray by tyrannically declaring that his 'will shall stand for law' (4.1.49). In the event, Titus Andronicus, a celebrated warrior, endorses Saturninus in an apparent vote of confidence for the more conservative principle of primogeniture.

Titus' belief that the eldest son of the previous ruler will 'ripen justice in this commonweal' is quickly undermined by the new ruler's sexual incontinence, just as Bassianus had feared. To reward Titus for his support, Saturninus announces that he will marry Titus' daughter Lavinia, 'Rome's royal mistress, mistress of my heart' (1.1.241). At the same time, Saturninus praises the beauty of his prisoner of war, Tamora, Queen of the Goths, whom he calls a 'goodly lady', of the 'hue / That [he] would choose were [he] to choose anew' (1.1.261–262). In short, it seems that Saturninus is admitting that although he is marrying Lavinia for political reasons, if he could 'choose' a wife based purely on sexual desire, it would be Tamora. Worse, Lavinia is already betrothed to Bassianus, who refuses to relinquish her to his brother in the name of 'right', 'justice', and 'lawful' ownership (1.1.279–281, 294). In the quarrel that erupts, Titus' sons take Bassianus' part, and Titus, enraged at their disobedience to the Emperor and himself, kills one of them. Moments after ascending to power, then, Saturninus' impulsiveness and sense of entitlement have precipitated a crisis that seems to revolve precisely around his inability to square continence with justice. Furious at having been so humiliated, Saturninus rejects Titus and his family and chooses Tamora instead of Lavinia as his spouse.

Saturninus' emphasis on Tamora's beauty hints at an imbalance in this royal marriage much like that between Henry VI and Margaret in the *Henry VI* plays. Both marriages are also similar in that a king marries a foreigner from an enemy nation. Saturninus acknowledges

Tamora's ethnic and racial differences even as he 'creates' her Empress of Rome:

> And therefore, lovely Tamora, Queen of Goths,
> That like the stately Phoebe 'mongst her nymphs
> Dost overshine the gallant'st dames of Rome,
> If thou be pleased with this my sudden choice,
> Behold, I choose thee, Tamora, for my bride,
> And will create thee Empress of Rome. (1.1.312–317)

In comparing Tamora to Pheobe (or Diana), the brightly shining goddess of the moon, Saturninus might be acknowledging a racial difference between the extremely fair-skinned Goths and the more moderately coloured Romans.[27] Titus' brother Marcus remarks the danger of so precipitously bringing an unknown foreigner and racial other into the centre of political power: 'the subtle Queen of Goths / Is of a sudden thus advanced in Rome' (1.1.389–390). Soon thereafter, Tamora employs her subtlety to convince Saturninus to 'be ruled by [her]' and to '[d]issemble all your griefs and discontents' until she can find an occasion to massacre Titus' family (1.1.439–440). Having been ruled by his lust in choosing Tamora for a wife, Saturninus quickly cedes political rule to her as well. In fact, his praise of Tamora as 'stately Phoebe 'mongst her nymphs' is an ominous sign that he has practically written himself out of political authority. A virgin goddess, 'stately' (of 'high rank; princely') Phoebe ruled over a community of female nymphs from which men were completely excluded.[28]

Saturninus' political subordination to Tamora is all the more disturbing because Tamora has a lover, Aaron the Moor, another racial outsider to Rome. In a soliloquy, Aaron boasts of his sexual control over the queen, whom he 'in triumph long / Hast prisoner held fettered in amorous chains, / And faster bound to Aaron's charming eyes / Than is Prometheus tied to Caucasus' (2.1.14–17). Whereas Saturninus figures Tamora as stately Phoebe, Aaron figures her as abject Prometheus, who was punished by being eternally chained to a mountain, where an eagle would devour his liver each day. Aaron claims to have sexually 'charm[ed]' Tamora, herself a 'siren' who will 'charm Rome's Saturnine / And see his shipwreck and his commonweal's' (2.1.21, 24–25). In ancient Greek texts, sirens are monstrous bird-woman hybrids, and in medieval texts they are mermaids who would lure sailors to their destruction by

Figure 2.2   'This siren that will charm Rome's Saturnine': monstrously seductive femininity. Aegidius Sadeler (II), 'Fabel van de zeemeermin' [fable of the mermaid]. (Prague: 1608). Rijksmuseum, Amsterdam.

singing an enchanting but deadly song (Figure 2.2). By calling Tamora a siren, Aaron suggests that her sexual allure has the power to ruin not only her husband, but an entire 'commonweal'. Like Suffolk in *2 Henry VI*, Aaron believes that he can use his sexual bond with the queen to control her and thereby seize political power for himself.

Tamora, like Margaret in *2 Henry VI*, foreshadows the destruction of the kingdom over which she rules through an allusion to Troy. In the *Aeneid*, Dido and Aeneas are hunting one day when a violent storm sends them scrambling for shelter in a cave, where they have sex for the first time. Like Dido and Aeneas, Tamora and Aaron are of different races and nationalities; when they become separated from their hunting party, Tamora similarly entices Aaron to a sexual encounter in the wilderness. Although Aaron shares African origins with Dido, he resembles Aeneas as a 'wand'ring prince': a traveller who achieves considerable political influence through a sexual bond with the queen of a powerful city-state (2.3.22). Just as Aeneas' relationship with Dido destabilizes Carthage through the circulation of damaging sexual rumours and the resentment of Dido's rejected African suitors, so Aaron's sexual relationship with Tamora threatens the stability of the Roman state under the ineffectual leadership of a cuckold.

When Lavinia and Bassianus discover Tamora and Aaron alone in the forest, they deride Tamora's sexual attraction to a Moor in terms that underline the larger political implications of royal adultery. Responding to Bassianus' mocking identification of her as Diana, goddess of virginity, Tamora says that she would transform him into a stag if she could, just as Diana did to the hunter Acteon, who was subsequently devoured by his hounds. Because of the folk belief that cuckolded husbands grew humiliating horns, Lavinia finds a different meaning in Tamora's threat to turn Bassianus into a horned beast:

> Under your patience, gentle Empress,
> 'Tis thought you have a goodly gift in horning,
> And to be doubted that your Moor and you
> Are singled forth to try experiments.
> Jove shield your husband from his hounds today—
> 'Tis pity they should take him for a stag.
> BASSIANUS   Believe me, Queen, your swart Cimmerian
> Doth make your honour of his body's hue,
> Spotted, detested, and abominable.
> Why are you sequestered from all your train,
> Dismounted from your snow-white goodly steed,
> And wandered hither to an obscure plot,
> Accompanied but with a barbarous Moor,
> If foul desire had not conducted you?   (2.3.66–79)

Being known as a cuckold, a figure of ridicule, has clearly compromised the Emperor's political authority. To the degree that Bassianus voices the early modern European antipathy to black skin as '[s]potted, detested, and abominable', public knowledge of Tamora's sexual preference for a Moor would be particularly humiliating to Saturninus. According to Lavinia, Tamora's unruly lust inverts the gender hierarchy of the Roman court: she identifies Saturninus in relation to Tamora as 'your husband', just as Aaron is 'your Moor'. Stressing Aaron's exotic identity as 'swart Cimmerian' and 'barbarous Moor', Bassianus hints at the danger of an alliance between the Gothic Empress and a non-white, non-European, foreigner. Although the Queen has evidently tried to 'obscure' her adultery, Bassianus observes that through their illicit sexual contact Aaron's black skin has corrupted Tamora's reputation, making it as foul as his hue. Tamora's rejection of the decorous and chaste ('snow-white') behaviour expected of a Roman Empress must be a consequence of 'foul desire': both wicked desire and desire for a 'foul' or 'raven-coloured' body (2.3.83).

Bassianus' fear of the infiltration of a 'detested' blackness into the heart of the Roman Empire almost literally comes to pass when Tamora gives birth to a black infant. To hide their adultery, Aaron plots to exchange his son with a white baby recently born to an interracial couple of his acquaintance: a black Moorish man and a white woman as 'fair as' Tamora's sons, which suggests that she is also Gothic (4.2.153). This white baby will be able to pass as the legitimate child of Tamora and the Emperor. As Francesca Royster observes, the result of this deception is that a boy who is half Moor and half Goth, without a drop of Roman blood, will secretly become the heir to the Roman Empire. Had Queen Margaret given birth to Suffolk's child in the *Henry VI* plays, that child at least would have combined noble French and English blood, just like King Henry VI himself, whose mother was a French princess. Since Aaron's changeling child has neither royal nor Roman blood, it would completely subvert the racial purity of the Roman imperial dynasty. Although Aaron is captured before he can carry out his plot, the possibility of its success reveals the intimate connection in early modern thought between sex unconstrained by dominant patriarchal values and the dissolution of 'justice, continence, and nobility' (1.1.15).

Anthony and Cleopatra also explores the political upheaval caused by a sexual bond between two leaders of different races and nations: Cleopatra, the queen of Egypt, and Anthony, one of the three rulers of the Roman Empire. The situation at the start of the play recalls the crisis in the Greek camp in *Troilus and Cressida*, where Achilles' refusal to fight is blamed, in part, on sexual desires that render him 'effeminate' (3.3.211). As the Roman Pompey reports, 'Mark Antony / In Egypt sits at dinner, and will make / No wars without doors' (2.1.11–13). The first lines of the play are spoken by Philo, a Roman soldier serving Anthony in Egypt, who similarly condemns his general's sexual indolence:

> Nay, but this dotage of our General's
> O'erflows the measure. Those his goodly eyes,
> That o'er the files and musters of the war
> Have glowed like plated Mars, now bend, now turn
> The office and devotion of their view
> Upon a tawny front. His captain's heart,
> Which in the scuffles of great fights hath burst
> The buckles on his breast, reneges all temper,
> And is become the bellows and the fan
> To cool a gipsy's lust. (1.1.1–10)

Philo's speech revolves around a stark antithesis between military discipline and amorous looseness. Anthony is revered for having once been a formidable commander whose eyes, glowing like the armour worn by the Roman god of war, used to survey the orderly lines of his soldiers. In this glorious past, the only powerful emotions Anthony experienced were the courage and rage that made his striving heart break through his chest armour during 'great fights'. Now, however, Anthony has 'turn[ed]' his 'devotion' from war to sexual 'dotage', and 'ben[t]' his view away from ranks of disciplined men and onto a 'tawny'-coloured 'gypsy'.[29] Submission to an African queen's lust, laments Philo, has made Anthony lose his masculine self-control: his desires now 'o[v]erflow' all limits of 'temper[ance]'. Since Europeans sometimes attributed to Africans an excessively lustful temperament, Cleopatra's race imparts a particular stigma to Anthony's sexual looseness.

Anthony's dotage carries serious political consequences. As we have seen with Queen Margaret in *2 Henry VI* and *3 Henry VI*, resourceful wives can step in to fill the power vacuum left by weak husbands; in the latter play, Margaret leads armies against King Henry's enemies. In *Anthony and Cleopatra*, while Anthony carouses in Egypt, his wife and brother make war against Octavius Caesar, a rival co-ruler of Rome. Realizing the risk of 'losing [him]self in dotage' to Cleopatra, Anthony returns to Rome to reestablish his political credibility with Caesar (1.2.106). Asserting his loyalty to Caesar, Anthony blames his wife, who has recently died, for her 'uncurbable' (uncontrollable—by him) 'impatience' to create havoc (2.2.71–72). To heal the rift between Anthony and Caesar, Agrippa proposes that Anthony marry Caesar's sister, Octavia, whose reputation for modesty and chastity is antithetical to Cleopatra's reputed wantonness. Despite agreeing to the marriage as a political expedient, Anthony has no intention of abandoning his sexual relationship with Cleopatra: 'I will to Egypt; / And though I make this marriage for my peace, / I'th'East my pleasure lies' (2.3.36–38). Marriage to a 'holy, cold, and still' European wife cannot compete with the luxurious sensual pleasures available in a generalized 'East' (2.6.120).

Along with Anthony's neglect of Octavia, the highly charged matter of political succession further sets Anthony and Caesar at odds. Caesar is appalled to learn that Anthony has staged a public ceremony in Alexandria intended politically to legitimize Cleopatra and her heirs, including the 'unlawful issue' of their lust (3.6.7). Through this ceremony, Anthony grants Cleopatra full possession of the Roman territories of Egypt, Syria, Cyprus, and Lydia. Moreover, he proclaims his sons 'the kings of kings' and gives them rule over other Roman provinces. As Caesar bitterly complains, 'He hath given his empire / Up to a whore' (3.6.66–67); Maecenas agrees that Anthony, 'most large / In his abominations', has given his 'potent regiment to a trull' (3.6.93–95). From a Roman perspective, Anthony's loss of self-control in the presence of his African 'whore' is inimical to manly 'poten[cy]' and the ability to advance the aims of Roman imperialism. Indeed, Anthony's continued dotage on Cleopatra contributes to his military failures, defeat by Caesar, and, finally, his suicide.

In its linkage of gender, sexual, and racial transgressions, *Anthony and Cleopatra* returns us to the unnatural and apocalyptic imagery of Drayton's *The Mooncalf*. Recall that the poem describes the mooncalf, the product of the devil's fornication with the world, as hermaphroditic: 'A fem'nine man, a woman masculine.' Likewise, in *Anthony and Cleopatra*, Caesar complains that Anthony and Cleopatra have inverted genders: Anthony 'is not more manlike / Than Cleopatra', nor she '[m]ore womanly than he' (1.4.5–7). The mooncalf is stranger than anything that 'ever Nile yet into light could bring'. According to popular belief, serpents were 'bred' from the extremely fertile mud of the Nile; hence Antony affectionately calls Cleopatra 'my serpent of old Nile' (2.7.25; 1.5.25). When Cleopatra discovers that Anthony has married Octavia, she furiously calls down ruin on her own kingdom, as if imagining Sodom liquified by flames: 'Melt Egypt into Nile, and kindly creatures / Turn all to serpents!' (2.5.78–79).

Throughout this chapter, we have seen how Shakespeare's plays represent transgressive forms of desire and embodiment—sodomy, rape, adultery, male indolence, female aggressiveness, extra-marital interracial partnerships—as engines of the ruin of cities (Sodom, Troy) and of the suffering and weakening of nations (England under Henry VI and Edward IV, Scotland under the Macbeths, Rome under Saturninus, Egypt under Cleopatra). The terrible vividness of these familiar stories from Biblical, ancient, and British history can help us to understand why early moderns sometimes responded to queer violations of sexual and gender propriety with such vehemence.

Shakespeare and Queer Studies. Mario DiGangi, Oxford University Press. © Mario DiGangi 2025.
DOI: 10.1093/9780191994951.003.0003

Queer Gender Transformations

In Chapter 1, we considered how Portia's male disguise facilitates queer erotic possibilities within marriage, as both Portia and Bassanio imagine having sex with her male alias 'Balthazar'. Although cross-gender performances can be powerful vehicles for sexual desires, fantasies, and intimacies, in this chapter I put less emphasis on sexuality in order to foreground ideas from transgender studies, which addresses 'gender's multiplicity and transformability'.[1]

Premodern cultures tended to stress the social fact of gender difference, even as they recognized that some bodies confounded binary gender categories. Now considered offensive, 'hermaphrodite' was the most common premodern term for intersex people: those born with sexual or reproductive features that do not correspond with binary gender. 'Hermaphrodite' could also be deployed as an insult to stigmatize those whose dress or behaviour flouted dominant gender expectations. For instance, an English satirical pamphlet called *Hic Mulier* (1620) excoriated as 'new *Hermaphrodites*' London women who wore short hair and male clothing. Although some early modern physicians acknowledged the natural diversity of gendered anatomical features, early modern medical, legal, and social institutions tended to impose binary gender categorizations upon individuals who were brought to their attention for having transgressed gender boundaries.[2] Intersex persons could be subjected to medical examinations to determine their dominant gender; they were then constrained to live in accordance with that official gender, as manifested through their name, clothing, profession, spouse, and sexual practices. When examining intersex individuals, 'physicians looked, in the final analysis, to the genitals and their functional capacities as the means for establishing norms and identities'.[3] The medical assignment of intersex persons to a single gender illustrates Jean Howard's trenchant claim that 'the Renaissance needed the idea of two genders, one subordinate to the other, as a key part of its hierarchical view of the social order and to buttress its gendered division of labor'.[4]

Given the importance of binary gender to early modern social order, Kathleen McLuskie is surely right to posit that Shakespeare's theatrical explorations of gender transformation depended on a shared understanding of commonly assumed gender differences.[5] McLuskie argues that the comedies'

> play with gender could not have achieved their narrative and theatrical pleasures without being based in some shared understanding of the discursive integrity of maleness or femaleness. Audiences and readers had to accept the coherence of maleness and femaleness and the way that distinction worked as a social category in order to participate in the plays' imaginary world where, for purposes of jokes or suspense, male and female behaviour could be put on and taken off as easily as farthingale or doublet and hose.[6]

McLuskie oversimplifies when she compares the adoption of gendered behaviour to the ease of putting on or taking off a piece of clothing. When women in Shakespeare cross-dress, they strategize about the male styles, speech patterns, mannerisms, and movements that they will need to perform in order to pass convincingly as men. Passing as a man is not a simple matter of donning doublet and hose: the voice, attitude, and body must be laboriously aligned with conventionally male gender traits.

Transgender scholar Sawyer Kemp has addressed the limitations of analyses that address theatrical cross-dressing as the sole manifestation of early modern transgender experience. Whereas Shakespeare's cross-dressed women are always perceived as male, he observes, contemporary transgender people often face 'anxiety, ambivalence, and danger' when attempting to pass in public or asking others to use their correct pronouns and names.[7] Kemp challenges early modern scholars to 'locate transgender identity in something other than clothing'—for instance, to identify dramatic characters who confront the kinds of difficulties familiar to contemporary transgender people, such as body dysphoria, police harassment, homelessness, and sexual violence—whether these characters are cross-dressed, such as Rosalind, or not, such as Hamlet.[8]

Following Kemp's lead, my aim in this chapter is to read the gender transformations of Shakespeare's female characters through a transgender lens that addresses gender dysphoria, harassment, homelessness, and sexual violence. In drawing parallels between Shakespearean drama and contemporary society, I do not intend to treat Shakespeare's characters as subjects of sociological analysis, as if they were real people with real problems instead of 'figures in a persuasive discourse or agents of a plot'.[9] A dramatic character's speeches and actions do not naturally or spontaneously derive from their life experiences, values, or psychology. Whatever Shakespeare's characters do or say has been deliberately arranged to develop the ideas or situations being explored in a particular play. Moreover, characters often correspond to dramatic types, such as the wilful lover or the witty page. Nonetheless, if we bear these caveats in mind, we can appreciate how the plays explore the emotional and social consequences of temporarily adopting a different gender identity in ways that resonate with contemporary transgender experiences.

Although Shakespeare's characters have very different motives for altering their gender than those of contemporary transgender people, who are often driven by the 'urgency of inner necessity', the affective stakes and consequences of cross-dressing in the comedies can still feel quite high.[10] Rosalind in *As You Like It*, Julia in *The Two Gentlemen of Verona*, and Viola in *Twelfth Night* articulate compelling reasons for temporarily adopting a male identity, and they experience both pleasure and anxiety in their unfamiliar gender roles. Because I wish to focus on what gender transformation feels like for these characters, I will devote less attention to discussing the erotic consequences of cross-dressing, which have been vigorously explored by scholars since the 1980s. I will also discuss the comedies out of chronological order, beginning with the one in which the gender-transforming woman experiences the most unadulterated pleasure (*As You Like It*) and ending with the one in which she faces the greatest risks (*Twelfth Night*). I conclude the chapter with an English history play, *1 Henry VI*, whose female protagonist, Joan la Pucelle (Joan of Arc), adopts a masculine military identity, including armour, without trying to pass as a man. My analysis of Joan most directly answers Kemp's challenge to engage with transgender identity in Shakespeare beyond clothing. The verbal, physical, and sexual violence that Joan suffers because of her queer gender, I will show, resonates with forms of abuse familiar to contemporary transgender people.

In each of the four plays I discuss, standards of beauty play an important role in the gendering of bodies, and racial ideologies affect which gendered features count as beautiful. Shakespeare's contemporaries predominantly defined feminine beauty in terms of 'fairness', which connoted whiteness, high status, and chastity. During the seventeenth century, whiteness became naturalized as 'the defining English complexion for both sexes', as opposed to the darker complexions associated with various foreign (e.g., Mediterranean, African, Middle Eastern, Southeast Asian, etc.) nationalities.[11] Kim Hall has argued that the praise of fairness typical of early modern lyric poetry such as Shakespeare's *Sonnets* signals and promotes this 'emergent ideology of white supremacy'.[12] Moreover, scholars have demonstrated how ideologies of gender and racial difference developed in tandem during the early modern period. I hope to contribute to these findings by reading gender transformation in Shakespeare's plays in terms of racial, sexual, and social differences.

Boy Actors and Female Parts

Before moving to the plays, it will be helpful to address one of the most sustained topics of debate in feminist and queer Shakespeare scholarship: the erotic appeal of the 'boys' (usually aged thirteen to twenty-one) who played women's roles on the London stage. Shakespeare's 'anti-theatrical' contemporaries excoriated the phenomenon of boys dressing, talking, and behaving like women for the entertainment—and sexual titillation—of male and female playgoers. In the *School of Abuse* (1579), for instance, Stephen Gosson objects that theatre offers 'effeminate gesture to ravish the sence, and wanton speache to whette desire to inordinate lust'.[13] Philip Stubbes in the *Anatomie of Abuses* (1583) charges that when a play is over, stimulated spectators get together to 'play the Sodomits, or worse'.[14] Granting clothes an almost magical power to alter gender and provoke lust, John Rainolds warns of the sexual allure of 'beautiful boys transformed into women by putting on their raiment, their feature, looks and fashions'.[15] According to Laura Levine, for these critics 'the hermaphroditic actor, the boy with the properties of both sexes, becomes the embodiment of all that is frightening about the self', particularly the belief that 'there is no such thing as an essential gender'.[16] Roberta Barker concurs that the boy actor destabilized 'normative codes of desire'.[17] Nonetheless, Bruce Smith cautions that the eroticization of boy actors is 'not a universal fact about boy actors playing female roles in all plays, in all circumstances', since some plays stressed the satiric, not the erotic or romantic, aspects of boys' cross-gender performances.[18]

As Smith and Barker reasonably argue from the meagre surviving evidence, responses to boy actors must have greatly varied depending on the playgoer, actor, play, genre, and style of performance on any given day. 'How could we ever hope to generalize about spectators whose numbers might run into the thousands?' asks Smith.[19] Simone Chess argues, however, that certain seventeenth-century boy actors developed a reputation for 'queer gender performances', even once they became adults and played exclusively male roles.[20] Often described as 'pretty' or 'beautiful' youths, these actors were recognized for their facility at embodying femininity or androgyny. Although the following analysis of Shakespeare's comedies does not specifically focus on boy actors' gender performances, it is useful to remember that whenever a female character draws specific attention to her body, clothing, or gender identity, original audience members might have become particularly attuned—whether erotically or not—to the presence of the boy who was embodying a woman's part on stage.

As You Like It

In what follows, I build on Chapter 1's account of the homonormative love between Celia and Rosalind in *As You Like It* by focusing on Rosalind's transformation into Ganymede. Banished by her uncle, Rosalind announces her plan to

> suit me all points like a man,
> A gallant curtal-axe upon my thigh,
> A boar-spear in my hand, and in my heart,
> Lie there what hidden woman's fear there will.
> We'll have a swashing and a martial outside,
> As many other mannish cowards have,
> That do outface it with their semblances.   (1.3.110–116)

Through a combination of clothing, weapons, and attitude, Rosalind will convey the 'martial outside' of a 'man', despite the 'woman's fear' lying 'hidden' in her 'heart'. Rosalind intends her display of weaponry and bravery to discourage assailants from accosting Celia and herself during their travels. However, Rosalind undermines the grounds of the seemingly essential gendered distinction between (brave) men and (fearful) women by modelling her 'swashing and martial outside' on the 'semblances' or mere appearances of courage adopted by 'mannish cowards': an oxymoron that yokes manliness with its opposite, cowardliness. To 'outface' means '[t]o disconcert, silence, or defeat (a person) by face-to-face confrontation or a display of confidence, arrogance, etc.', or 'to maintain (something false or shameful) with boldness or effrontery; to brazen out'.[21] Cowardly men successfully confront brave men by performing a false confidence; through a similarly brazen performance, Rosalind will project a convincing show of manhood. That either a man or a woman might outwardly seem 'like a man' implies that manhood involves the creation of a semblance—or, at the least, suggests that it is impossible to tell the difference between 'true' and 'false' manhood, which is always dependent on the performance of conventional traits such as courage. The manliest man might be hiding a 'woman's fear' in his heart. Shakespeare here seems to anticipate Judith Butler's theory (discussed in the Introduction) of gender as an imitation of an imitation, not as an authentic manifestation of some natural, original biological condition.

Even if it is a fiction, manhood is nonetheless useful. Self-consciously using her 'swashing and martial outside' to comfort Celia and herself when they become exhausted by travel, Rosalind again admits that her woman's heart should make her cry:

I could find in my heart to disgrace my man's apparel and to cry like a woman. But I must comfort the weaker vessel, as doublet and hose ought to show itself courageous to petticoat; therefore, courage, good Aliena! (2.4.3–6)

Proposing that 'man's apparel' can impart a 'courageous' heart—the word 'courageous' in fact derives from *cor*, Latin for 'heart'—Rosalind reveals that gendered behaviour is not necessarily tied to gendered anatomy, at the same time that she ironically cites the conventional gender binary that makes women (here, Aliena) the 'weaker vessel'.

As Oliver will later advise Ganymede, a boy who 'lack[s] a man's heart' can still take 'good heart, and counterfeit to be a man' (4.3.163–164, 171–172). In short, some women (or boys) can display male 'heart'—spirit, vigour, character—without literally possessing a man's 'heart'—the biological organ imagined as the seat of thought and emotion.[22] As Rosalind's attribution of courage to 'doublet and hose' suggests, male clothing can certainly help a woman to feel and to display the 'heart' of a man. Jennifer Drouin refers to such moments of self-consciousness about the relationship of clothing to gender in Shakespeare as 'drag', a performance style that 'exposes rather than conceals its own artifice'.[23] Yet is it important to remember that clothing is only one element involved in Rosalind's convincingly embodied gender performance.

In fact, despite often joking with Celia about the artifice of her 'man's apparel', Rosalind relies more on a naturalized, racially inflected, ideal of feminine beauty in order to pass herself off as Ganymede, who is demonstrably not yet a 'man' (3.2.208). That Orlando perceives Ganymede as a 'pretty youth' and a 'fair' boy of 'female favour' certainly facilitates his willingness to court Ganymede as if he were Rosalind, and thus serves Rosalind's goal of secretly developing intimacy with the man she loves (3.2.303, 4.3.84–85) (Figure 3.1). By contrast, to succeed in her disguise as Aliena, Celia uses umber to 'smirch' or darken her otherwise fair complexion, thus rendering herself a less attractive target to potential assailants (1.3.106).

Whereas elite European women typically wore masks to protect their skin from the sun, common women, especially those who worked outside, might be recognized by their tanned skin, unless they used cosmetics to whiten their complexions.[24] That Aliena is noticeably 'browner than her brother' enhances Ganymede's fair feminine beauty by contrast (4.3.87).[25] Likewise, Rosalind draws upon the warrant of Ganymede's fair femininity to mock in racialized terms the shepherdess Phoebe's unappealing 'inky brows', 'black silk hair', 'bugle eyeballs', 'leathern hand', and 'Ethiop words' (3.5.47–48; 4.3.24, 35).[26] Nonetheless, Phoebe falls for the feminine beauty of the 'pretty youth' who insults her, citing the 'pretty redness in his lip' and the paler red of his cheek (3.5.114, 121). Ganymede's fairness thus gives Rosalind erotic leverage over both men and women, and enhances her control over the terms of her male impersonation.

Polydorus de Carauagio Jn .

Figure 3.1   'Pretty youth': Jupiter embracing Ganymede. Cherubino Alberti after Polidoro da Caravaggio, 'Jupiter en Ganymedes' [Jupiter and Ganymede]. (Italy: 1590–1600). Rijksmuseum, Amsterdam.

Rosalind decides when playing Ganymede no longer serves her turn. When Orlando expresses envy that Oliver and Aliena will marry the next day, Ganymede asks him, 'Why, then, tomorrow I cannot serve your turn for Rosalind?' (5.2.43–44). Declaring 'I can live no longer by thinking', Orlando prompts Rosalind to end her charade: 'If you do love Rosalind so near the heart as your gesture cries it out, when your brother marries Aliena shall you marry her' (5.2.55–57). Notably, this solution not only secures Rosalind the husband she desires, but affirms her love for Celia through the symbolism of a double wedding. Although the queer temporality of Rosalind's leisurely, improvisational, homoerotic play as Ganymede has seemingly come to an end through the advent of a wedding that must occur 'tomorrow', the play's marital conclusion incorporates both Rosalind's longstanding homonormative bond with Celia and her frequently homoerotic transgender performance as Ganymede (5.2.59). A stage direction in the First Folio (1623) printing of *As You Like It* indicates that, in the final scene, Hymen, the classical god of marriage, enters with 'Rosalind, and Celia'. As Jennifer Drouin notes, subsequent editors have often added stage directions specifying that the women have abandoned their personas and costumes as Ganymede and Aliena: for instance, '*Rosalind in Woman's Cloths*' (Rowe, eighteenth century); or Rosalind and Celia '[*as themselves*]' (*The Norton Shakespeare*). Drouin argues that 'the onstage lookers' recognition that Ganymede had been Rosalind indicates, however, that Rosalind must have some vestiges of the clothes in which she was passing in order for them to recognize Ganymede in Rosalind'.[27] Although Drouin's theory is ingenious, theatrical convention might simply dictate that other characters recognize Rosalind as Ganymede by her face, stature, or speech, not because she wears any remnants of her male disguise.

Still, when Hymen instructs the Duke, in the words of the First Folio, to receive his 'daughter' and to 'joyne his hand with his, / Whose heart within his bosome is', the marriage of Rosalind and Orlando appears to incorporate a remnant of Ganymede after all (Figure 3.2).

Most modern editors assume that the first *his* of 'ioyne his hand with his' is a print-shop misreading of the word *hir* ('her') in the manuscript. Marriage, they reason, must join a 'his' with a 'her', not with a 'his'. Jeffrey Masten, however, cautions that 'we would not want to exclude too quickly the possibility of two male hands joined in the last scene of a play that repeatedly directs attention to the boy actor playing the part of Rosalind'—a character who has performed under the 'homoerotically charged name "Ganymede"' and who has already taken Orlando's hand in a 'version of this same marriage'.[28] Moreover, despite his role as the god of marriage, Hymen has a queerer pedigree than we might suspect. In one ancient tradition, Hymen was a 'very handsome youth who disguised himself as a girl among others in order to be near his beloved', and in another he was a remarkably

Enter Hymen, Rosalind, and Celia.
Still Musicke.
Hymen. *Then is there mirth in heauen,*
When earthly things made eauen
attone together.
Good Duke receiue thy daughter,
Hymen from Heauen brought her,
Yea brought her hether.
That thou mightst ioyne his hand with his,
Whose heart within his bosome is.

Figure 3.2 'his hand with his': *As You Like It*, First Folio (1623). William Shakespeare, *Mr. William Shakespeares Comedies, Histories, and Tragedies* (London: [Isaac Jaggard and Ed. Blount], 1623), folio 206, sig. S1 verso. Call#: STC 22273 Fo.1 no.09. Folger Shakespeare Library.

beautiful boy whom the god Apollo fervently loved—just as Jove loved Ganymede.[29] Delivered by this queer god to her father and her husband, Rosalind offers herself in identical terms to each of the men she loves: 'To you I give myself, for I am yours', she says twice (5.4.105–106).[30] This queerly double giving which hints at multiple selves can serve as a reminder that marriage not only marks the 'begin[ning]' of a projected future of 'true delights', but also maintains a temporal continuity with the queer affections, identities, and intimacies of the past (5.4.186–187).

The Two Gentlemen of Verona

The Two Gentlemen of Verona illustrates Sawyer Kemp's concern that cross-dressing in Shakespeare often has little connection with contemporary transgender experiences. Unlike those who transition in order to express their authentic gender identity, Julia adopts a temporary male identity only to travel more safely from Verona to Milan, where Proteus, her betrothed, is living. Whereas transgender people disproportionately suffer from sexual assault and homelessness, Julia disguises herself as a man to *prevent* sexual assault (the 'loose encounters of lascivious men') during a provisional and volitional state of homelessness (2.7.41). Her reasons for taking on a male identity, in short, are the conventional ones that Shakespeare draws upon in several comedies.

At the same time, Julia's gender change is motivated by an emotional urgency conveyed through heightened religious metaphors. Julia tells her maid Lucetta that she pines for the 'soul's food' of Proteus' loving glances, and that to quell her spiritual hunger she welcomes the physical discomforts of a temporary homelessness: 'A true-devoted pilgrim is not weary / To measure kingdoms with his feeble steps' (2.7.15, 9–10). Once reunited with Proteus, at which time she presumably intends to abandon her male disguise, Julia anticipates that she will 'rest as after much turmoil / A blessèd soul doth in Elysium' (2.7.37–38): a goal perhaps roughly analogous to a transgender person's hope of finally 'rest[ing]' in an authentic gender identity after the emotional 'turmoil' of dysphoria.

Through a kind of gender dysphoria, Julia certainly displays an awareness of the turmoil involved in adopting a male gender identity, no matter how temporary and instrumental. From our vantagepoint, it might seem as if Julia is gender transitioning 'in reverse', eschewing the comfort of her assigned gender identity for the discomfort of a new one. In Julia's command that Lucetta 'fit' her with clothes that 'may beseem some well-reputed page', 'fit' means both to tailor clothes to a body and to wear socially seemly or appropriate clothes (2.7.42–43). But how could clothes fit for a young man's body be either physically or socially fit for a young woman's?[31] For Lucetta to ask what style of breeches Julia requires 'fits as well' as asking a man what kind of farthingale (petticoat) he would like—in other words, it's not a fitting or seemly question (2.7.50). Worst of all, wearing a codpiece—a bag-like appendage or a phallic protrusion used to cover and, in the latter instance, to emphasize a man's genitals—strikes Julia as 'ill-favoured', meaning to have an 'unpleasing appearance' or to be 'offensive'.[32] According to Will Fisher, the codpiece was often represented as a 'crucial component of masculine identity' at the same time that its detachability and transferability could be read as 'destabiliz[ing] patriarchal gendered relations'.[33] Far from destabilizing patriarchal gendered relations, Julia's ultimate goal in donning a codpiece is to marry Proteus, establishing him as the patriarch of their household. That goal would be jeopardized should her male persona bring 'scandal' to her name, hence staining her reputation for chastity (2.7.61). Caught in the paradox of using a potentially transgressive means to an orthodox end, Julia ultimately leaves it to Lucetta to prepare an outfit that is 'meet and most mannerly'—a difficult task considering that clothing that is 'mannerly' (appropriate for a *man*) might not be 'mannerly' (modest, showing good manners) on a young woman.

Although Julia's gender transformation might be motivated by self-protection, when she arrives in Milan to discover that Proteus has transferred his affections to Silvia, she invents (or possibly retains and elaborates from her travels?) a male persona as the page 'Sebastian', a decision that creates a different kind of emotional turmoil. Overhearing Proteus assure Silvia that Julia has died, Julia experiences the disorientating feeling of being both alive and dead, as if the presence of the youth Sebastian has relegated the woman Julia to a faded past:

> PROTEUS   I grant, sweet love, that I did love a lady,
>   But she is dead.
> JULIA [*aside*]   'Twere false if I should speak it,
>   For I am sure she is not burièd . . .
> SILVIA   Go to thy lady's grave and call hers [her love] thence,
>   Or, at the least, in hers sepulchre thine.
> JULIA [*aside*]   He heard not that.   (4.2.98–100, 109–111)

For Sebastian to speak of Julia's death would be 'false', but for Julia (as Julia) to speak of it would be absurd, or uncanny: only a ghost returned from the dead, such as Hamlet's father, could relate the demise of the 'burièd' body of which it is a manifestation. Moreover, even as Julia quips that Proteus hears only what he wants to hear, she is queerly hearing what she should not—the news of her own body's internment in a faraway grave. Through asides, Julia can express her pained feelings, but that she can share them only with the theatre audience puts her in the position of a ghost who can be perceived only by some. Thus, the very ease of her passing as Sebastian pains Julia by preventing her from exerting agency as *Julia*, whether by declaring her love to Proteus, confronting him with his treachery, joining forces with Silvia to shame him, and so on. Moreover, Julia suffers from a state of queer temporality due to the postponement of her marriage and to Sebastian's relegation of her to a past available only as an occasion of sad remembrance and regret (4.2.26). Experiencing what Susan Stryker calls the 'abrupt, often jarring transitions between genders', Julia struggles to align her sense of self with a past (female) identity she has left behind, a present (male) identity she is publicly performing, and a future in which she hopes to inhabit a new (female) identity as a wife.[34]

In another aside, Julia articulates this queer temporality as the feeling of being turned into an ephemeral 'shadow' as a result both of Proteus' neglect and of her adopting the 'shadow' role of Sebastian in response to that neglect. Rejected by Silvia, Proteus uses the common Shakespearean antithesis of substance/shadow to justify his desire to worship her portrait:

> To that I'll speak, to that I'll sigh and weep;
> For since the substance of your perfect self
> Is else devoted, I am but a shadow,
> And to your shadow will I make true love.
> JULIA [*aside*] If 'twere a substance, you would sure deceive it
> And make it but a shadow, as I am.   (4.2.115–120)

Because Silvia has devoted her 'substance' (or 'perfect self') to another man, Proteus has become a 'shadow' (a nothing), and must be content courting her 'shadow' (her artificial image). Picking up Proteus' metaphor, Julia defines her male persona as a 'shadow': an artificial reflection of her true self. At the same time, Julia refers to her 'authentic' female self ('as I am') as a shadow, a kind of nothing in this new world where Proteus has rescinded the spiritual nourishment of his love. Julia reasons that if Silvia were to give Proteus not her 'shadow'—a portrait of herself—but her very 'substance'—her actual body—he would certainly 'deceive' her as well, turning her into another abandoned 'shadow'.

Julia's sadness at having become nothing to Proteus is only intensified by the intimacy they achieve as master and servant. Proteus employs Sebastian as his page because he recognizes 'good bringing up, fortune, and truth' in the youth's face and comportment, even as he cannot recognize Julia's face in Sebastian's (4.4.61). Although Proteus' inability to recognize Julia is consistent with the theatrical convention that renders any gender disguise impenetrable, in the world of the play it compounds Julia's suffering. Instead of seeing through the false Sebastian (the 'shadow') to the actual Julia (the 'substance') whom he used to love, false Proteus registers only the reality of the shadow. Another way to put this is that in mistaking the shadow (Sebastian) for the substance (Julia), Proteus confirms Julia's sense that she has become a shadow or ghost. Indeed, Julia continues to experience the relationship between her female and male selves as painfully divided. When Proteus admits to Sebastian that Julia still lives, we might expect her to feel comforted; instead, Sebastian pities Julia as an abandoned woman who 'dreams on him that has forgot her love' (4.4.74). As if recounting a fairy tale, Sebastian implies that Julia will remain frozen in the stasis of a dream world until Proteus' memory of her love miraculously revives her. If pitying herself offers Julia relief, it comes at the price of ceding her vitality to Sebastian—an illustration of Marjorie Garber's claim that the cross-dressed stage figure becomes an 'instated presence' with 'subjectivity and agency'.[35]

Julia's self-division peaks when Proteus asks Sebastian to give Silvia the betrothal ring that Julia had once given him, thereby making Julia complicit in a ritual gesture of forgetting:

> This ring I gave him when he parted from me,
> To bind him to remember my good will.
> And now am I, unhappy messenger,
> To plead for that which I would have refused;
> To praise his faith, which I would have dispraised.
> I am my master's true-confirmèd love,
> But cannot be true servant to my master
> Unless I prove false traitor to myself.   (4.4.91–98)

Julia articulates a deeply incoherent sense of self, framed by the contradiction between her past gift of the ring and her duty 'now' to convey the ring, along with Proteus' love, to Silvia. Julia's 'I's—'I' gave the ring, 'I' am the 'unhappy messenger', 'I' would have Silva refuse him, 'I' would dispraise his faith—seem clearly to align with her female self until the statement, 'I am my master's true-confirmèd love'. Even though that 'I' in some way refers to Julia as faithful lover, not Julia but Sebastian would address Proteus as 'my master'. Hence Sebastian cannot be a 'true servant' to his master unless Julia becomes a 'false traitor' to herself. It seems odd that Julia should care about being a 'true servant' to Proteus as the fictional page Sebastian. Perhaps Julia's compulsion to faithfully serve Proteus as Sebastian is justified by her resigned admission, 'Because I love him, I must pity him' (4.4.89). In any case, Julia's acknowledgment that she no longer possesses a single 'self' makes the closing 'myself' of her soliloquy especially poignant.

When Julia encounters Silvia, however, her relationship to her male persona changes. Facing her rival emboldens Julia to speak as and for herself, thus narrowing the gap between her female and male selves. For the first time, Sebastian claims to know Julia 'almost as well as I know myself' and to have wept 'a hundred times' over her 'woes' (4.4.135–137). When Silvia asks Sebastian to describe Julia's appearance, he claims that Proteus' neglect has darkened Julia's once 'fair' beauty:

> When she did think my master loved her well
> She, in my judgement, was as fair as you.
> But since she did neglect her looking-glass,
> And threw her sun-expelling mask away,
> The air hath starved the roses in her cheeks
> And pinched the lily tincture of her face,
> That now she is become as black as I. (4.4.142–148)

Rejected by Proteus, Julia neglected her appearance, allowing the sun and wind to parch and darken her skin. In early modern England, a black complexion was usually (but not always) regarded as the antithesis of an ideal 'fair' feminine beauty. Julia's blackness, manifested in the spoiling of the blended red ('rose') and white ('lily') cheeks praised as signs of beauty in conventional love poetry, signals her despair at having lost Proteus' love. Sebastian's blackness ('she is become as black as I') is probably meant to convey his labours as a messenger exposed to the elements; men, unlike women, did not protect their skin with masks.[36] Moreover, Sebastian has been characterized by a typically 'black' melancholy. Julia thereby points to a similarity in both emotional and physical complexion that unites her female and male selves, even if their shared 'blackness' carries mainly negative associations of unattractiveness and sadness. Howsoever we understand the meaning of this blackness, it signals a merging of Julia's gendered identities.

By self-consciously embracing the rhetorical power of the actor (or 'shadow') that she has become, Julia is also able to exploit the more pleasurable and agential possibilities of her male persona. In response to Silvia's curiosity about Julia's height, Sebastian might have simply replied, 'She is as tall as I'. Instead, he tells an elaborate tale about a supposed episode from their shared past in which Sebastian borrowed Julia's gown in order to play the tragic role of Ariadne, the foremost classical example of an abandoned woman. Sebastian's performance made Julia weep; he, in turn, felt her 'very sorrow' (4.4.164). There is a vertiginous conflation of male and female selves here, as Julia, watching a version of herself (Sebastian in her gown) act an abandoned woman's sorrow, weeps, conveying her sorrow to Sebastian (and compelling him to weep on stage 'for real?'). Through Sebastian, who pretends simply to be recounting a true event, Julia improvises this account of her past empathy for Ariadne via her current perspective as a woman who has been similarly abandoned. In response to Sebastian's masterful account of his cross-gendered performance as Ariadne, Silvia both identifies Julia with Ariadne as a 'poor lady, desolate and left', and also empathetically identifies *with* Julia, weeping for her just as Julia had wept at Sebastian's performance (4.4.166). We can imagine a performance of this scene in which Silvia is moved to weep by Sebastian's own weeping in the process of telling this story, thus demonstrating Julia's formidable acting skills. Pamela Brown and Sophie Tomlinson concur that Julia exercises significant emotional and rhetorical agency through this self-conscious performance.[37] Tomlinson astutely concludes that '[a]lthough, or perhaps *because* she is alienated from herself by her disguise, Julia's conversation with Silvia helps her surmount her distress at Proteus's perjury'.[38]

From this point forward, Julia takes greater pleasure in her role as Sebastian. Having just told Silvia of Julia's ruined beauty, Julia, now alone on stage, scrutinizes Silvia's portrait and decides that she is as fair, if not more fair, than her rival. In a more triumphant key, Julia returns to the shadow/substance antithesis that she had once evoked to express her sorrow at Proteus's neglect:

Come, shadow, come, and take this shadow up,
For 'tis thy rival. O, thou senseless form,
Thou shalt be worshipped, kissed, loved, and adored;
And were there sense in his idolatry,
My substance should be statue in thy stead.   (4.4.189–193)

Despite continuing to refer to herself as a 'shadow'—both the ghost Julia and the actor Sebastian—Julia exercises a satisfying control over her rival's 'shadow' (portrait), even indulging an aggressive fantasy of 'scratch[ing] out' the portrait's eyes (4.4.196). Indignantly addressing Silvia's image, Julia protests that if Proteus were thinking rationally, 'My substance should be statue in thy stead'. Julia imagines her 'substance' (female self) in the privileged and adored place of the 'statue' (crafted image or idol) kissed by Proteus. Julia no longer despairingly regards her true substance—her past, authentic and loved, female self—as negated by her inauthentic shadows—her present, ghostly, female self and male alter-ego. Instead, she projects herself into a more hopeful, just, future in which she, not Silvia, is the object of Proteus' erotic 'idolatry'.

When we next see Julia, she is using asides not to express her sadness at having been transformed into a shadow, but to take evident pleasure in insulting Sir Thurio, a suitor of Silvia whom Proteus is pretending to assist in his courtship. Julia's disdain for Thurio is curious; if anything, she should be pleased that Proteus has a rival for Silvia. A psychological interpretation might posit that Julia's scorn for this inept lover displaces onto him through humour the pain and confusion of her own amorous misadventures. As Sebastian, Julia displays the confidence and wit often associated with knavish adolescent boys—the stereotypical 'cheeky page'—to heal her own sorrow.[39] For instance, when Thurio declares that he will wear boots to make his legs more appealing to Silvia, Julia quips, 'But love will not be spurred to what it loathes', a possible acknowledgement that her own strategic male garb has done nothing to spur Proteus' love or soften his loathing (5.2.7). By mocking Thurio's 'cowardice', Julia might be propping up her own failure to confront Proteus with his betrayal (5.2.21). Julia also significantly returns to a racialized discourse of beauty defined by the poles of fairness and blackness. When Thurio asks how Silvia regards his face, Proteus responds, 'She says it is a fair one'. Thurio replies:

THURIO   Nay, then, the wanton lies. My face is black.
PROTEUS   But pearls are fair; and the old saying is,
          'Black men are pearls in beauteous ladies' eyes'.
JULIA [*aside*] 'Tis true, such pearls as put out ladies' eyes,
          For I had rather wink than look on them.   (5.2.9–14)

By describing his face as 'black', Thurio perhaps alludes to a melancholy humour that darkens his complexion, but the play has also
explicitly referred to ethnic or geographical blackness, most pointedly
in Proteus' musing that Silvia's fairness '[s]hows Julia but a swarthy
Ethiope' (2.6.26).[40] Perhaps seeing in 'black' Thurio a reflection of her
own loss of beauty in Proteus' eyes, Julia eagerly affirms her own dis-
taste for black skin. Julia's mockery of Thurio for his failure to meet
standards of masculine valour and beauty is a good reminder that supposedly 'queer' practices (here, passing as another gender, possibly at
the risk of scandal) can sometimes have retrogressive ethical or political effects.

Twelfth Night

Whereas Rosalind, Julia, and *Twelfth Night*'s Viola all adopt the
identity of a page, Viola deliberately models her male persona after
her twin brother, Sebastian, whom she believes to have drowned in
the shipwreck that has stranded her in Illyria. Viola asks, 'And what
should I do in Illyria? / My brother he is in Elysium': the 'heaven' of
classical mythology (1.2.2–3). 'Illyria' and 'Elysium' sound similar and
different enough to suggest Viola's despair at being separated from
the person who is a kind of double. To survive in a foreign land as a
kinless, homeless young woman, Viola enlists a Captain's help to procure her male clothing and to present her 'as an eunuch' singer to
Duke Orsino, Illyria's ruler (1.2.52). Viola later reveals that this male
clothing is only one component of an effort to imitate not only how
Sebastian dressed, but also how he looked and behaved: 'Even such
and so / In favour was my brother, and he went / Still in this fashion,
colour, ornament, / For him I imitate' (3.4.344–347). For Viola, mirroring
her brother's appearance and mannerisms as the page 'Cesario' might
emotionally compensate for his loss, but it also, I will argue, provokes
unintended erotic and disciplinary responses from others, which take

an emotional toll. From a contemporary perspective, we might say that Viola experiences early modern forms of transphobia.

Although the play never clarifies whether or not Viola actually presents herself to Orsino as a eunuch, that allusion significantly connects Viola's gender transition to a particular kind of racialized embodiment (1.2.52). When Viola asks the Captain to conceal her true identity, he replies, 'Be you his [Orsino's] eunuch, and your mute I'll be', referring to the Ottoman Empire's practice of employing eunuchs to guard harems and 'mutes' (deaf men) to attend at court (1.2.58).[41] According to Abdulhamit Arvas, the eunuch constitutes a 'distinct gender category' that 'productively demonstrates the ways that gender and race were co-constituted' in the early modern period.[42] In early modern Ottoman writing, Arvas shows, black African eunuchs were sometimes derided as ugly and wicked in contrast to white European eunuchs; English travellers to the Ottoman Empire tended to replicate this association of 'gender nonconformity' with 'racial otherness'.[43] In *Twelfth Night*, Shakespeare evokes this 'exoticized' figure of 'gendered, racial, and corporeal otherness' perhaps to signal Viola's alienation from her former gender, status, and national identities.[44] Particularly because eunuchs are figures of anatomical and reproductive deprivation, in identifying as a eunuch Viola might be understood to be denying herself 'in favor of her lost male alter ego', Sebastian.[45] In this sense, Viola resembles *The Two Gentlemen of Verona*'s Julia, who relegates her own selfhood to the past in order to pass as a male servant also named Sebastian.

To better understand the significance of Viola's gender transformation, it is worth further scrutinizing Arvas' account of the eunuch as a distinct gender category. According to Arvas, early moderns regarded eunuchs as 'non-men' who 'existed beyond the gender binary altogether': as transgender figures, they were 'neither masculine nor feminine' or 'both masculine and feminine'.[46] Whereas I agree that eunuchs disrupt gender binarism, to describe them as 'non-men' is somewhat misleading. Instead, I would argue that the eunuch, who was always a castrated man, never a woman, is necessarily understood in relation to embodied masculinity. Because eunuchs were without testicles and hence incapable of sexual reproduction, they were not considered 'men' in the fullest sense of that term, but precisely that judgment of their deficiency indicates that they were evaluated as people on the male side of the gender binary. As Katherine Crawford explains, 'castrates were men, but their effeminization made them like women'.[47]

Like the eunuch, Cesario is perceived by others as a male-bodied person with some woman-like traits. Although, as we will see, this tempered manhood will later expose Cesario to harassment, it initially enhances his access to the nobles Orsino and Olivia. An 'alluringly androgynous youth', Cesario is what Simone Chess calls a 'genderqueer type', who is perceived as attractive through the 'very queerness of the entire gender presented'.[48] Orsino's confidence in Cesario's ability to woo Olivia on his behalf suggests that he sees his servant as a kind of 'gender informant who decodes and interprets masculine and feminine rules and norms'.[49] Explaining to Cesario why Olivia will welcome him, Orsino keeps Cesario's maleness in view even as he compares his features to the 'parts' of women:

> Diana's lip
> Is not more smooth and rubious; thy small pipe
> Is as the maiden's organ, shrill and sound,
> And all is semblative a woman's part. (1.5.30–34)

Just as eunuchs are regarded as men who are *like* women in certain ways, Cesario is a boy who is *like* or 'semblative' of women in appearance and voice. If Viola's identification of herself with the racialized figure of the eunuch possibly signifies her alienation from her former social, family, and gender identities, Orsino's comparison of Cesario to the white, virgin goddess Diana suggests that Viola's hopes of marriage depend on projecting through Cesario's male body an unambiguously chaste, feminine fairness.

Orsino rightly predicts that the feminine Cesario will appeal to Olivia. Unintentionally sparking Olivia's curiosity, Malvolio describes Cesario in similarly genderqueer terms as a male-bodied person who falls in between categories: he is '[n]ot yet old enough for a man, nor young enough for a boy' (1.5.139–140). Searching for the right metaphor to describe this odd being, Malvolio tries liquids—''Tis with him in standing water between boy and man…One would think his mother's milk were scarce out of him'—as well as vegetables and fruit: he is like 'a squash is before 'tis a peascod, or a codling when 'tis almost an apple' (1.5.140–144). If 'standing water' means a 'swamp between the states of land and water', then Malvolio has found an excellent metaphor for 'the inability to categorize Cesario' in gendered terms, even *within* the gendered terms of masculinity.[50] Significantly, although Sebastian is identical in appearance to Cesario as a lovely, somewhat feminine young man, nobody in the play anatomizes his gender or remarks upon his body as they do with Cesario. This discrepancy suggests that for Shakespeare the phenomenon of a woman passing as male prompted thinking about non-binary gender in a particularly intense or urgent way.

The attention that Orsino and Malvolio pay to Cesario's genderqueer body resonates with the contemporary phenomenon of 'inappropriate curiosity': the intrusive fascination that people sometimes direct towards a transgender person's body, particularly through speculation or questions about their genitalia. Inappropriate curiosity can have serious negative effects on transgender people, especially when it interferes with the provision of appropriate medical care.[51] Orsino's and Malvolio's suggestive descriptions of Cesario's 'upper body' (his lips, voice, face) might be regarded as decorous or unconscious displacements of an urge to discern the 'truth' of his sex/gender from the evidence of his lower body. The red lip of Diana, maiden's organ, and woman's part might all refer to a vagina; the small pipe might refer to a boy's penis or a clitoris; the peascod and codling might refer to testicles.[52] Moreover, Malvolio's comparison of Cesario to 'standing water' might be a 'phallic insult', in that water cannot 'stand' or get an erection.[53] Might Orsino and Malvolio be speculating about whether this boy's body in which 'all is semblative a woman's part' has a vagina or a penis? Or if Cesario might be a hermaphrodite with *both* a vagina (and/or clitoris) and a penis? Or if he might be a eunuch after all? Whereas Orsino might be motivated by erotic fascination and Malvolio by malice, the urge to know Cesario's anatomy is not only invasive, but complicit with misogynist and colonialist logics of discovering the secrets of female bodies and foreign lands, as Patricia Parker argues of *Othello*.[54] Nonetheless, whatever curiosity Orsino or Olivia might feel about Cesario's body seems only to enhance their desire for further intimacy with him, putting Cesario in a position of favour and advancement.

When Viola discovers that she has unintentionally seduced Olivia, however, she ruefully reflects on Cesario's gender queerness not as a source of agency, access, and empowerment, but of regrettable deceit.

'Disguise', she pronounces, 'I see thou art a wickedness / Wherein the pregnant enemy does much' (2.2.25–26). Although we might interpret 'disguise' simply as clothing—'a garb assumed in order to deceive'—it can also mean 'any artificial manner assumed for deception'.[55] As we have seen, Viola's gender passing involves much more than covering her body with male clothes: 'Even such and so / In favour was my brother, and he went / Still in this fashion, colour, ornament, / For him I imitate' (3.4.344–347). Along with the 'fashion' and 'colour' of her brother's garb, Viola resembles him in his accessories ('ornament'), face ('colour', 'favour'), gait ('he went'), and bearing ('in this fashion').[56] Likewise, Olivia cites the embodied assemblage of Cesario's 'tongue', 'face', 'limbs', 'actions', and 'spirit' as evidence of his (male) gentility (1.5.262). Referring to the 'pregnant enemy' (meaning the 'quick/resourceful devil'), Viola possibly recalls the original act of deception, in which Satan used the embodied disguise of a serpent's shape and voice to tempt Eve to sin, just as Viola's embodied disguise has tempted Olivia to feel 'mistaken' desire for a woman (2.2.33). Early moderns believed that the devil continued to use 'disguise' to deceive human beings into committing sin. If Viola had initially associated her embodied maleness with the strangeness of the eunuch's black body, she now seems to identify it with the 'wickedness' of the devil's black body.[57] The pun on 'pregnant' as 'with child' suggests a non-binary Satan, which further confirms Viola's identification with him in the role of Cesario. Viola, in short, thinks of herself in this moment as a 'white devil': a wicked (morally 'foul') woman mispresenting herself in the body, appearance, and behaviour of a fair/white boy.

Admittedly, the gravity of this claim is hard to reconcile with *Twelfth Night*'s comic tone; its implausibility is suggested by the fact that I have not come across this interpretation in any scholarship on the play. This reading is corroborated, however, by the play's insistent return to the figure of the 'white devil'. Just moments before, Viola had warned Olivia that beneath her lovely 'red and white' complexion lurked the foul sin of pride: 'you are too proud. / But if you were the devil, you are fair' (1.5.219–220). Olivia later refers to Cesario as a presumably fair or physically attractive devil: 'Fare thee well. / A fiend like thee might bear my soul to hell' (3.4.192–193). Finally, Antonio will accuse Cesario, whom he mistakes for Sebastian, of using his boyish fairness as a cover for wickedness: 'Virtue is beauty, but the beauteous evil / Are empty trunks o'erflourished by the devil' (3.4.333–334). Antonio's image of the whited sepulchre, significantly, is the exact inverse of the image that the Duke of Venice in *Othello* uses to praise Othello's uprightness to Brabantio, who has wrongly accused his daughter's new husband of devilish practices: 'If virtue no delighted beauty lack, / Your son-in-law is far more fair than black' (1.3.288–289). The inverse of the white devil is the black angel, beautiful only on the inside. The unavoidable racial connotations of that sentiment in *Othello* suggest that ideas of racial difference also inform Viola's identification with the devil in *Twelfth Night*.

I am not arguing that *Twelfth Night* here confirms the worst fears of Renaissance anti-theatricalists: that the public theatre is a playground for devilish deception and sodomitical lust. Antonio, after all, turns out to be wrong about Sebastian, who hasn't betrayed him and whose affection is genuine. I am suggesting that among the many occasions of agency, pleasure, and humour afforded Viola by passing as a male, she is also made to confront—and to confess to—some genuine emotional, physical, and even theological perils.[58] Following her self-comparison to the 'pregnant enemy', Viola refers to herself as a 'poor monster', a term that associates her gender transformation with the embodied transgressions of the hermaphrodite and the tribade.[59] Although the epithet 'poor' has an affective charge closer to self-pity than self-condemnation, the early modern idea of monstrosity carries weighty associations of the unnatural that are hard to ignore. In a classic essay, transsexual writer Susan Stryker uses the metaphor of Frankenstein's monster to convey the subjective experience of gender transition: '[t]ranssexual embodiment, like the embodiment of the monster, places its subject in an unassimilable, antagonistic, queer relationship to a Nature in which it must nevertheless exist.'[60] Although Viola's experiences might be incommensurate with those of contemporary transgender and transsexual people, Stryker's provocative claim can push us to think about Viola's vulnerability in a way that has not often been acknowledged. Shakespeare gives us a glimpse into what it feels like for Viola to occupy a queer, antagonistic, relationship to nature. Significantly, this queer relationship to nature also involves a queer relationship to temporality: Viola ends her soliloquy by asking 'time' to untangle the impossible erotic knot that her male impersonation has created (2.2.38).

Twelfth Night prompts our continued reflection on Viola's affective experience of transgender embodiment by exposing her to physical peril. Whereas Viola doesn't experience anything comparable to the police harassment that Sawyer Kemp includes among the dangers faced by contemporary transgender people, she does face harassment on account of Cesario's boyish femininity. Fabian and Sir Toby engineer a fight between Cesario and Sir Andrew Aguecheek because they anticipate the hilarity of terrorizing two cowardly males. Toby goads Andrew into a duel as a means of proving his 'valour' and 'manhood' to Olivia, thus making him a more attractive suitor (3.2.32, 3.4.160). Andrew's manhood quickly vanishes, however, when Toby warns him of Cesario's fierceness, and Toby likewise drives Cesario 'into a most hideous opinion' of Andrew's 'rage, skill, fury, and impetuosity' (3.4.171–172). Knowing that 'oxen and wain-ropes cannot hale' these two cowards together, Toby employs other forms of coercion (3.2.51). When a shaken Cesario seeks to return to Olivia's house for a safe escort, Toby detains him and threatens to fight him on the spot if he refuses to face Andrew. Offering Cesario no escape from this ritual test of male prowess, Toby makes a familiar pun on the sword as penis: 'Therefore on, or strip your sword stark naked, for meddle you must, that's certain' (3.4.222–224). As a woman, Viola lacks a man's naked 'sword', as she quips when she considers revealing her imposture to escape physical harm: 'Pray God defend me! A little thing would make me tell them how much I lack of a man' (3.4.268–269).

Viola's failure to improvise her way out of physical danger is significant because, as Phyllis Rackin observes, 'armed combat' is the 'only arena in *Twelfth Night* where Viola's true sex seems to make a difference'.[61] Viola's aversion to physical violence once again reveals the risks of gender passing: for the first time, Cesario confesses a deficiency in his manhood: 'I am one that had rather go with Sir Priest than Sir Knight—I care not who knows so much of my mettle' (3.4.240–242). Having already written a play featuring Joan of Arc, Shakespeare knew that women were capable of fighting—and beating—men in combat. In *Twelfth Night*, however, the supposed naturalness of women's tender 'mettle' serves to confirm not only Viola's feminine subjectivity, ultimately securing her fitness as Orsino's wife, but also the dangers and limitations, as well as pleasures and possibilities, of occupying a queerly antagonistic relationship to nature.

1 Henry VI

In *1 Henry VI*, Joan la Pucelle's antagonistic relationship to nature is the source both of her strange power and of attempts to delegitimize that power.[62] As she explains, the Virgin Mary authorized her extraordinary advancement from poor shepherdess to prophet and 'warlike mate' of the French nobility (1.3.71). Tending her lambs one day under the 'sun's parching heat', Joan was transformed by a vision of the Virgin (1.3.56):

> In complete glory she revealed herself—
> And whereas I was black and swart before,
> With those clear rays which she infused on me
> That beauty am I blest with, which you may see.   (1.3.62–64)

Dark-skinned from working outdoors, Joan is miraculously whitened by an 'infus[ion]' of the Virgin's 'clear rays'.[63] 'Clear' refers to 'brightly shining' or 'brilliant' light, but was also commonly used to describe 'fair' skin of 'bright, fresh, and ...pure colour'.[64] This miraculous whitening of Joan's formerly black skin possibly alludes to the racist trope of 'washing the Ethiope white', a proverbial description of an impossible task that depicts African skin as an indelible layer of dirt. Joan's incredible bodily transformation enhances her feminine beauty even as it paradoxically authorizes her transformation into a belligerent 'woman clad in armour' (1.7.2).[65] Elsewhere in Shakespeare, virginity is itself described as a kind of armour: in *Romeo and Juliet*, for instance, Rosaline is 'well armed' in 'strong proof of chastity' (1.1.203). The metaphorical armour of embodied virginity thus serves as the foundation and justification for the actual 'male' armour that Joan wears over her body (Figure 3.3).

Joan recognizes the Virgin Mary as the source of her ability both to defeat men in combat—'Christ's mother helps me, else I were too weak' (1.3.85)—and to resist male seduction—'I must not yield to any rights of love, / For my profession's sacred from above' (1.3.92–93). Boasting that she 'exceed[s] [her] sex', Joan embodies a supernaturally enhanced femininity combined with certain masculine traits (valour, aggression) rarely displayed by women (1.3.69).

The responses of the men in the play to Joan's queerly excessive gender are in themselves excessive.[66] As if searching for a historical

LA Pucelle ennoyée de Dieu au secours de la France, entre dans Orleans assiegé par les Anglois : et par la liberté de cette Ville donne commencement à la delivrance de l'Estat. Annales Galliæ . . . en . . . invent. *Mariotte excud . cum privil. Regis.*

Figure 3.3 'A woman clad in armor': Joan la Pucelle. Peter Le Moyne, *The Gallery of Heroick Women* (London: [R. Norton], 1652), plate facing page 119. Call#: 131–611f, image 9287. Folger Shakespeare Library.

precedent that would explain Joan's anomalous combination of female virginity and male valour, Charles promiscuously names various male and female classical, Hebrew, Muslim, and Christian figures as her spiritual, physical, and military exemplars: Amazon warriors; Deborah, a Biblical prophetess and warrior; the prophet Mahomet; France's patron saint, Denis; St. Helen, the mother of Emperor Constantine; St. Philip's prophetic daughters; Venus, the goddess of love; Darius, the king of Persia; and Astraea, the goddess of justice. Several of these female exemplars were known for exceptional modes of embodiment: Amazons cut off a breast to better wield their bows; Venus was a paragon of feminine beauty; St. Philip's four daughters were all virgins. Charles' rapid and jumbled citations, however, do not encourage any sustained reflection on what these female figures might reveal about Joan's body or sexuality. Since the French benefit from fostering the narrative that Joan's sanctity as a 'sweet virgin' underlies her success as a transgender warrior, it would be counterproductive to draw attention, say, to the racial and masculine connotations of an Amazon, or to the phallic sexual aggression suggested by the 'sword of Deborah' (3.7.16; 1.3.84).

The French, in short, want Joan's reputation for chastity to be as unimpeachable as the reputations of the three young women in the comedies discussed above. While impersonating men, Rosalind, Julia, and Viola must preserve their female modesty so that they might finally marry. Although Julia initially worries that cross-dressing will harm her reputation, once she arrives in Milan as Sebastian she never explicitly raises this worry. Rosalind's chastity is never compromised by the connotations of her moniker, Ganymede, which in contemporary slang referred to a youth who sexually services men.[67] The gentility of Rosalind, Julia, and Viola plays an important role in the preservation of their chastity.[68] As we have seen, whereas Proteus and Olivia read gentility in the bodies and behaviours of Sebastian and Cesario, respectively, Ganymede conveys his gentility through his wealth, 'fine' accent, and courtly discourse (3.2.284).

Unlike Rosalind, Julia, and Viola, Joan is not only known to be a woman appropriating a conventionally male role, she also lacks the gentility that might enhance her reputation for chastity, thus making her vulnerable to degradation. In early modern London, cross-dressing was commonly associated with sexual transgression: lower-status women apprehended in male clothing were usually accused of sexual misdemeanours. Through boastful and mocking language that would be highly indecorous for an elite woman, Joan only confirms her enemies' accusations of incivility. Responding to one of Joan's bitter taunts, the Duke of Burgundy scolds, 'Scoff on, vile fiend and shameless courtesan' (3.4.5). The prototypically masculine Lord Talbot likewise calls Joan a 'high-minded strumpet' and 'railing Hecate' (1.7.12; 3.4.24). Talbot refutes Joan's claims to holiness by reading back from the unnaturalness of a belligerent woman clad in armour to the promiscuity of the body beneath: 'Devil or devil's dam, I'll conjure thee. / Blood will I draw on thee—thou art a witch— / And straightway give thy soul to him thou serv'st' (1.7.5–7). Since 'dam' is a common word for an animal's mother, and since the devil was thought to be black, 'devil's dam' animalizes, racializes, and sexualizes Joan's body, as well as re-gendering her as traditionally female. We could describe this animosity as a kind of transphobia: an aversion to or hatred of transgender people expressed through derogatory language or the disciplinary imposition of binary gender categories.

In another manifestation of transphobia, Joan's enemies engage in hostile speculation about her genitalia. When the Duke of Bedford wonders how a 'maid' could be 'so martial', Burgundy responds, 'Pray God she prove not masculine ere long. / If underneath the standard of the French / She carry armour as she hath begun—' (2.1.22–24). For Burgundy, Joan's male armour accentuates her embodiment of an exceptionally queer femininity, raising the unholy and unnatural possibility that she will be discovered to be 'masculine': either a biological man who has been passing as a woman, or an intersex person with male and female genitalia. Burgundy might also be charging Joan with sexual promiscuity. Since Joan has lain 'underneath' the 'standard[s]' or penises of the French (whose weight in intercourse she has 'carr[ied]' on top of her body), she might 'ere long' become pregnant with a boy, and hence 'prove masculine'. Joan is literally imagined here as the 'pregnant enemy' with whom Viola identifies in her deceptive male role. Even when Joan is imagined to possess a male or intersex body, the most degrading thing that can be said about her is that she is a whorish woman: 'devil's dam' implies that a female demon was pregnant with and gave birth to Satan. To insist on Joan's ability to bear a child is to radically reduce the complexity of her gender identity to the typical sign of biological womanhood.

The image of a pregnant Joan returns in her final scene, just before her English captors hale her off to be burned at the stake. Although the English lords do not rape Joan, their delight in enumerating her sexual transgressions immediately preceding her execution can be considered a form of sublimated sexual violence. After Joan claims to be pregnant in order to get a legal stay of execution, the Duke of York condemns her promiscuity with Charles. Whereas the First Folio prints the Duke of York's line as 'She and the Dolphin have bin iug-ling', some modern editions render it as 'She and the Dauphin have been ingling' (5.6.68).[69] 'Dauphin' is the traditional title of the King of France's eldest son; retaining the English variation 'Dolphin', however, makes available a rather bizarre charge of bestiality.[70] Talbot had earlier evoked the animalistic connotations of Charles's title as 'Dolphin or dog-fish' (First Folio p. 100). Furthermore, the Folio's ambiguous 'iugling' can be read as two different words: *juggling*, meaning 'conjuring', 'cheating', or 'deceiving'; and *ingling*, meaning 'to fondle or caress lov-ingly', particularly in the context of a man's sexual use of a younger male.[71] The conflation of *juggling/ingling* thus covers a panoply of Joan's actual or imagined crimes: witchcraft (conjuring), cross-dressing (deceiv-ing), bestiality, and sexual promiscuity, with the additional implication that she and Charles have committed sodomy (ingling), and that this act of non-reproductive sex has unnaturally resulted in her pregnancy.[72]

Consequently, the English lords' eagerness to burn Joan at the stake can be regarded as a displaced form of sexual violence against an 'unnatural', sexually promiscuous, transgender woman. When the English gloat about murdering Charles' bastard child in Joan's womb, Joan claims that the child's father is actually the Duke of Alençon; she then ascribes paternity to René, King of Naples. The English lords delight in rehearsing Joan's sexual transgressions and desperate rhet-orical evasions:

WARWICK   A married man?—That's most intolerable.
RICHARD DUKE OF YORK Why, here's a girl; I think she knows not well—
    There were so many—whom she may accuse.
WARWICK It's sign she hath been liberal and free.
RICHARD DUKE OF YORK   And yet forsooth she is a virgin pure!
    [*To* Joan] Strumpet, thy words condemn thy brat and thee.   (5.6.79–84)

Although the Duke of York had earlier condemned Joan for the theological crimes of being a 'witch' and 'miscreant' (heretic), he now suggests that she is being 'condemn[ed]' for adultery and fornication, which were not felonies punishable by death in medieval or early modern England (5.4.5, 14). The determination to reduce Joan's body to ashes perhaps expresses a desire to purge the world of a monstrously gendered and sexed being. An incident from sixteenth-century history offers a curious parallel: a report of the 1578 execution in Rome of eight men convicted of sodomy claimed that their trial records and bodies were 'burned in the place where they were arrested in order to erase all memory of them'.[73]

Transgender studies directs our attention to the ways in which gender transformations can paradoxically centre the body as a constraint upon the fluidity and slipperiness that queer approaches often attribute to sexual language and identity. To be sure, the boundary-crossing identities of Ganymede, Sebastian, Cesario, and Joan render attempts to define them excessive, ambiguous, and confused. At the same time, however, the desire for legibly gendered bodies persistently authenticates the existence of a 'world that needed the idea of two genders', in Jean Howard's words. In *Twelfth Night*, for instance, Orsino and Malvolio scrutinize Cesario's feminine male body as if assured that discovering his anatomical secrets would settle the question of who he really is. Sir Toby disciplines the supposed gender deficiencies of Cesario and Andrew by orchestrating a humiliating spectacle of failed manhood. At the same time, Viola casts herself as the sharply dichotomized figure of the white devil, a woman darkly deceiving others beneath the alluring appearance of a fair boy. Whatever private moral dilemma Viola might be experiencing, however, the legibility of Cesario's fair boyishness is essential to establishing Viola's chastity and thus her eligibility to marry Orsino. In *1 Henry VI*, Joan offers both the palpable fact of her transformed fairness—'That beauty am I blest with, which you may see' (1.3.65)—and the sacred armour of her touted virginity as authorization for engaging in warfare. Yet despite Joan's ability to 'exceed her sex' by defeating men in combat, her enemies accuse her of embodying a typically unruly femininity manifested as lust and the capacity to give birth. Joan is ultimately condemned not for religious heresy, but for violating the strictures of feminine modesty, chastity, and gentility. To lay claim to the presence of transgender characters in Shakespeare, then, is both to celebrate the agency that might come from crossing 'the boundaries constructed by…culture to define and contain' gender, *and* to acknowledge that such crossings can carry great risks and harsh consequences.[74] Beneath the queer ebb and flow of gender transformation we can still detect the stubborn undertow of the desire for an authentically embodied gender.

Shakespeare and Queer Studies. Mario DiGangi, Oxford University Press. © Mario DiGangi 2025.
DOI: 10.1093/9780191994951.003.0004

| 4

Queer Asexuality

So far, our exploration of queer gender and sexuality in Shakespeare has largely addressed the intimacies of loving couples, friendship networks, throuples, adulterous lovers, and spouses. This chapter considers another kind of queerness, namely, the refusal of sex, marriage, or sexual reproduction: what J. Jack Halberstam, in a contemporary context, has called 'queer failure'. Halberstam argues that if heteronormativity defines success as the achievement of marriage and children, then resistance to heteronormativity might take the form of failing to fulfil that expectation.[1] As I explained in the Introduction, although neither heterosexuality nor sexual norms were operative concepts in early modernity, Christian marriage was vigorously promoted as the only institution for legitimizing male-female reproductive sex. In Protestant early modern England, the married state was theoretically the most honourable and also brought many social and economic privileges; nonetheless, many men and women remained unmarried for significant periods of their lives, whether because they were young people who had not yet found a spouse, widows or widowers who had not remarried, or lifelong single people. Unmarried or celibate people would not necessarily have been stigmatized or considered 'queer' unless a particular circumstance drew suspicion to them.[2]

Shakespeare does, however, depict situations in which resistance to sex or marriage provokes consternation, censure, and even violence. Because the notion of queer failure seems to presume a deliberate or conscious rejection of social norms, a more capacious way of understanding someone's lack of interest in sex or marriage is asexuality. Asexuality is generally defined as the condition of not experiencing sexual attraction to others. Nonetheless, in their essay 'Asexual Resonance', Ela Przybylo and Danielle Cooper argue that a narrow biological account of asexuality as a life-long condition excludes forms of asexuality that might be considered queer, in the sense of non-heteronormative or non-gender normative. Rejecting the common binary of celibacy as choice and asexuality as nonchoice, Przybylo and Cooper offer the helpful notion of asexual 'resonances': 'traces, touches, [or] instances' that 'can accommodate the elusive and ephemeral fragments of asexuality'.[3] The concept of resonance allows us to identify moments in literary or historical texts in which asexuality appears, even if as a temporary or freely chosen condition.

Most importantly, Przybylo and Cooper argue that a focus on asexuality 'encourages skepticism of any approach to sexuality that does not question the sociocultural centrality of sex'.[4] In other words, a queer approach that does not question why sexual relations are valued in the first place can contribute to a cultural bias that represents non-sexual people as strange, deficient, or incapable of achieving fulfilment. Kristina Gupta defines this cultural bias as 'compulsory sexuality': 'the assumption that all people are sexual', which serves to 'marginalize various forms of non-sexuality, such as a lack of sexual desire or behavior', and to 'compel people to experience themselves as desiring subjects, take up sexual identities, and engage in sexual activity'.[5] To the extent that compulsory sexuality validates any kind of sexual intimacy, from an asexual perspective a same-sex couple might seem no more queer than a married male-female couple with children.

This chapter will explore the motives and consequences of choosing celibacy, declining sex, or rejecting marriage in Shakespeare's narrative poem *Venus and Adonis* and in five plays: *A Midsummer Night's Dream*, *Romeo and Juliet*, *Measure for Measure*, *Love's Labors Lost*, and *All's Well that Ends Well*. Sometimes in these texts the absence of sexual desire is depicted as constitutional, not just volitional. In commenting on others' refusal of sexual intimacies, that is, characters will sometimes attribute to them an innate 'coldness', or physiological inability to feel sexual passion, as if they were made of stone instead of flesh. That in Shakespeare's texts asexuality is often an attribution imposed from without rather than a conscious self-identification indicates how it could be perceived as a queer disruption of social and physiological expectations—a subject of wonder, ridicule, and invidious analysis instead of an expression of authentic selfhood.

Venus and Adonis

The first thing that the narrator of *Venus and Adonis* tells us about Adonis is that '[h]unting he loved, but love he laughed to scorn' (4). Although capable of loving a pleasurable activity, Adonis regards 'love'—feelings of romantic or sexual desire—as ridiculous. If this claim alerts us to Adonis' asexuality, it does so by attributing to him not merely an inability or disinclination to love but an active, even impassioned, rejection of love. Justifying her description of Adonis as 'actively asexual rather than passively presexual', Simone Chess rightly points to his 'successfully articulated disinterest in sex and romance'.[6] Yet it is significant that we do not hear Adonis' reasons for his disinterest in sex and romance until quite late in the poem; instead, both the poem's narrator and Venus, who is unsuccessfully attempting to seduce Adonis, proffer various explanations for behaviour depicted as anomalous. Presumably, had Adonis eagerly consented to have sex with Venus from the start, the poem would not have provided detailed rationales for his desire.

Even as the narrator shows Adonis to be capable of a wide range of feelings, he also attributes Adonis' sexual resistance to a cold, hard, constitution, as if Adonis had no feelings at all. Through his descriptions of Adonis' physical reactions—'lour[ing]', 'fret[ting]', 'burn[ing]', 'blush[ing]', and 'pout[ing]' (75, 49, 33)—the narrator suggests that Adonis responds to sexual seduction with embarrassment, annoyance, contempt, discomfort, and distress. The narrator also attributes to Adonis a wide range of specific emotions: 'sullen[ness]', 'shame', 'anger', 'disdain', and 'bashful[ness]' (75–76, 33–34, 49). When he describes Adonis as 'frosty in desire', however, the narrator offers coldness as a *physiological* symptom of virginity or asexuality (36). According to the humoral theory that informed early modern understandings of bodily function, heat was essential for sexual reproduction: semen was heated blood. The narrator's attribution to Adonis of a 'leaden appetite' connects sexual craving to the 'desire to satisfy the natural necessities, or fulfil the natural functions, of the body', such as food (34).[7] Although 'leaden' carries the metaphorical meaning of 'heavy' or 'spiritless', it also literally means '[c]onsisting or made of lead'.[8] 'Leaden appetite' therefore implies that Adonis' cold, stony, body is constitutionally 'unapt to toy'—or to feel *any* form of desire, even the natural desire to survive (34). The *OED* supplies an early usage of 'unapt' in a specifically sexual context from Chacuer's *Troilus and Creseyde*: 'Was neuere man ne woman yet bygete, / That was vnapt to suffren loues hete Celestial.'[9] Although *Venus and Adonis* offers other, more contingent, reasons for Adonis' sexual inaptitude, including inexperience and youth, it thus raises the possibility that his inherent frigidity, *pace* Chaucer, makes him unable to feel love's heat.

This suggestion of innate asexuality is bolstered by Venus' claims of Adonis' coldness and hardness, since these states could imply a physiological inaptness for sexual stimulation. Frustrated by Adonis' denials, Venus describes his warm and impressionable flesh as dead and unyielding matter: 'Art thou obdurate, flinty, hard as steel? / Nay, more than flint, for stone at rain relenteth' (199–200). 'Obdurate', which means 'hardened in wrongdoing or sin', might imply that Adonis has (wrongfully) resisted sex for so long that he has made himself incapable of pitying a lover's pleas.[10] Consequently, he experiences fewer sensations than even a stone, which will 'relent' or yield to the pressure of water. Developing the lithic metaphor, Venus calls Adonis a 'lifeless picture, cold and senseless stone, / Well painted idol, image dull and dead, / Statue contenting but the eye alone' (211–213). Like a statue, Adonis is pleasant to look at but unresponsive to the touch, which Venus defines as the primary sign of sentience.

Along with defining Adonis as a lifeless statue, Venus attempts to diagnose what is wrong with him, a depressingly familiar experience for asexual people. Through Venus' efforts to interpret Adonis' sexual disinterest, the poem engages our own lurid curiosity about why a young man would not want to have sex with the beautiful goddess of love. Venus would understand Adonis' disinterest if she were old, ugly, and dried up, but she is fresh, lovely, and juicy. Perhaps Adonis is just a shy boy 'ashamed to kiss' who needs reassurance that nobody will witness their love-making (121). Less sympathetically, Venus diagnoses Adonis with suicidal narcissism:

> Is thine own heart to thine own face affected?
> Can thy right hand seize love upon thy left?
> Then woo thyself, be of thyself rejected;
> Steal thine own freedom, and complain on theft.
>   Narcissus so himself himself forsook,
>   And died to kiss his shadow in the brook.   (157–162)

Venus warns Adonis that to love yourself is to be not self-sufficient but self-divided, to have your right hand futilely try to 'seize love' from your left hand, to be caught in a fruitless circuit of self-wooing and self-rejecting like the mythical Narcissus, who fell in love with his reflection. Such self-regard leads to death, the antithesis of life-generating sex. Later, Venus will refer to the 'fruitless chastity' of '[l]ove-lacking vestals and self-loving nuns' (752). Whether nuns are faulted for loving nobody, loving only themselves, or loving only each other, the result is the same: a chaste refusal of fruitful sexual reproduction that paradoxically 'would breed a scarcity / And barren dearth' of children (753–754). Figured as perversely reproducing only dea(r)th, asexuality becomes the queer enemy of what Lee Edelman calls 'the cult of the Child': the 'compulsory narrative of reproductive futurism', which mandates the production of children as a way to ensure the viability of the social order and the future of the species.[11] Had Adonis' mother refused sex, Venus reminds him, '[s]he had not brought [him] forth' but 'died unkind', having unnaturally and cruelly deprived him of life (203–204).

Venus' allusion to Adonis' mother in fact ironically offers another possible reason for the boy's 'unnatural' rejection of sex. Shakespeare read Ovid's tale of Venus and Adonis in the *Metamorphoses*, which recounts the longer 'history of inbreeding and unnatural sexuality' in Adonis' family.[12] Whereas Venus reminds Adonis that by 'law of nature thou art bound to breed' (171), his family history reveals that breeding can also take unlawful and 'unnatural' forms. This history begins with the sculptor Pygmalion, who, disgusted by the promiscuity of prostitutes, rejects women and falls in love with the statue of a woman he has carved. After Venus has given the statue life, Pygmalion conceives a child with her called Paphus. Paphus' son, Cinyras, has sex with his daughter, Myrrha, who gives birth to Adonis after having been transformed into a tree. By animating Pygmalion's statue, Venus herself sets in motion the chain of 'unkind' sexuality that produces Adonis, who, much like his ancestor Pygmalion, is repelled by female promiscuity (187). Venus' attempt to shame Adonis for his disinterest in sex by accusing him of being 'like a man, but of no woman bred' is literally true, for he was born of the tree into which his mother had been changed (214) (Figure 4.1).

Figure 4.1 'Like a man, but of no woman bred': Adonis' birth from a tree.
Philips Galle after Anthonie Blocklandt, 'Geboorte van Adonis' [birth of
Adonis]. (Antwerp: c. 1577–c.1581). Rijksmuseum, Amsterdam.

If *Venus and Adonis* suggests that Adonis bears in his body a long
family history of sexual anomalies, it also allows a more conventional
interpretation of his asexuality: the possibility that his resistance constitutes an erotic game, an attempt to prolong or to intensify Venus'
courtship. This possibility is conveyed by Venus' claim that Adonis
might feel 'proud' of his remarkable power to resist the goddess of love
(113). In early modern love poetry, such pride is often represented as
coyness: an insincere display of scornful reluctance meant to inflame a
wooer. Venus uses the term 'coy' to describe her own skill at sexual
manipulation. When the god Mars wooed her, Venus reduced him to
a 'servile' condition with her 'coy disdain'; only then did she yield to
sex (112). Coyness was usually a female trait, due to the expectation
that men would woo women, and that women would modestly resist
being seduced. *Venus and Adonis* provides another example of female
coyness in the jennet (a mare in heat) that attracts Adonis' male horse.
'[P]roud' to be wooed, the jennet 'puts on outward strangeness, seems

unkind, / Spurns at his love, and scorns the heat he feels' (309–311). Having sufficiently tormented the horse, the jennet grows 'kinder'—both less cruel and more 'natural'—and welcomes his sexual advances (318). Like the coy jennet, perhaps, Adonis might be putting on an 'outward strangeness' to provoke the desire he 'seems' to 'scorn' (310–311). At this moment in the poem, we might wonder if Adonis will finally pity Venus' suffering and consent to sex.

The possibility that Adonis has adopted the role of the coy woman aligns with Venus' interpretation of his behaviour as a deficiency of virility. Venus urges Adonis to conform to conventional manliness by manifesting a propensity to sexual pursuit: 'Thou art no man, though of a man's complexion, / For men will kiss even by their own direction' (214–216). Adonis might have the outward appearance or 'complexion' of a man, but in the early modern meaning of 'complexion' as the body's mixture of humours, he appears to lack the greater corporeal heat that typically distinguished men from women and that fuelled their sexual drives. Men should naturally 'kiss even by their own direction', without prompting or cajoling. When Adonis' horse behaves with typical male ardour by pursuing the jennet, Venus takes the opportunity to teach Adonis a lesson about self-directed sexual response. A man who spies his lover naked in bed, she explains, will feast his 'eye' on her beauty until his 'other agents' (possibly hands, mouth, etc., but certainly penis) become enflamed to 'aim at like delight', through direct contact with the beautiful object (399–400). 'Who is so faint that dares not be so bold / To touch the fire, the weather being cold?' Venus asks (401–402). A man who is not bold enough to 'touch the fire' when he feels cold must possess a 'faint' or unmanly disposition. Hence Subha Mukherji suggests that Venus takes Adonis' 'unresponsiveness to be a sign of his androgyny'.[13] If so, it is an androgyny represented as a shameful manifestation of 'effeminacy' or unmanliness.

Adonis does finally justify his sexual disinterest in Venus, yet his explanations are no less equivocal and indeterminate than those offered by the narrator and Venus. Even his straightforward declaration, 'I know not love ... nor will not know it', is double-edged, since 'know' has both an intellectual meaning—i.e., 'I don't know what love is and I don't want to learn more about it'—and a physiological meaning—i.e., 'I have not experienced and will not experience "carnal knowledge," or sexual intimacy with another person' (409). Despite disavowing any knowledge of love, however, Adonis admits that he knows enough to know that he wants nothing to do with it: ''Tis much to borrow, and I will not owe it / …For I have heard it is a life in death' (411, 413). Although he never reveals the source of his information, Adonis seems convinced that experiencing love would destroy the peace he enjoys while single: 'My heart longs not to groan, / But soundly sleeps, while now it sleeps alone' (785–786).

Whatever the source of Adonis' knowledge, he confidently expresses the conviction that he is too young to experience sexual intimacy, prompting some readers to argue that he is not asexual but simply in a 'pre-sexual' stage of life. We might instead understand Adonis' rhetorical argument about the relationship of sexuality to time as rejection of the queerly accelerated temporality produced by Venus's importunate desire. Venus attempts to initiate Adonis into the 'adult' world of male-female reproductive sexuality before he is ready:

> Measure my strangeness with my unripe years.
> Before I know myself, seek not to know me.
> No fisher but the ungrown fry forbears.
> The mellow plum doth fall, the green sticks fast.
> Or, being early plucked, is sour to taste.   (524–528)

Whereas the narrator had attributed to Adonis a constitutionally 'leaden appetite' for sex, Adonis here argues that one's appetite should be appropriately calibrated to the time: fish and fruit should be eaten only once they have fully grown (34). By 'stick[ing] fast' to the tree, 'green' or unripe fruit naturally resists being too 'early plucked'. Moreover, when Adonis urges, 'Before I know myself, seek not to know me', he implies that, as an adolescent, he has not yet achieved an adequate understanding of his own identity; it would be wrong for Venus to 'know' him (sexually) before he knows himself morally, intellectually, temperamentally, or perhaps even sexually, through masturbation (525). Whereas Venus diagnoses what is wrong with Adonis, he instead implies that there is something wrong with *her* for seeking sexual intimacy with an immature, unripe, inexperienced boy. Why would anyone want to eat unripe fruit that 'is sour to taste' (528)? Moreover, plucking a flower before it has bloomed can irreparably damage it: 'Who plucks the bud before one leaf put forth? / If springing things be any jot diminished, / They wither in their prime, prove nothing worth' (416–418). Adonis might genuinely fear that to experience sex before his mind and body are ready for it could cause him harm.

When Adonis agrees to kiss Venus goodbye, however, the narrator seizes on this moment of yielding to suggest that what has changed is not Adonis' willingness to consent to sex, but the physiological temperament of his body: 'What wax so frozen but dissolves with temp'ring / And yields at last to every light impression?' (565–566). Previously compared to implacable flint, steel, and stone, Adonis is now a frozen wax ball that can be tempered or softened by heating.[14] The imprint of a signet on soft wax was a classical metaphor for sexual reproduction: in penetrative sex, a man left a 'foetal imprint' in a woman's womb.[15] Because a softened wax ball cannot help but 'yield' to whatever is impressed upon it, that metaphor renders Adonis' body prototypically feminine, 'designed' to be penetrated. I am not arguing that Adonis is feminized because he can be sexually penetrated. Men as well as women can be sexually penetrated, and being penetrated does not feminize a man. Still, the particular gendering of sexual reproduction through the metaphor of penis as signet and uterus as wax associates Adonis with a penetrable female body. Recall Martin Luther's justification of human sexuality: 'A woman does not have complete mastery over herself. God so created her body that she should be with a man and bear and raise children…the members of her body sufficiently show that God himself formed her for this purpose.'[16] In being rendered sexually penetrable, Adonis is also deprived of 'mastery' over himself:

> What though the rose have prickles, yet 'tis plucked!
> Were beauty under twenty locks kept fast,
> Yet love breaks through, and picks them all at last.   (574–576)

A rose cannot avoid being plucked; a lock cannot refuse to be picked. Venus had anticipated this figuration of Adonis as passive object of her pleasure when she reasoned that despite being physically 'unripe'— too young to desire sex? too young to penetrate her?—he could still be 'tasted' by her, evidently regardless of his consent (128). It as if the narrator has finally solved the 'problem' of Adonis' asexuality by removing the need not only for his consent, but for his sexual stimulation in achieving an erection. Adonis' asexuality would no longer be an obstacle to Venus' sexual satisfaction if she decided to penetrate *him* in an act of nonconsensual rape.

Perhaps because *Venus and Adonis* is not a tragic poem in the mode of *The Rape of Lucrece* but one that precariously balances the humorous, titillating, lyrical, satirical, and elegiac, it never occurs to Venus to act on this possibility. To be sure, after Adonis grants her a kiss, Venus preys upon his mouth in a 'blindfold fury' of lust that the boy cannot possibly resist (554). Still, Venus does not follow through on the narrator's line of thought—that Adonis, like a warmed ball of wax, can be 'impressed' (penetrated); that Adonis is a rose that can be plucked or a lock that can be picked (554). In the end, Venus 'takes all she can, not all she listeth'—what she 'lists' or desires presumably involves more than kissing, as the following episode suggests (564). When Venus learns that Adonis plans to hunt the boar, she panics, grappling him closely to her so that she falls on her back and he lands on her belly:

> Now is she in the very lists of love,
> Her champion mounted for the hot encounter.
> All is imaginary she doth prove.
> He will not manage her, although he mount her,
> > That worse than Tantalus' is her annoy,
> > To clip Elysium, and to lack her joy. (595–600)

'Lists' are enclosed fields for jousting matches in which male 'champions' battle with long lances, here a metaphor for the erect penis.[17] Thrilled that Adonis finally seems ready for the 'hot encounter' of penetrative sex, Venus is bitterly disappointed to discover that he 'will not manage her, although he mount her'. Adonis can mount the mare but will not or cannot ride her. Consequently, the narrator concludes, Venus 'hath assayed as much as may be proved' (608). How can we understand the limitation that Venus (or Shakespeare) imposes on her sexual enjoyment of Adonis? It might be that Venus' 'love' for the boy will not admit the violence of non-consensual sex. It might be that she desires only to be penetrated, not to penetrate. Or perhaps from an early modern perspective penetrative rape is virtually unthinkable in the absence of a male perpetrator: women might be imagined as forcibly kissing, groping, grasping, or immobilizing a male object of desire, but not as penetrating him with, say, a finger or dildo.[18]

Adonis' fate is to be fatally penetrated by a male boar, whose violent insertion of a tusk into his groin Venus allegorizes as a sexual act. Venus identifies with the boar's supposed intention merely to kiss Adonis: 'nuzzling in his flank, the loving swine / Sheathed unaware the tusk in his soft groin' (1115–1116). Uninterested in or incapable of penetrative sex, Adonis is killed by violent penetration. What Venus would or could not do to satisfy her desire for him, the boar does without thought or hesitation. From an asexual perspective, Adonis' death, at least in Venus' interpretation of it, might seem like a punitive symbolic imposition of compulsory sexuality.[19]

A Midsummer Night's Dream

In *Venus and Adonis*, as we saw, Venus contemns the 'fruitless chastity' of '[l]ove-lacking vestals and self-loving nuns' (752). In *A Midsummer Night's Dream*, Duke Theseus elaborates Venus' portrait of the nunnery as a place of emotional and physical barrenness: a place where only the truly asexual might be content. Egeus has appealed to Theseus to render judgment on his daughter Hermia, who has refused to marry Demetrius, the man Egeus has chosen for her spouse. According to Athenian law, unless she obeys her father, Hermia must either suffer death or join a convent, but the difference between the two options collapses when Theseus depicts an asexual existence among other women as a living death:

> Therefore, fair Hermia, question your desires.
> Know of your youth, examine well your blood,
> Whether, if you yield not to your father's choice,
> You can endure the livery of a nun,
> For aye to be in shady cloister mewed,
> To live a barren sister all your life,
> Chanting faint hymns to the cold fruitless moon.
> Thrice blessèd they that master so their blood
> To undergo such maiden pilgrimage;
> But earthlier happy is the rose distilled
> Than that which, withering on the virgin thorn,
> Grows, lives, and dies in single blessedness. (1.1.67–78)

Through images of hardship ('endur[ance]'), darkness ('shade'), sterility ('barren', 'fruitless'), quietness ('faint'), and 'cold', Theseus represents what compulsory asexuality will feel like for a sexually desirous young woman. Since a 'mew' is a cage for birds or poultry, to be 'mewed' in the cloister is a particularly chilling, claustrophobic, image.[20] As Alison Findlay observes, the nuns' 'maiden pilgrimage' takes place within the walls of the convent, which 'physically recreate the impenetrable body of the Virgin [Mary], separating nuns from the world of men like an architectural hymen'.[21] Theseus' portrait of the convent as a place of deprivation and enclosure makes it an ill-suited place for a young woman's 'blood', a word he stresses twice at the end of verse lines. Hermia must 'examine' her 'blood'—meaning 'temperament' as well as 'passions' or 'base and fleshly appetites'—to determine if she is capable of emotionally, spiritually, and physically 'master[ing]' her sexual appetites: the only hope of surviving such an anemic existence.[22]

In addition to his chilling description of the cloister, Theseus deploys the metaphor of sex as rose-plucking which we have already encountered in *Venus and Adonis*. As Theodora Jankowski shows, this metaphor also appears in a familiar sixteenth-century text that stages a debate between the value of virginity and marriage, Erasmus' colloquy 'The Wooer and the Maiden'. Courting a resistant young virgin named Maria, Pamphilus argues that just as a fruit tree's value comes not from its beauty but from its fruit, a woman's value comes not from her beauty but from the children she produces in marriage. Countering Pamphilus' dismissal of aesthetic worth, Maria asks if 'a rose gleaming white on its bush' isn't more beautiful than one 'plucked and gradually withering'.[23] Whereas the untouched virginal body remains a fair and fresh rose, the sexually active or 'plucked' woman loses her beauty along with her vitality. Although Pamphilus doesn't respond to Maria's implication that having children prematurely ages women, he observes that aging is inevitable for all women. Nonetheless, the wife is superior to the virgin because her loss of virginity benefits her *husband*: the 'plucked rose that delights a man's eyes and nostrils is better than one that grows old on a bush'.[24] Pamphilus concludes by asking 'what's more naturally unnatural than an old maid?'[25] Erasmus uses the Latin 'prodigiosius'—meaning 'more monstrous or unnatural'—to convey Pamphilus' disgust at a queer temporality that thwarts reproductive futurism. For a woman to age from young virgin to old virgin constitutes an unnatural refusal to give a man both sexual pleasure and children.

Theseus uses the same botanical image of the rose to make a different argument in favour of marriage and sexual reproduction. In Erasmus' colloquy, Maria argues that the plucked rose—the sexually active wife—will 'wither' faster than the unplucked virginal rose. Theseus instead asserts that the *unplucked* rose will 'wither[ ] on the virgin thorn', while the plucked rose, 'earthlier happy', will remain fresh through distillation into perfume. 'Earthlier happy' means both more fortunate in life and enjoying more earthly or fleshly, as opposed to spiritual, pleasures. Whereas Pamphilus shows concern only for the pleasure that a wife can give her husband, Theseus' image of the 'earthlier happy' rose preserved as fragrance suggests the longevity of the wife's capacity to give and to *receive* sensual pleasure. Theseus, in sum, advocates marriage as the sole source of erotic pleasure for women. By contrast, he describes the nun's state as one of 'single' blessedness not only because she remains unmarried, but also because he evidently believes that communities of women are incapable of deep friendships or physical intimacies. An existence without men must be dark, cold, and lonely.

To enforce Hermia's compliance with her father's wishes, Theseus omits from his account any acknowledgment of the possibility of intimacy and sexual pleasure among virgins. As Valerie Traub observes, Hermia's 'appropriation of Theseus' rhetoric' when responding to his cautionary image of the rose that '[g]rows, lives, and dies in single blessedness'—'So will I grow, so live, so die, my lord' (1.1.79)—affirms the 'possibility of growth and life within a religious sisterhood'.[26] Early modern writers did, in fact, acknowledge that 'queer virgins could live with sexual pleasure and without men'.[27] For instance, Andrew Marvell's ode 'Upon Appleton House' recounts a sexually suggestive episode from a country estate's past use as a Catholic convent. Tempting the young Isabel Thwaites to join their order, a nun promises her nightly '[d]elight' and 'pleasure':

> Each night among us to your side
> Appoint a fresh and virgin bride;
> ....
> Where you may lie as chaste in bed,
> As pearls together billeted.
> All night embracing arm in arm,
> Like crystal pure with cotton warm.[28]

Whereas Theseus depicts the cloister as 'barren' and 'cold', the nun offers Isabel a 'fresh' virgin 'bride' to 'warm' her bed every night. Since newly married couples generally consummated their marriage by having sex on their wedding night, Isabel is invited to take the role of husband with new 'brides' on consecutive nights. Although the nun specifies that such intimacy will be 'chaste', her description of virgins 'embracing arm in arm' like warm cotton cradling 'pure' crystal implies the compatibility of sexual heat and spiritual virtue. In early modern England, sexual contact between women could be considered both virginal and chaste to the degree that the most significant, consequential, sexual act was reproductive sex with a man. Although Marvell is satirizing the hypocritical chastity of Catholic nuns, 'Upon Appleton House' suggests that a 'celibate' single life without men does not necessarily rule out the possibility of same-sex intimacy and pleasure.

Romeo and Juliet

Whereas Hermia is threatened with forced celibacy, in *Romeo and Juliet* a young woman willingly takes a vow of chastity. At the start of the play, Romeo is lovesick for Rosaline, a young virgin who is evidently immune to Cupid's lust-inducing arrows. Comparing his courtship of Rosaline to a military assault, Romeo represents his 'loving terms' as the aggressive 'siege' of a fortified city or castle:

> she hath Dian's wit,
> And, in strong proof of chastity well armed,
> From love's weak childish bow she lives unharmed.
> She will not stay the siege of loving terms,
> Nor bide th'encounter of assailing eyes,
> Nor ope her lap to saint-seducing gold.   (1.1.202–207)

Although the armour of 'Diana's wit'—an unshakable devotion to virginity—passively protects Rosaline from being 'harmed' by Cupid's 'weak childish bow', she declines to use that armour actively to defend herself in the love games that Romeo's metaphors require (Figure 4.2). Disengaging from Romeo's amorous assaults, she 'will not stay' or 'bide' his attempts to initiate her into compulsory sexuality. Rosaline's refusal to 'open her lap to saint-seducing gold' underscores the purity of her commitment to virginity. The allusion to the myth of Danae,

I nuc, CVPIDO, nil 'que iaclita tuis
Mortale poste uiribus resistere.
Adiuta summi te fautore numins,

Nil nostra per quem non potest infirmitas,
Pede proterit; tuas et extinquit faces,
Arcum'que, pharetram, ac tela frangit CASTITAS.

Figure 4.2 'From love's weak childish bow she lives unharmed': Chastity defeating Love. Pieter Jalhea Furnius, 'Kuisheid overwint Liefde' [Chastity conquers Love]. (1550–1625). Rijksmuseum, Amsterdam.

a woman impregnated by Jove via a shower of inseminating gold that falls into her lap, also signifies Rosaline's rejection of reproductive futurism: she has 'sworn that she will still live chaste' (1.1.210).

Romeo depicts Rosaline's refusal of sexual reproduction as deeply antisocial, as if she were rejecting not just him—or even all men—but all humankind. By 'sparing' her body from reproductive sex, Rosaline wastes her great 'store' of beauty, which will fade away without having ever been replicated in a child (1.1.211, 209). The idea of beauty as a kind of social good that one is obliged to preserve, invest, and pass on is also articulated in Shakespeare's *Sonnets*. Scolding an aristocratic young man for refusing to produce a child who would embody his exceptional fairness, the speaker accuses him of antisocial narcissism. Instead of hoarding his beauty, the speaker insists, the young man should 'use' it—with a pun on usury or loaning money at interest—by finding a woman to marry and impregnate. Just as Romeo objects that Rosaline cuts off her beauty from 'all posterity', the speaker asks the young man why he would want to be 'the tomb / Of his self-love to stop posterity?' (3.7–8). Such arguments for reproductive futurism burden single people with being stewards, not owners, of their beauty, which is understood as a gift of Nature to be carefully tended and multiplied for the benefit of the world. Through this logic, asexuality and celibacy constitute the queer neglect of a duty to society and humanity.

Measure for Measure

Unlike *Venus and Adonis* and *A Midsummer Night's Dream*, which briefly refer to nuns in arguments against virginity, *Measure for Measure* features a central character, Isabella, who is about to join the Order of St. Claire. Although the play takes place in the Catholic city of Vienna, Shakespeare makes no effort to depict the city's history or customs accurately, instead drawing upon his knowledge of London to represent urban life as rife with sexual exploitation, betrayal, and disease. The scoundrel Lucio, for instance, refuses to support a prostitute with whom he has had a bastard child. Temporarily advanced by the Duke as the chief authority in Vienna, Angelo enforces a long neglected law against illicit sex that shutters brothels and punishes fornication (sex between the unmarried) with death. Claudio and Juliet, a young unmarried couple, are arrested under the fornication law because Juliet has become visibly pregnant. It is under these conditions that the deeply devout Isabella seeks out a life in the convent.

What Isabella desires is not a leisurely escape from the dangers of urban life; judging the discipline of the Claires to be too lax, she wishes for a 'more strict restraint' to be imposed on the sisters (1.4.4). It is not clear what kind of restraint Isabella desires, or why. The Claires already limit nuns' interactions with men: nuns may talk with men only in the presence of the Prioress, and even then they must not show their faces. This rule seems aimed at protecting the sexual purity of the nuns, since it is unlikely that such a highly mediated encounter would provoke erotic desire either from the nuns or from their male visitors. When Isabella visits Angelo to persuade him to pardon her brother Claudio, the combined force of her beauty and eloquence does, in fact, kindle his sexual desires, leading to a terrible dilemma: if she does not consent to have sex with him, Angelo threatens, he will execute her brother under the fornication law. In the world of the play, a 'strict restraint' might well be necessary to protect a woman like Isabella not from her own sexual desires, but from the predatory desires of men.

Some critics have argued that Isabella expresses an erotically 'masochistic desire for restraint'.[29] Central to such interpretations is Isabella's insistence to Angelo that she would rather undergo physical torture and death than yield to sexual blackmail:

> were I under the terms of death,
> Th' impression of keen whips I'd wear as rubies,
> And strip myself to death as to a bed
> That longing have been sick for, ere I'd yield
> My body up to shame.   (2.4.100–104)

Isabella's ardent denunciation of the 'shame' of sex, particularly her comparison of gory welts to gorgeous rubies and her 'longing' to strip herself naked for death, have led some readers to conclude that she expresses a subconscious sexual longing.[30] Celibacy theorist Benjamin Kahan might cite such interpretations as attempts to 'decode' queer content from evidence that is not explicitly sexual, thereby rendering asexuality invisible.[31] Other readers have interpreted the passage as evidence of Isabella's singular commitment to celibacy, expressed through a vehement rejection of male sexual coercion. Theodora Jankowski observes that virginity might involve not just abstention from sex, but a spiritual incapacity for desire and pleasure: 'The virgin's bodily integrity is usually reinforced by a similar spiritual integrity, a purity of thought as well as deed, which suggests that she herself is neither desired nor desiring.'[32] According to Jankowski, any pleasure we might detect in Isabella's speech derives not from an eroticization of pain but from an empowering awareness that 'she herself is responsible—through the exercise of her own free choice—for the preservation of her virginity'.[33] Melissa Sanchez concurs that 'however much she aestheticizes or eroticizes her imagined martyrdom, the point of the comparison is to render torture or death superior to unwanted sex'; hence, what has been interpreted as a masochistic sexuality may instead be asexuality.[34]

If some critics have read Isabella through the lens of eroticism instead of asexuality, Angelo does as well, for his own self-interested reasons. When Isabella excuses Claudio's crime of fornication by attesting to his human frailty, Angelo assents, 'We are all frail' (2.4.122), thus assuming 'the universality of the sexual drives' and rendering 'asexuality not only unnatural but also unthinkable'.[35] Rendering asexuality unthinkable enables Angelo to call upon Isabella's capacity for sexual transgression despite her spiritual purity: 'Nay, women are frail too', he darkly hints (2.4.124). Without confirming Angelo's insinuation, Isabella confesses women's frailty only in terms of their vanity—their tendency to admire their beauty in the mirror, long a symbol of the sin of pride—and their vulnerability to male exploitation. If weak women require the help of heaven, she insists, it is not to fortify their resistance to sexual temptation but to protect them from men's tendency to 'profit' from their weaknesses:

> ANGELO   Nay, women are frail too.
> ISABELLA   Ay, as the glasses where they view themselves,
> Which are as easy broke as they make forms.
> Women? Help, heaven! Men their creation mar
> In profiting by them. Nay, call us ten times frail,
> For we are soft as our complexions are,
> And credulous to false prints.
> ANGELO   I think it well,
> And from this testimony of your own sex,
> Since I suppose we are made to be no stronger
> Than faults may shake our frames, let me be bold.

> I do arrest your words. Be that you are;
> That is, a woman. If you be more, you're none.
> If you be one, as you are well expressed
> By all external warrants, show it now
> By putting on the destined livery. (2.4.124–138)

In Isabella's confession of frailty, which Angelo 'arrest[s]' by twisting to his own intentions, Angelo hears an admission of susceptibility to sexual temptation. His interpretation may well be facilitated by Isabella's imagery of women as fragile mirrors or as pieces of warm wax that readily accept the 'prints' of other objects. As we saw in *Venus and Adonis*, the stamping of a seal upon malleable wax can serve as a metaphor for sexual intercourse. Because this metaphor is so familiar, when Isabella describes women as 'soft' and 'credulous to false prints', Angelo can claim that Isabella has conceded women's destiny to be sexually 'printed' by a man in the act of sex.

Angelo's argument reveals how lifelong asexuality might be considered strange or queer in terms of both sexuality and gender. Although virginity was the cultural expectation for unmarried women in early modern England, a permanent state of virginity could mark a woman as 'deviant', because it removed her from patriarchal sexual, marital, and reproductive economies.[36] Angelo expresses precisely this view in objecting that if Isabella strives to be 'more' than a woman by spiritually transcending her inborn sexual capacities, she is no longer a woman at all. Relevant here is Martin Luther's contention that the lifelong virgin was 'neither a man nor a woman' because virgins, arrogantly confident in their ability to resist sexual temptation, regarded themselves as more than human—a blasphemous lie 'contrary to God and his ordinance'.[37] Luther argued that women in particular were incapable of maintaining vows of virginity:

A woman does not have complete mastery over herself. God so created her body that she should be with a man and bear and raise children…the members of her body sufficiently show that God himself formed her for this purpose. Just as eating, drinking, waking, and sleeping are appointed by God to be natural, so God also wills that it be natural for a man and woman to live together in matrimony.[38]

According to Protestant orthodoxy, God made humans capable of feeling sexual desire so that they could marry, procreate, and raise children in the Christian faith. Hence, explains Melissa Sanchez, Luther and Jean Calvin consider the true celibate an extremely rare exception to this divine purpose: both theologians deem 'the lack of sexual desire a unique divine gift afforded only a minority of believers'.[39] Angelo echoes this position when he instructs Isabella that 'we are made to be no stronger / Than faults may shake our frames'. That God gave humans imperfect 'frames' (bodies) that could be 'shake[n]' by 'faults' indicates that he did not expect them to resist fleshly temptations. From this perspective, sexual desire is the essence of humanness.

Even though the severe Angelo and the liberal Lucio take antithetical positions on the question of sexual freedom, Lucio seems equally vexed by Isabella's exceptional purity. Lucio believes that Isabella's extreme 'renouncement'—of sex, but presumably also of wealth, freedom, and other bodily pleasures—has transformed her into something 'enskied and sainted' (1.4.33–34). In Angelo's terms, Lucio makes Isabella 'more' than a woman: an angelic creature who has miraculously transcended the bodily urges that human beings, according to Renaissance philosophy, shared with animals. If Lucio is thereby attributing a kind of asexuality to Isabella, he seems to regard that condition with wonder: 'astonishment mingled with perplexity or bewildered curiosity.'[40] Wonder can disturb as much as fascinate. It is not surprising that Isabella accuses Lucio of mocking her.

Just as Lucio defines Isabella as radically subordinating the desiring body to the spirit, he defines Angelo as radically subordinating the desiring body to the mind. Because of Angelo's hostility to sexual liberty, Lucio describes him as

> a man whose blood
> Is very snow-broth; one who never feels
> The wanton stings and motions of the sense,
> But doth rebate and blunt his natural edge
> With profits of the mind, study, and fast.   (1.4.56–60)

By honing his mind with 'study' and disciplining his body with 'fast', Angelo 'rebate[s] and blunt[s]' the 'natural edge' of sexual desire. The image of a dulled edge recalls two sexually charged images from Shakespeare's *Sonnets*. Sonnet 52 describes a miser 'blunting the point' of pleasure by frequently unlocking his treasure chest with a key (4). Sonnet 95, which recounts the youth's 'lascivious' behaviour, warns that the 'hardest knife ill used doth lose his edge' (6, 14). Through overuse, the key becomes blunted and the knife becomes dulled. Given the roughly phallic shape of those objects, these images appear to warn against the decline in sensation caused by too much sex. Yet according to Lucio, Angelo *pre-emptively* blunts his senses in order to reinforce his asexual constitution. If sensual 'stings and motions' constitute the 'natural edge' of the body's senses, however, then to preventatively quell them as Angelo does seems unnatural. Moreover, Angelo's very blood, which, according to Renaissance physiology should be warm, is 'snow-broth'. As with Isabella, Lucio hints at something inhuman about Angelo, a man who seemingly 'never feels'.

Lucio explains the unnaturalness of Angelo's asexuality by attributing it to his strange conception. Reporting the gossip that Angelo 'was not made by man and woman, after this downright way of creation', Lucio offers that either 'a sea-maid spawned him' or that 'he was begot between two stockfishes' (3.1.349–351, 353–354). Whereas the distinctly gendered couple of 'man and woman' represents the familiar or 'downright' mode of sexual reproduction, 'spawning' refers to reproduction without intercourse, when a male fish inseminates eggs laid by a female fish. Lucio reasons that a cold, passionless act of generation has created a man incapable of sexual passion, who urinates 'congealed ice' and who is more fish than flesh (3.1.355). Fish were often associated with women, flesh or meat with men. Describing Angelo as a 'motion generative', a wooden puppet capable of sexual reproduction, Lucio both acknowledges and denies Angelo's paradoxical humanity (3.1.356). In an emendation accepted by many modern editors, eighteenth-century editor Lewis Theobald tried to resolve this paradox by changing Lucio's phrase to 'motion *un*generative', thus making the wooden puppet properly sterile.

Like Adonis in *Venus and Adonis*, Angelo articulates his own perspective on his asexuality, in response to his shock at finding himself attracted to Isabella—a kind of ad hoc queer sexuality that Paul Morrison cleverly calls 'same-saint desire'.[41] Angelo muses that even the most seductive women have failed to stimulate him:

> Never could the strumpet
> With all her double vigour—art and nature—
> Once stir my temper; but this virtuous maid
> Subdues me quite. Ever till now
> When men were fond, I smiled, and wondered how.   (2.2.187–191)

Angelo's framing of his sexual history through the absolute temporalities of 'never' and 'ever till now' implies that he has never experienced sexual desire for *any* woman. Even the 'double vigor' of prostitutes, who marshal the power of 'art' (cosmetics, clothing) and 'nature' (beauty), has failed to 'stir' him. Perhaps more revealing is his confession that whenever he has encountered a 'fond' man—one 'subdue[d]' by erotic desire—he 'smiled and wondered how'. Angelo's smug derision of lovers implies that he has never himself been attracted to a woman, no matter how 'virtuous' or otherwise appealing; he has only judged other men's desires to be ridiculous and demeaning. Describing Angelo as one who 'scarce confesses / That his blood flows, or that his appetite / Is more to bread than stone', the Duke seems aware of his asexual history (1.3.51–53). In refusing to confess that his blood flows, Angelo exhibits 'the sinful pride that Protestant Reformers associated with the Catholic celibate's denial of, as Luther put it, human "nature and disposition."'[42] That flowing blood and nourishing food are essential to human life once again associates asexuality with the queerly inhuman and unnatural.

From a contemporary perspective, the most recognizably queer aspect of Angelo's asexuality might be his hostility to reproductive futurism. It is as if asexuality as a frigid denial of human vitality naturally produces in Angelo a desire to punish sexual activity with death. Angelo's first act as deputy governor is to sentence Claudio to death and Juliet to prison for having conceived a child before marriage. The anti-reproductive cast of Angelo's severity is noted by the bawd Pompey, who predicts that after ten years of executing sexually active citizens, the city will 'be glad to give out a commission for more heads' (2.1.214–215). Angelo himself proudly boasts of the abortive power of the fornication law, which

> Takes note of what is done, and, like a prophet,
> Looks in a glass that shows what future evils,
> Either raw, or by remissness new-conceived
> And so in progress to be hatched and born,
> Are now to have no successive degrees,
> But ere they live, to end.   (2.2.96–101)

Angelo's fantasy of the law as a prophet predicting and preventing 'future evils' recalls Philip K. Dick's science fiction thriller 'The Minority Report', in which the police prevent as yet uncommitted crimes predicted by psychics. Angelo reasons that if citizens fear the law, they will restrain themselves from committing the sexual crimes they previously would have committed with impunity. By deterring potential evildoers from acting on their illicit desires, the law effectively aborts illicit sexual acts 'in progress to be hatched and born'. The metaphor of the law as an aborting prophet could apply, of course, to any kind of crime and to any kind of sentence: the point is that fear of punishment prevents criminals from acting on—giving 'successive degrees' or stages to—their wicked thoughts. That this particular law punishes *sexual activity* with death, however, collapses the metaphor of the law as aborting prophet into the literal meaning of abortion as the termination of a pregnancy.[43]

Love's Labors Lost

In *Measure for Measure*, Lucio affirms that Angelo's asexuality results from his dedication to 'profits of the mind, study, and fast' (1.4.60). Although Angelo never explains what role mental discipline has played in developing or maintaining his chastity, *Love's Labors Lost* provides just such an explanation. When the comedy opens, the King of Navarre and three of his courtiers are about to embark on a three-year retreat of study, fast, and celibacy. By turning Navarre into a 'little academe', a courtly version of all-male colleges such as Oxford or Cambridge, the men hope to prove their ability to conquer their 'own affections' and the 'huge army of the world's desires' (1.1.13, 9–10).[44] Were these men asexual, forgoing erotic pleasures for three years would be easy; the point of the academe is to make Navarre 'the wonder of the world' for their extremely difficult sacrifice (1.1.12). Nonetheless, it is possible to understand the court's intention as the accomplishment, through mental discipline, of an asexual temperament for an extended period of time.

In imagining the conditions necessary for the success of this asexual academy, the play recalls the language associated with celibacy and asexuality in other texts we have considered. Just as Rosaline in *Romeo and Juliet* and Isabella in *Measure for Measure* vow to avoid male society, the French courtiers have 'sworn' oaths to 'keep those statutes' that the king has devised to maintain their chastity (1.1.16–17). These 'statutes' recall Angelo's reliance on laws to repress sexual desires through fear. The courtiers must be 'armed' against sexual desires, just as Rosaline is in 'strong proof of chastity well armed' against Romeo's courtship (*LLL* 1.2.22; *RJ* 1.1.203). The technique of bolstering chastity through fasting, which Lucio attributes to Angelo, is endorsed by Longueville:

> Tis but a three years' fast.
> The mind shall banquet, though the body pine.
> Fat paunches have lean pates, and dainty bits
> Make rich the ribs but bankrupt quite the wits.   (1.1.24–27)

According to Longueville, the mind and body thrive in inverse relation to each other: the courtiers will 'banquet' their minds through study while starving their bodies (and desires) through fasting. Whereas such discipline might appeal to someone like *Measure for Measure*'s Isabella, who finds her strict religious order too permissive, Biron has little faith in his ability to obey the academy's rules: 'O, these are barren tasks, too hard to keep— / Not to see ladies, study, fast, not sleep' (1.1.47–48). Biron laments the sexual 'barren[ness]' of an all-male academy, much as *A Midsummer Night's Dream*'s Theseus portrays the nunnery as a lonely, 'fruitless' place (*MSND* 1.1.72)

Biron also articulates the view, which we have encountered several times already, that asexuality is antithetical to human nature. He predicts that he and his companions will repeatedly break their vows of chastity:

> Necessity will make us all forsworn
>   Three thousand times within this three years' space;
> For every man with his affects is born,
>   Not by might mastered, but by special grace.
> If I break faith, this word shall speak for me:
> I am forsworn on mere necessity.   (1.1.147–152)

The bookending of this speech with the word 'necessity' emphasizes the claim that since 'affects'—emotions, but more specifically erotic passions—are inborn, taking an oath of celibacy is futile. Biron echoes Luther's belief that human beings do not have the 'might' to repress or 'master' their fleshly desires, and that the only true celibates are a tiny minority who have been given that capacity through 'a special miracle of God'.[45] Biron turns out to be right. When the French princess and her ladies arrive, the courtiers quickly fall in love with them. Even as it depicts long-term celibacy as an aspiration of high-minded noblemen, then, *Love's Labors Lost* makes it very difficult to imagine asexuality as a viable condition for fleshly beings born with 'affects'.

All's Well that Ends Well

All's Well that Ends Well and *Measure for Measure*, generally considered Shakespeare's final comedies, stretch and destabilize the conventions of the genre. Whereas *Measure for Measure* associates sexual desire with disease, corruption, and death, *All's Well that Ends Well* inverts the more familiar situation in which a young woman, such as Hermia in *A Midsummer Night's Dream*, is coerced to marry against her will. In *All's Well that Ends Well*, the King commands a nobleman, the Count Bertram, to marry a poor dependent of Bertram's family, Helena, to reward her for having cured his illness. Horrified at having to marry a commoner whom he does not love, Bertram emphatically refuses to have sex with his wife: 'Although before the solemn priest I have sworn, I will not bed her' (2.3.253–254). Even though Bertram has been constrained through the marriage ceremony to swear to love his wife, he has subsequently 'sworn' another oath to the contrary: 'I have wedded her, not bedded her, and sworn to make the "not" eternal' (3.2.21). The latter oath recalls the ritual commitments to lifelong celibacy that *A Midsummer Night's Dream* and *Measure for Measure* associate with the convent. Hence Jordan Windholz argues that Bertram's oath represents 'male chastity as a queer mode of asexual life'.[46]

Just as vows of celibacy provide women entry into the same-sex community of the convent, Bertram's vow to avoid conjugal sex prompts his escape into the same-sex community of the military. 'I'll to the Tuscan wars and never bed her', he insists to his friend Paroles (2.3.257). Paroles endorses Bertram's decision to seek out military glory among men rather than to debilitate himself through sex with a woman:

> To th'wars, my boy, to th'wars!
> He wears his honour in a box unseen
> That hugs his kicky-wicky here at home,
> Spending his manly marrow in her arms,
> Which should sustain the bound and high curvet
> Of Mars's fiery steed. To other regions!
> France is a stable, we that dwell in't jades.
> Therefore to th'war.   (2.3.262–269)

Remaining at home to 'hug' his 'kicky-wicky'—a nonce-word possibly meaning a slight or unimportant woman—a man hides his honour in a box instead of displaying it on the battlefield for other men to witness and endorse. Paroles' graphic imagery activates a pun on the vagina as the 'box' in which a husband might 'spend his manly marrow', or expend his semen.[47] The meaning of 'spend' as 'to exhaust or consume by use' implies that sex with a woman saps one's manhood.[48] It's possible, therefore, to understand Paroles as recommending for Bertram (and possibly himself) a kind of asexuality in which precious 'manly marrow'—the source of a man's 'vitality and strength'—will not be depleted through orgasm but rather channelled into controlling a 'fiery' horse of Mars, the god of war.[49] As Windholz explains, '[s]emen preserved in the testicles fired the bodily heat soldiers might project not in sex, but in battle'.[50] Thus the man who refuses to ride a horse into battle becomes himself a worn-out horse or 'jade', a word commonly used to insult women.[51]

Having won military honour in Florence, Bertram pursues a local virgin named Diana who is 'wondrous cold' and 'armed' with chastity to repel his seduction (3.6.103; 3.5.70). A young virgin might well be expected to defend her chastity by responding to a suitor with 'cold' indifference or unfriendliness.[52] As we have seen with Adonis and Angelo, however, the metaphor of coldness might also suggest a constitutional asexuality based on one's complexion or mixture of bodily humors.[53] Frustrated by Diana's refusals, Bertram asks if she lacks the capacity for sexual desire:

> But, fair soul,
> In your fine frame hath love no quality?
> If the quick fire of youth light not your mind,
> You are no maiden but a monument.

When you are dead you should be such a one
As you are now, for you are cold and stern,
And now you should be as your mother was
When your sweet self was got.   (4.2.3–10)

Bertram defines humanness here in terms of the 'quick' or enlivening 'fire' that turns a virgin into a mother; lacking such heat, Diana is either a corpse or a cold, hard monument. In *Venus and Adonis*, Venus similarly associates asexuality with death when she calls Adonis 'life-less picture, cold and senseless stone' (211). Whereas Venus complains that the stony Adonis must have no mother, Bertram advises Diana to imitate her mother when she was engaged in the sexual activity through which Diana herself was conceived. That such a comparison actually puts Diana in the incestuous position of having sex with her father and queerly begetting herself doesn't seem to occur to him. Bertram attributes a queer temporality to Diana in which what she is 'now'—cold and stern—befits a *future* time, when she will be dead; and what she should be 'now'—warm and available—follows the pattern of her mother's sexual *past*, which gave Diana life. Bertram's questioning the existence of love in Diana's 'frame' or body also recalls Angelo's insistence, in *Measure for Measure*, that God created human beings with the resilience to commit the sexual sins that might 'shake' but not destroy their 'frames' (2.4.133).

When Diana finally addresses her own sexual disposition, she suggests that asexuality is the basis of her rejection of Bertram. Because of her experience with Bertram, Diana avers, she will remain a virgin: 'Since Frenchmen are so braid, / Marry that will; I will live and die a maid' (4.2.73–74). Diana offers a very strange justification for lifelong virginity. Although her mother has warned her that 'all men' swear false oaths, Diana has experienced the deceit of only a single 'Frenchman', not all Frenchmen, let alone Florentine men or men in general (4.2.71). Why would her disillusionment with Bertram rule out all other potential husbands? Neither Helena nor the King anticipates that Bertram's wickedness would forever sour Diana on the prospect of marriage. By promising to give Diana a dowry, Helena evidently believes that marriage might be in her future; at the end of the play, the King concurs: 'If you be'st yet a fresh uncroppèd flower', he promises Diana, '[c]hoose thou thy husband and I'll pay thy dower' (4.4.19;

5.3.323–324). Diana's weak logic might indicate not that her experience with Bertram has made her averse to marriage but that she has found a way to justify a prior inclination or decision to remain a virgin. Given the familiar argument we have encountered that asexuality in lovely young people (Adonis, Rosaline, Isabella, the youth of the *Sonnets*) is selfish, anti-social, and unnatural, we can understand why a young woman might latch on to an external justification for her queerness. Dramaturgically, however, the insight that Shakespeare gives us into Diana's psychology is puzzling, since there is no compelling reason for us to know that Diana has decided to remain a virgin, and her decision has no bearing upon the plot. It might simply be that Shakespeare capitalizes on Diana's queer asexuality as one more way to distance *All's Well that Ends Well* from comedic conventions, which typically require that young marriageable women marry.

Although an erotic preference for women might offer another explanation for Diana's rejection of marriage, the play offers little in support of that interpretation.[54] As we saw in Chapter 1 with Emilia in *The Two Noble Kinsmen*, Shakespeare sometimes connects a woman's disinterest in marriage to her exclusive affection for women. In *All's Well that Ends Well*, however, Diana's devotion to Helena is the only hint of her possible same-sex affections: 'Let death and honesty / Go with your impositions, I am yours, / Upon your will to suffer' (4.4.28–30). As long as she can preserve her 'honesty' or chastity, Diana will perform whatever Helena asks of her, even at the price of death. 'I am yours' might well signal a complete dedication of one's body to a lover. Bertram courts Diana in similar terms: 'my life be thine, / And I'll be bid by thee' (4.2.53–54). But unlike *As You Like It*, *A Midsummer Night's Dream*, or *The Two Noble Kinsmen*, all of which develop a richly metaphorical and imagistic language of female same-sex love, Diana says nothing further to suggest an erotic attachment to Helena or other women. For this reason, we would be justified in regarding Diana as an asexual character who is still capable of deep emotional commitment and solidarity, particularly to other young virgins like herself.

We have seen a pattern in Shakespeare in which lovely young men and women are deemed selfish and unnatural for resisting sexual intimacy. To conclude, it is worth stressing how racialized this perspective is. As Bertram asks Diana, '[F]air soul, / In your fine frame hath love no quality?' (4.2.3–4). The alliterative sequence of 'fair', 'fine', and 'frame' depicts Diana's white body as something refined and well-composed that is meant to be admired, enjoyed, and reproduced. Precisely because Rosaline is 'fair' and 'rich in beauty', Romeo regrets that 'with beauty dies her store' (*RJ* 1.1.199, 208–209). Isabella, according to Angelo, is a 'fair maid' who must prove her womanhood by submitting to sex with him (*MM* 2.4.30). Finally, the youth of the *Sonnets*, as the first line of the sequence asserts, is one of those 'fairest creatures' from whom 'we desire increase' (sexual reproduction) so that its beauty might live on (1.1). Inversely, as the speaker admonishes the youth, 'Let those whom nature hath not made for store, / Harsh, featureless, and rude, barrenly perish' (11.9–10). In other words, those who are naturally rough, ugly, and 'rude'—meaning not impolite but 'uncivilized or barbarous'—should die without reproducing themselves (1.1).[55] Why, the speaker implies, would 'we' want more of such people in the world? The asexuality of fair young people is so troubling in Shakespeare's texts not only because others tend to crave sexual intimacy with them, but also because of the ideological imperative to reproduce whiteness as an engine of civility.

Shakespeare and Queer Studies. Mario DiGangi, Oxford University Press. © Mario DiGangi 2025.
DOI: 10.1093/9780191994951.003.0005

Queer Heteroeroticism

In *The Two Gentlemen of Verona*, Julia imagines herself as a 'statue' or idol that is 'worshipped, kissed, loved, and adored' by her lover Proteus (4.4.191). Julia's fantasy equates a woman and a religious icon as plausible objects of male adoration—romantic in the former case and spiritual in the latter. But what if a man worshiped, kissed, loved, and adored a statue romantically, not spiritually? Shakespeare and his contemporaries were familiar with ancient stories about such men, such as the Athenian nobleman who scandalized citizens by embracing and kissing a female statue situated in a public space.[1] Another Greek man gained notoriety for leaving a stain on a statue of Aphrodite after a night of love-making.[2] In *Metamorphoses*, Ovid recounts the tale of the sculptor Pygmalion, who carved an ivory figure of a lovely woman and subsequently developed amorous feelings for it (Figure 5.1). Venus, the goddess of love, fulfils his desires by transforming the statue into a living woman. Shakespeare alludes to the Pygmalion myth at the end of *The Winter's Tale*, when Leontes responds sensually to a stone statue of his dead wife Hermione. Prompted by the statue's life-like beauty, Leontes declares: 'Let no man mock me, / For I will kiss her' (5.3.79–80).

In early modernity, the queer vagaries of male-female lust were regularly acknowledged. In *The Hospital of Incurable Fools* (1600), for instance, Tomaso Garzoni catalogues notorious instances of sexual 'folly' from the ancient world: several men were known to love female animals, including a goat, a mare, an ass, and a doe; the queen Semiramis desired a bull; Pygmalion and Alchiades adored 'dumb statue[s]'; and Periander had sex with a dead prostitute.[3] Although none of these practices—bestiality, statue love, or necrophilia—requires the participants to be of different gender (if one can even speak of a statue

Corpore vt insignem sculpsit faciéque puellam, Imponensque toro, fiat precor hæc mea coniunx, Pygmalion, operis captus amore sui est. Dixit, et alma Venus viuere iufsit ebur.
Crifpin van de Pafse figurauit et excud. *Ouid. Metam. libr. 10.*

Figure 5.1 'Let no man mock me, / For I will kiss her': Pygmalion and his statue. Crispijn van de Passe, 'Pygmalion die verliefd wordt op zijn beeld' [Pygmalion falling in love with his statue]. (1602–1607). Rijksmuseum, Amsterdam.

having gender), in each of these instances Garzoni specifies a male-female coupling, as if to stress that these foolish loves are distorted versions of more conventional pairings. Whereas Garzoni is writing satire, Protestant minister William Gouge's didactic guide to household government, *Of Domestical Duties* (1622), also includes various illicit couplings as counter-examples to proper Christian marriage. According to Gouge, a Christian who wishes to marry must choose 'one of the same kind or nature' to avoid 'buggery with beasts'; 'one of the contrary sex' to avoid 'those unnatural commixtions of parties of the same sex'; 'one beyond those degrees of consanguinity and affinity which are forbidden by the law of God' to avoid incest; and 'one that is free', meaning neither married nor betrothed to another, to avoid bigamy and polygamy.[4] Such lists encourage readers to distinguish unreasonable or illicit sexual practices from reasonable or licit kinds of sexual union between men and women. Still, they have the effect of suggesting that such illicit practices are familiar, available, and pleasurable, and that one must therefore vigilantly guard against the temptations of queer desires.

This chapter addresses the emotional and social significance in Shakespeare's texts of various manifestations of queer heteroerotic (male-female) desire.[5] Acknowledging the broad range of queer male-female sexual desires, acts and relations in Shakespeare can help to historicize 'heterosexuality', which, as I argued in the Introduction, was not a concept available to early moderns. In early modernity, sexual relations between men and women were not categorically distinguished from same-sex relations as the naturalized norm of erotic compatibility, harmony, or mutuality. When explaining what constitutes a Christian marriage, Gouge doesn't distinguish heterosexual from homosexual couples; rather, he disqualifies same-sex couples along with marriages between humans and animals, between men and women who are already married, and between close kin. Even within a legitimate Christian marriage, desire was considered illicit if it led to sodomy (non-reproductive sex) or 'unchaste' lust for one's spouse.

My focus in this chapter falls on Shakespeare's depictions of queer heteroeroticism, some forms of which were recognized by contemporary thinkers such as Gouge, and others of which have been identified in queer scholarship as productive sites of exploration. As I have argued throughout this book, queer desires and practices do not always challenge socially orthodox beliefs or institutions. Likewise, I will examine here the various ways in which queer heteroerotic desires and practices are involved in men's attempts sexually to control, humiliate, or censure women, whether such men are love objects, future spouses, husbands, fathers, or sons. Masochistic women in *A Midsummer's Night Dream*, *All's Well that Ends Well* and *Measure for Measure* seek affection from men who degrade and reject them; prospective husbands in *Henry V* and *The Taming of the Shrew* use the threat of anal penetration to bolster their patriarchal power; a father in *Pericles* corrupts his obedient daughter into an incestuous bond; and a disobedient wife in *A Midsummer Night's Dream* is magically compelled by her husband to love an animal. This is not to say that women in Shakespeare never pursue or enjoy queer pleasures with men. In *Hamlet*, for instance, there is no suggestion that Gertrude was reluctant to marry her former husband's brother; to the contrary, Hamlet feels that he must urge his mother to renounce the incestuous pleasures of Claudius' bed. Even more explicitly, Venus in *Venus and Adonis* and Nell in *The Comedy of*

Errors sexually cajole and grope the physically smaller men who resist their advances.

Yet even when these texts foreground female agency and pleasure, sexually expressive women are often subject to male mockery and censure. Hamlet shames Gertrude, not Claudius, for the sin of incest; Adonis decries Venus' passion as vicious lust; and Dromio degrades Nell as a dirty beast. Though we need not assent to such denunciations, they draw significant authority from dominant cultural views about the inherent unruliness of female sexuality. Courtships or marriages characterized by highly evident bodily differences between men and women—whether of size (*Venus and Adonis*, *The Comedy of Errors*), ability (*Richard III*), or race (*Othello*)—provoke reactions of disgust, ridicule, or fear based on the belief that erotic and emotional compatibility require a consonance of culture, age, appearance, or status. Lady Anne in *Richard III* and Desdemona in *Othello* choose husbands in opposition to this paradigm of spousal compatibility. Lady Anne's ability to overcome her initial revulsion to Richard's physical deformity is revealed as a fatal error, for the play continually reiterates the idea that Richard's crooked body manifests his twisted mind. Although Venetian Desdemona and African Othello share a genuine bond of love, Iago destroys that bond by convincing Othello that the physical and cultural differences between him and his wife guarantee her sexual betrayal. The forms of queer heteroeroticism I explore in this chapter thus seem to involve either the subordination of women's sexual wills or the expression of women's sexual wills at the price of their dignity, reputation, or safety.

Masochism

In the three instances of masochism I discuss from *A Midsummer Night's Dream*, *All's Well that Ends Well* and *Measure for Measure*, Shakespeare does not represent the conjoining of desire with pain as a deeply rooted sexual inclination that one might consensually act out with a partner. Instead, women suffer when they romantically pursue men who despise and neglect them. If these women experience pleasure, it is only from sustaining an emotional connection with a man who wishes to be left alone. Being scorned, rejected, or debased by someone you love is preferable, it seems, to having no contact with them at all. In this sense, we can attribute an erotic masochism to these queerly one-sided heteroerotic relations.

Perhaps the most explicit scene of erotic masochism occurs in *A Midsummer Night's Dream*, in which Demetrius bristles at Helena's refusal to be dissuaded by his rejection. When Demetrius insists that he 'cannot love' her, Helena avers that the more he rebukes her, the more she desires him (2.1.201):

> HELENA   And even for that do I love you the more.
> I am your spaniel, and, Demetrius,
> The more you beat me the more I will fawn on you.
> Use me but as you use your spaniel: spurn me, strike me,
> Neglect me, lose me; only give me leave,
> Unworthy as I am, to follow you.
> What worser place can I beg in your love—
> And yet a place of high respect with me—
> Than to be usèd as you use your dog?   (2.1.199–210)

In an important analysis of this episode, Melissa Sanchez argues that because 'to use' could mean 'to have intercourse with', Helena's wish to be used as Demetrius' dog might voice a desire for 'bestial' sex— possibly anal intercourse, since early moderns 'saw bestiality as a form of sodomy'.[6] According to Sanchez, then, Helena is actively negotiating the terms of the sexual intimacy she desires: she attempts to persuade Demetrius that a sexual encounter could fulfil both his desire to 'beat' her and her desire to be roughly 'used'. Consequently, Sanchez argues that even as Helena abases herself, she simultaneously 'upsets clear distinctions between domination and submission' by 'co-opt[ing] the male role of lover and the male prerogative of refusing to take no for an answer'.[7]

Although Sanchez's emphasis on the complex power dynamics of Helena's aggressive masochism is salutary, one might also argue that Helena's desire for Demetrius to 'beat', 'spurn', 'strike', and '[n]eglect' her derives from what we would now call low self-esteem. Of course, 'kinky' practices such as beating or bondage can be negotiated in a healthy way between partners who enjoy such sexual play. Helena, however, asserts that Demetrius' *dislike* fuels her desire: 'And even for that do I love you the more.' If Helena takes pleasure from the thought of Demetrius spurning and striking her like a dog, she also believes that such abuse is justified by her 'unworth[iness]' to be his partner. Her sense of inferiority emerges most sharply in her claim that she could 'beg' no 'worser place' in Demetrius' love than to serve as his dog—an abjection that she would regard as below neither her dignity nor her humanity but instead as a 'place of high respect'. Moreover, Helena understands Demetrius' romantic preference for Hermia as a consequence of her own unattractiveness:

> No, no, I am ugly as a bear,
> For beasts that meet me run away for fear.
> Therefore no marvel that Demetrius
> Do, as a monster, fly my presence thus.   (2.2.100–103)

In short, then, Helena's masochism seems to eroticize feelings of unworthiness and ugliness that are confirmed and exacerbated by Demetrius' hatred.

In *All's Well that Ends Well*, another Helena's similar feelings of unworthiness are heightened by a discrepancy in social rank. An orphaned commoner raised by the Countess of Roussillon, Helena cures the King of France of an illness, in recompense for which he promises her a husband of her choice. Helena selects the Countess' son Bertram, who is horrified at having to marry a poor commoner whom he doesn't love. As with her namesake in *A Midsummer Night's Dream*, Helena's desire is fuelled by her sense of inferiority to a man who scorns her. James Kuzner offers a compensatory reading of Helena's masochism as granting her a degree of control over a painful situation. Adopting Gilles Deleuze's account of masochism as not simply an emotional or sexual disposition but 'an art comprised of elaborate scenes, ones that merely mobilize pain as a precursor to pleasure and that are structured by "disavowal, suspense, waiting, fetishism, and fantasy"', Kuzner argues that Helena artfully fashions masochistic scenes as a way of exerting power through submission.[8] His account is consistent with Sanchez's notion that female masochism might sometimes be an expression of agency and pleasure.

The scene in which Helena seems divided between craving and deferring erotic satisfaction from Bertram illustrates the masochistic dynamic that Kuzner describes. As Bertram takes his leave from his new wife, Helena frames her request for a kiss in a way that gives him good reasons to deny it:

> HELENA   I am not worthy of the wealth I owe,
>   Nor dare I say 'tis mine—and yet it is—
>   But like a timorous thief most fain would steal
>   What law does vouch mine own.
> BERTRAM   What would you have?
> HELENA   Something, and scarce so much: nothing indeed.
>   I would not tell you what I would, my lord. Faith, yes:
>   Strangers and foes do sunder and not kiss. (2.5.75–81)

Since in early modern English 'owe' meant both 'owe' and 'own', when Helena claims to be unworthy of the wealth she owes, she doubly undermines the validity of her conjugal claim to Bertram: because she *owes* him deference and gratitude as his social inferior, she *owns* him unworthily as a husband. According to Protestant orthodoxy, Helena could legitimately demand that Bertram pay the marital 'debt' of sex that spouses owed to each other, yet as a former dependent in his household she does not 'dare' press her claim. Helena therefore obliquely requests '[s]omething' and '[n]othing'; she 'would not' tell him what she 'would'. At the moment of specifying her desire for a kiss, Kuzner observes, Helena allows Bertram to regard himself as a 'stranger' or 'foe' who would have no reason to kiss her: she 'asks for proximity and for distance, and for distance in proximity, a state of suspension'.[9] As if taking up the role Helena offers him, Bertram not only refuses to kiss Helena, but also makes himself a stranger to her by swearing that he will never have sex with her and fleeing France to fight in the Tuscan wars.

Helena achieves a similarly masochistic distance in proximity through the infamous 'bed trick' that she arranges to sexually consummate her marriage without Bertram's knowledge. Helena convinces Diana, a young Florentine virgin whom Bertram has been courting, to grant Bertram's request for a sexual liaison on the condition that it take place in complete darkness and silence. Through this ruse, Helena takes Diana's place in bed, simultaneously preventing her husband from committing adultery and fulfilling her own desire for sexual intimacy. As Kuzner notes, however, Helena achieves her sexual desires only by putting herself in the humiliating and self-erasing position of 'cheating on herself': 'Bertram will only bed Helena if he thinks she is someone else', and she can enjoy him only 'if she disavows herself, is with him as Helena in fact but not in fantasy'.[10] Masochistically, Helena orchestrates things such that she and her husband are 'apart even in bed'.[11]

Like Helena, Mariana in *Measure for Measure* desperately loves a man, Angelo, who has cruelly abandoned her. As the Duke recounts, Angelo had broken off his engagement to Mariana after her dowry was lost in a shipwreck. Worse, Angelo justified his abandonment by slandering Mariana as unchaste. Angelo thus 'bestowed her on her own lamentation, which she yet wears for his sake; and he, a marble to her tears, is washed with them, but relents not' (3.1.222–224). Breaking his betrothal vow, Angelo instead 'bestows' Mariana—gives her in marriage—to her sadness. Yet Mariana seems to eagerly embrace that sadness in lieu of her husband. Why else would she wilfully continue to 'wear' her 'lamentation' for Angelo's 'sake', as if it were a keepsake or precious gift from him? Why does Mariana continue to wash Angelo with the tears shed in response to his betrayal if, like a block of marble, he will never soften? Unlike the two Helenas, Mariana does not explicitly describe herself as unworthy of the man she loves, but both the loss of her dowry and Angelo's slander have surely lowered her worth as a marriageable woman. Nonetheless, like *A Midsummer Night's Dream*'s Helena, Mariana finds that abuse intensifies desire. According to the Duke, Angelo's 'unjust unkindness, that in all reason should have quenched her love, hath, like an impediment in the current, made it more violent and unruly' (3.1.233–235). Mariana's 'violent' masochistic response to Angelo's cruelty strikes the Duke as both highly unreasonable and entirely natural.

Mariana's first appearance in the play confirms the Duke's portrait of her as one who has wilfully embraced her sadness. A boy has been singing to Mariana a mournful song in which a false lover is asked both to 'take those lips away' and 'my kisses bring again', demonstrating the masochistic paradox of distance in proximity that we saw in Helena's equivocal request for a kiss from Bertram (4.1.1, 5). Mariana apologizes to the Duke for listening to music, as if experiencing aesthetic pleasure betrays her commitment to grief: 'My mirth it much displeased, but pleased my woe' (4.1.13) When modern editions gloss 'pleased my woe' as 'soothed my woe' (Arden) or 'helped to soothe my melancholy' (Oxford), they mean that the music eases Mariana's suffering, since 'soothe' means to allay or dispel. But Mariana's claim that the music 'pleased' her woe implies the *opposite* of soothe: the music gratified or indulged her woe. A pleasing woe could be taken as an aptly oxymoronic definition of masochism, as could the Duke's somewhat cryptic description of music's power to 'make bad good' (make sorrow pleasant?) or 'good provoke to harm' (make pleasure hurtful?) (4.1.15).

As in *All's Well that Ends Well*, a bed-trick brings an abandoned woman into a masochistically distanced proximity with the man she loves: Mariana will secretly take the place of Isabella, a virgin whom Angelo is blackmailing into sex. In the play's conclusion, the Duke publicly reveals Angelo's failed attempt to sexually exploit Isabella, forces him to marry Mariana, sentences him to execution, and then estates Mariana with her new husband's wealth so that she might 'buy' a 'better' husband after his death (5.1.417). Despite Angelo's declaration that he desires nothing more than death as punishment for his shameful crimes, Mariana insists that she seeks no better husband than Angelo and begs the Duke to pardon him. The best men, she avers, are 'moulded out of faults' (5.1.41). Although Mariana's constancy to Angelo and faith in his capacity for redemption might seem admirable, Angelo never expresses any affection for Mariana; the play leaves us with the disquieting sense that their marriage will offer Mariana many more opportunities to 'please her woe'.

Anal Eroticism

As with these three instances of female masochism, a significant power imbalance between men and women also informs the two allusions to anal eroticism I turn to now. In Chapters 1 and 2, allusions to anal eroticism or 'sodomy' arose in contexts involving intimate male bonds (e.g., between Romeo and Mercutio in *Romeo and Juliet* or Achilles and Patroclus in *Troilus and Cressida*). But the possibility of anal pleasure between men and women was also acknowledged by early modern writers.[12] Recall that Mercutio punctures the conventional idealism of Romeo's desire for Rosaline, a sworn virgin, by imagining her as an 'open arse': an anus available for penetration. Mercutio might be crudely implying that Rosaline's commitment to virginity would not rule out sexual acts that would not jeopardize her maidenhead. In any case, Mercutio seems to be suggesting that beneath Romeo's idealization of Rosaline is the desire—however sublimated or unacknowledged—for a particularly carnal or beastly kind of sex; what Rosaline would prefer to do (or not do) with her body seems completely beside the point. Similarly, the husbands-to-be in *Henry V* and *The Taming of the Shrew* rhetorically deploy the threat of anal eroticism as a way to assert their unquestioned patriarchal authority.

As we saw in Chapter 2, just before King Harry invades France in *Henry V*, he uses the language of sodomy to condemn his former bed-fellow, Lord Scrope, for having betrayed him to the enemy. Following a decisive military victory in France, Harry's allusion to anal intercourse—the sexual act most commonly associated with sodomy—underscores his command of matters both political and sexual, as epitomized in his demand to marry King Louis' daughter Katherine. Although Shakespeare writes an extensive scene in which Harry courts Katherine, it seems clear that, given her importance in the political alliance between England and France, she has little power to refuse him. Immediately following this courtship scene, the Duke of Burgundy jokingly advises Harry on how to make Katherine amenable to sex once they are married. Burgundy observes that although Katherine is now a modest virgin, if Harry takes good care of her and keeps her 'warm', she will come to resemble flies in August, which are sluggishly 'blind' and hence easily caught. Harry quips that even though he might have to wait until late summer to enjoy sexual intimacy with his wife, he will catch 'the fly, your cousin, in the latter end, and she must be blind too' (5.2.289–290). The 'latter end' means 'at last', but it also has a sexual connotation, as the place on Katherine's body that Harry will finally 'catch' or take possession of. The 'latter end' is glossed by the Norton Shakespeare as 'in the backside', by the New Cambridge Shakespeare as 'in Katherine's sexual organ'—presumably the vagina, although the anus might also be considered a 'sexual organ'—and by the Arden Shakespeare as 'in the lower part of her body'.[13] The editors' hesitancy in the latter two instances to gloss 'latter end' as 'backside' or 'anus' is perhaps understandable, in that it is difficult to understand why Harry would refer to anal sex with Katherine in the presence of the princess and her parents.[14]

Harry's indecorous remark makes sense, however, when we consider that he is speaking of Katherine's body not (merely) literally, but 'perspectively', or metaphorically, as a symbol or 'stand in' for the French territories that he intends to govern as the inheritor of the French throne:

> KING HARRY   And you may, some of you, thank love for my blindness, who cannot see many a fair French city for one fair French maid that stands in my way.
>
> KING CHARLES Yes, my lord, you see them perspectively, the cities turned into a maid—for they are all girdled with maiden walls that war hath never entered.
>
> KING HARRY   Shall Kate be my wife?
>
> KING CHARLES So please you.
>
> KING HARRY   I am content, so the maiden cities you talk of may wait on her: so the maid that stood in the way for my wish shall show me the way to my will.   (5.2.292–302)

Harry and Charles agree that unconquered French cities might be considered 'maids' or virgins in the sense that their walls have never been 'entered' or penetrated by enemy soldiers. Because he loves Katherine, Harry claims, he is willing to marry her as the primary condition of peace between England and France—as long as he also gains control of all those maiden cities that he left uninvaded during the war. Harry's joke about taking Katherine 'in the latter end' seems a warning about his capacity violently to 'enter' French cities should Louis not yield to his territorial stipulations.[15]

Aggressive male sexuality also informs the indecorous allusion to anal eroticism in *The Taming of the Shrew*, another play in which a Katherine is coerced to marry a man whom she has just met and who seeks her large dowry. During Petruccio's sole attempt to woo Katherine before their wedding day, he chides her for responding angrily to his mocking and boisterous language:

> PETRUCCIO Come, come, you wasp, i'faith you are too angry.
>
> KATHERINE If I be waspish, best beware my sting.
>
> PETRUCCIO My remedy is then to pluck it out.
>
> KATHERINE Ay, if the fool could find it where it lies.

PETRUCCIO Who knows not where a wasp does wear his sting? In his tail.

KATHERINE In his tongue.

PETRUCCIO   Whose tongue?

KATHERINE Yours, if you talk of tales, and so farewell.

PETRUCCIO What, with my tongue in your tail?   (2.1.207–214)

Countering Katherine's threat to 'sting' him with her 'tongue', Petruccio imagines *his* tongue in her 'tail', a word broadly used at the time to refer to the vagina, penis, or buttocks (*OED*, tail *n*1, 5c).[16] Petruccio seems to ask Katherine how she could walk away while he was performing cunnilingus (oral-vaginal sex) or anilingus (oral-anal sex) on her. James Bromley prefers to regard Petruccio's quip as a reference to anilingus, which 'is titillating and comic, part of the sexualized wordplay of this couple's version of courtship'.[17] If the 'sexualized wordplay' of this unusual courtship is humorous, however, it also marshals combative energies that might remind us of 'angry sex': the raw, 'animalistic' sex that sometimes follows an argument.[18] Petruccio seems to be warning Katherine that he is prepared to subdue her by degrading her or exerting complete control over her body—which he in fact proceeds to do in the play's scenes of marital 'taming'. My point is not that women cannot take sexual pleasure from either anilingus or anal intercourse, or that a man's offer of either kind of sex to a woman would necessarily be met with disgust or horror, as opposed to indifference, enthusiasm, or any number of responses.[19] However, in this particular moment Katherine and Petruccio are not negotiating which sexual acts they would like to perform with each other as husband and wife. Petruccio is aggressively courting Katherine in order to establish his dominance over her as her future husband. Immediately after the above exchange, Katherine strikes Petruccio for the first time, as if to convey that his aggressive tactics have finally gone too far.

Cross-Species Desire

The animalistic sex alluded to throughout much of Petruccio's courtship receives its fullest, and most literal, expression in *A Midsummer Night's Dream*. At several points during the play, Oberon, the King of

Fairies, uses a magical love juice derived from a flower to manipulate the desires of various (human and fairy) characters, thus producing a kind of physiological cross-species intimacy between plants and different kinds of sentient beings. Moreover, *A Midsummer Night's Dream* conveys the intense passions associated with sexual yearnings, anxieties, and betrayals by comparing human lovers to dogs, cats, bears, deer, tigers, birds, and snakes, as we saw above with Helena's masochistic demand to be used as Demetrius' spaniel. Sorting out the four confused young lovers into two marriageable couples, the impish fairy Robin Goodfellow assures us that 'Jack shall have Jill', and that—more remarkably—'the man shall have his mare again' (3.3.45, 47). Most spectacularly, Titania falls in love with the weaver Bottom, after Robin has mischievously transformed his head into that of an ass. Rick Rambuss has compared Titania's desire for this half-man, half-ass to the contemporary kink of 'pony play', in which a partner submits to being 'harnessed, ridden, [and] groomed' by their master.[20]

Whereas pony play is a consensual kink, the 'bullying Oberon' engineers this 'bestial prank' on Titania in order to reduce her to what he considers proper wifely submission.[21] Oberon gloats that the love juice will make Titania desire the first creature she sees upon awaking, be it 'lion', 'bear', 'wolf', 'bull', or 'monkey' (2.1.180–181). As Laura Levine has pointed out, because the juice overrides Titania's ability to consent to sex, Oberon essentially creates the conditions for his wife to be raped by an animal. In the event, Titania falls in love with the ass-headed Bottom, and although it is not clear if the two have a sexual encounter, Titania expresses shame and disgust when, released from the drug's effects, she discovers that she had been 'enamoured of an ass': 'O, how mine eyes do loathe his visage now!' (4.1.73, 76). In an argument about women's ability to enjoy anal eroticism, Jonathan Goldberg proposes that we understand 'ass' anatomically and thereby acknowledge 'Titania's love for her ass'.[22] Yet Goldberg doesn't acknowledge that whatever sexual pleasures Titania has experienced with her 'ass' have been coercively produced by Oberon in a plan to punish and subdue her. So even if her queer dalliance with Bottom has given Titania sexual or other forms of pleasure, such pleasure has come at the price of squelching her resistance to Oberon's patriarchal authority.

Incest

Whereas *A Midsummer Night's Dream* makes a magical juice responsible for a fairy's dotage on a strange human-animal hybrid, the disturbing sexual coercion depicted in *Pericles* arises from the most familiar domestic relations. Because *Pericles* is based on the *Confessio Amantis* of medieval poet John Gower, the play casts Gower as a choral figure who introduces and comments on its events. Gower begins with the story of Antiochus, King of Antioch, who developed sexual feelings for his (unnamed) daughter after his wife's death. This daughter was

> So buxom, blithe, and full of face
> As heav'n had lent her all his grace,
> With whom the father liking took,
> And her to incest did provoke.
> Bad child, worse father, to entice his own
> To evil should be done by none.
> By custom what they did begin
> Was with long use account' no sin.   (Scene 1.23–30)

Whereas in the *Confessio Amantis* Antiochus clearly rapes his daughter, in *Pericles* the daughter shares the guilt for a 'sin' that is initiated by a man with enormous authority as both father and king.[23] The play's etiology of incest thus both acknowledges and occludes the coercion involved in Antiochus' 'provok[ing]' and 'entic[ing]' his daughter into a sexual relationship. Although the daughter's age is not given, Gower's description of her as 'buxom' is telling. Deriving from *bow* ('to decline the head or body'), 'buxom' means '[o]bedient, pliant,... [s]ubmissive, humble...[f]lexible', as well as '[f]ull of health, vigour, and good temper'.[24] The daughter's submissive nature suggests the probability of her yielding to Antiochus' enticements, even if she had initially accounted incest a 'sin'. As a patriarch obliged to regulate his passions and raise his daughter virtuously, Antiochus is justly condemned as 'worse' than his merely 'bad' daughter. Nonetheless, because early moderns 'understood passion as integral to women's nature', they 'barely distinguished' seduction and rape.[25] Howsoever physically or emotionally coerced we might imagine the daughter to have been, she is still stigmatized as a 'sinful dame' (1.31).

Adding to the daughter's guilt, Antiochus' riddle, which suitors must solve in order to win the daughter's hand in marriage or else suffer death, explicitly makes her the active agent of incest. To solve the riddle, a suitor must be able to read the daughter as a vicious, pleasure-seeking perverter of familial structures:

> I am no viper, yet I feed
> On mother's flesh which did me breed.
> I sought a husband, in which labour
> I found that kindness in a father.
> He's father, son, and husband mild;
> I mother, wife, and yet his child.
> How this may be and yet in two,
> As you will live resolve it you.   (1.107–114)

In this version of events, Antiochus does not seduce his daughter. Rather, she 'sought a husband' and 'found' a father; consequently, she 'feed[s]' on her 'mother's flesh' as her father's second wife. Charles Forker observes that the riddle's characterization of the father as 'kind' and 'mild' implies the daughter's enjoyment of their sexual intimacy. Describing the daughter as a 'fair viol' that was 'played upon before [her] time', Pericles, however, excoriates the queer temporality of Antiochus' sexual appropriation of his daughter, which prevents her from making 'lawful music' with an exogamous husband. Pericles perhaps intuits this queer temporality from the implied parallelism of the familial roles in the sequence '[h]e's father, son, and husband mild', which states that, in relation to his daughter, Antiochus is a father (biologically) and a husband (functionally), but also a 'son'. Through the unnaturalness of incest, the daughter has not only sexually replaced her own mother, but somehow become Antiochus' mother.[26] It is as if the daughter has undergone the untimely symbolic 'labour' of giving birth to her own father because she has been prevented from undertaking the timely social 'labour' of finding an exogamous spouse. Blaming Antiochus for the incestuous relationship, Pericles recognizes the riddle as Antiochus' displacement of sexual guilt from himself onto his daughter.

Like Antiochus, Hamlet draws upon a dominant cultural belief in women's voracious sexual appetite to blame incest on a woman. Hamlet excoriates the 'wicked speed' with which his mother Gertrude 'post[ed] / With such dexterity to incestuous sheets' when she married her brother-in-law Claudius mere months after her husband's death (*Ham* 1.2.156–157). Like Pericles queasily contemplating Antiochus' premature removal of his daughter from an exogamous martial economy, Hamlet is disgusted by the queer temporality of his mother's desire, which has propelled her too quickly into a corrupted conjugal bed. Hamlet minimizes the personal and political considerations that have driven Claudius and Gertrude to marry by focusing on his mother's wicked sexual desire. When the Ghost of the murdered King Hamlet relates to his son the true story of his death at Claudius' hands, he complicates Hamlet's view of Gertrude by describing Claudius as the 'adulterous beast' who 'seduce[d]' Gertrude to 'his shameful lust' (1.5.42, 45). At the same time, the Ghost affirms that had Gertrude been 'virtu[ous]', she would have resisted Claudius' seduction; as an embodiment of 'lust', Gertrude was all too eager to devour the 'garbage' of Claudius' body (1.5.53, 55, 57). When he confronts Gertrude, Hamlet adopts the Ghost's metaphor of incestuous lust as perverted appetite. Comparing sexual intimacy to grazing, Hamlet asks Gertrude how she could 'leave to feed' on the 'fair mountain' of King Hamlet's body to 'batten on the moor'—both a piece of 'waste ground' and a black African—of Claudius' body.[27] Gertrude's lust is so indiscriminate, Hamlet implies, that even a black man would sate it. Like *Titus Andronicus'* Queen Tamora, who destabilizes Rome through her adulterous desire for a treacherous Moor, Gertrude is blamed for destabilizing Denmark by authorizing, through her bestial appetite, the sovereignty of a fratricide and adulterer.

Differences of Size, Ability, and Race

So far, we have addressed erotic dispositions, practices, and relations that could be considered queer because they are non-marital, non-reproductive, forbidden by religion or law, or, in minister William Gouge's words, 'unnatural commixtions'. In addition to defining Christian marriage in opposition to such queer unions, Gouge attests that for legitimate 'matrimonial society to prove comfortable' there should be 'some equality' between the husband and wife 'in age, estate, condition, [and] piety' (188). Gouge concedes that certain kinds of inequality between spouses can be accommodated by or even bolster orthodox gender hierarchy, such as a marriage between an older man and a younger woman: 'it is very meet that the husband should be somewhat elder then his wife, because the husband is an head, a governour, a protector of his wife' (189). Nonetheless, he cautions, extreme age differences between spouses will lead to misery, as the younger spouse inevitably ends up loathing the older: 'inequality in years occasions of many mischiefs' (189). A contemporary Dutch print portrays the inevitable 'mischief' of a marriage based on inequality in years: a young wife finds in a young lover the sexual pleasure she cannot get from her elderly husband (Figure 5.2).[28] Conversely, marriages between older widows and younger men were sometimes denounced not because the younger husband might be unfaithful, but because the wife would presumably attempt to rule her less experienced, financially dependent partner. As Gouge warns, 'if a rich woman marry a poor man, she will look to be the master, and to rule him: so as the order which God hath established will be clean perverted' (190).

Another Protestant minister, William Whately, stresses the particular importance of spouses' religious and racial conformity: 'It cannot be thought, that anything should make cohabitation more tedious, than difference of faith.'[29] Moreover, the modest conjugal affections of a 'Christian husband' and a 'Christian wife' should be 'of a more divine and heavenly nature, than those that may be found amongst Pagans and Infidels', such as a 'Turk' or a 'woman of China' (36–37). Stressing the spirituality of conjugal affection, Whately instructs Christian husbands to love a physically or mentally disabled wife no less heartily for her lack of 'good conditions and amiable qualities':

as a man which seeth more wit and beauty, and other good parts, in his neighbor's son or daughter than his own—yea, whose own child is deformed, crooked and dull-witted, yea also shrewd [railing], untowardly, rebellious, when his neighbor's child is not alone comely, straight-bodied, quick-witted, but also meek, gentle, loyal, dutiful, and obsequious—doth yet love the person of his own ill-qualified child, above the person of his neighbor's well-qualified [child],…even so should it be betwixt husband and wife. (40–41)

For the true Christian husband, any defects of 'person' will be immaterial to the love he bears towards his wife, whom he will honour as 'the only woman in the world' (40).

La corne dabondance il porte sur sa teste
Et la pour se vanger si qlqun le frappoit
Se men vay doncq dicy car si il me happoit
Jl me pourroit hurter (coe'un boeuf) de sa creste.

Das Ceres horn so treget er
Auff seinem kopf für sein gewehr:
Jch mag hinschleichen als ein fuchs,
Das mich nit stoß der grimmig ochs.

Figure 5.2 'inequality in years occasions of many mischiefs': sexual incompatibility. Crispijn van de Passe, after Jacques Bellange, 'Een jonge vrouw bedriegt haar oude echtgenoot' [a young woman cheats on her old husband]. (1574–1637). Rijksmuseum, Amsterdam.

Whatever wisdom actual spouses might have taken from Whately's advice, early modern imaginative writers recognized that stressing physical differences between sexual partners could be a source of humour, wonder, horror, or titillation. A madman in Middleton and Rowley's *The Changeling* 'ran mad for a chambermaid, yet she was but a dwarf neither' (3.3.48–49). In Brome's play *The Mock-Marriage*, a rake boasts of having sexually enjoyed women representing all ages '[f]rom sixteen unto sixty', all complexions 'from the white flaxen to the tawny Moor', all statures 'between dwarf and giantess', all ranks 'from the doxie [poor] to the dowsabell [gentle]', and all shapes 'from the huckle-backed bum-creeper / To the straight spiny shop-maid' (3.4.61–68). The rake's indiscriminate lust for women of 'all sorts and sizes' signifies his immorality, even if it generates delight or envy for playgoers (3.4.69). Aside from the large pool of differently shaped, coloured, and textured bodies from which the rake chooses his lovers, Brome leaves us to imagine whether or not such variety implies his enjoyment of a comparably broad range of sexual acts.

In *Venus and Adonis*, Shakespeare does suggest that an extraordinary body might offer extraordinary pleasures. Using her large stature to make Adonis her 'sexualized plaything', the goddess Venus can 'promote the pleasure of extended erotic exploration' rather than 'penetration and climax'.[30] Venus enjoins Adonis to taste the vast landscape of her body, from her lips down to her 'hills' (breasts) and lower 'fountains' (vagina):

> I'll be thy park, and thou shalt be my deer.
> Feed where thou wilt, on mountain or in dale;
> Graze on my lips, and if those hills be dry,
> Stray lower, where the pleasant fountains lie.   (231–234)

As we have already seen, Hamlet portrays Gertrude as a grazing animal who, having once fed on the pure mountain of King Hamlet, now feeds on the filthy moor of Claudius. Venus sexually tempts Adonis with the unfettered freedom that he, as her 'deer' (dear), would have to feed 'where [he] wilt' on the wide regions of her body, from 'mountain' to 'dale'. In addition to authorizing non-penetrative, non-reproductive sexual acts such as cunnilingus, Venus flirts with the sexual taboos of cross-species desire in imagining Adonis as an animal hungrily feasting on her flesh.[31]

Whereas Venus describes her own body as a copious and luscious landscape, Dromio of Syracuse in *The Comedy of Errors* depicts the body of the obese kitchen maid Nell as filthy, bestial, and foreign. Dromio of Syracuse laments to his master Antipholus that Nell, having mistaken him for his twin brother Dromio of Ephesus, has sexually accosted him: 'I am an ass, I am a woman's man' (3.2.77). Nell has laid claim to his body 'as you would lay to your horse; and she would have me as a beast—not that, I being a beast, she would have me, but that she, being a very beastly creature, lays claim to me' (3.2.85–88). Whereas Venus casts Adonis as a hungry deer freely enjoying her ample flesh, Dromio represents Nell's voracious, bestial, desire as a diminishment of both his manhood and humanity. According to Holly Dugan, Dromio's panic constitutes a recognition 'that he is sexually vulnerable to penetration'.[32] Clearly repulsed by Nell's excessive corporeality, Dromio depicts her as grotesquely wet and dirty: she is 'all grease', sweats 'grime', and her face is 'swart' or black 'like [his] shoe', although not as clean (3.2.95, 101, 103). Dromio elaborates this racialized description of Nell's swarthy complexion through an extended joke about the foreign lands that comprise her 'globe' of a body (3.2.113). Unable to locate in Nell's blackened teeth the 'chalky cliffs' of England, Dromio finds the bogs of Ireland in her buttocks, the spices of Spain in her hot breath, and the gems of the Indies in her red nose (3.2.125). When Antipholus asks where the Netherlands ('low lands') are, Dromio replies that he 'did not look so low', implying his aversion to seeing Nell's genitalia. Dromio imagines Nell's lower body with dread, not as the source of the 'pleasant fountains' that Venus offers to Adonis for his refreshment. Not only does this account of a fat, labouring, and sexually desirous woman's body mobilize racist, nationalist, classist, and misogynist tropes of abject and uncivilized otherness, the fact that Nell never appears on stage eliminates any chance of a self-representation that might humanize her or counter Dromio's hyperbolically disgusted characterizations.

In *Richard III*, self-representation is crucial to our experience of the disabled body of Richard, Duke of Gloucester. In the play's opening soliloquy, Richard describes himself as a figure of queer temporality, physically deformed because born prematurely and currently living during a 'weak piping time of peace' for which those deformities make him unsuited (1.1.24):

> But I, that am not shaped for sportive tricks
> Nor made to court an amorous looking glass,
> I that am rudely stamped and want love's majesty
> To strut before a wanton ambling nymph,
> I that am curtailed of this fair proportion,
> Cheated of feature by dissembling nature,
> Deformed, unfinished, sent before my time
> Into this breathing world scarce made up—
> And that so lamely and unfashionable
> That dogs bark at me as I halt by them—   (1.1.14–23)

Whereas Dromio expresses disgust at the prospect of sexual intimacy with Nell's 'beastly' body (*CE* 3.2.87), Richard pre-emptively excludes himself from any 'sportive' or 'amorous' pursuits. How could any 'wanton ambling nymph'—a lustful, young, spry woman—be attracted to a man so lacking in 'fair' (white) beauty; so poorly 'shaped', 'stamped' and 'made'; so 'lamely and unfashionabl[y]' 'curtailed', 'cheated', 'deformed', and 'unfinished'? Even dogs evince a natural repugnance for his deficiencies. Having convinced himself that he 'cannot prove a lover', Richard determines 'to prove a villain / And hate the idle pleasures of these days' (1.1.30–31). Drawing on his natural attributes, Richard schemes not to secure a wife but to become a king.

Nonetheless, in the following scene Richard engages in precisely the activity he has rejected as unsuited for his deformed body: wooing a fair young woman, the Lady Anne, to be his wife. Richard's interest in marrying Anne is purely political, since as the daughter-in-law of the previous king, she would help to legitimize his questionable claim to the throne. In the early modern period, not love or sexual attraction but political expediency was of paramount concern in the fashioning of royal dynastic marriages. In *The Tempest*, for instance, the King of Naples marries his 'fair' daughter Claribel to the King of Tunis despite her evident 'loathness' to marry a black African (2.1.129–130). Although Claribel subordinates her racialized disgust to her filial obedience, Lady Anne vigorously expresses disgust at the prospect of allowing Richard, the murderer of both her husband, Prince Edward, and her father-in-law, King Henry VI, access to her 'bedchamber' (1.2.111). Anne excoriates Richard as a 'foul devil', 'lump of foul deformity', 'beast', 'diffused infection of a man', 'devilish slave', 'hedgehog', and 'toad' (1.2.50, 57, 71, 78, 90, 102, 147). Several of these insults—particularly 'foul' (the antithesis of 'fair'), 'devil', 'slave', and 'toad'—evoke black complexions, which the English commonly associated with ugliness. As an English nobleman, Richard is, unlike *The Tempest*'s King of Tunis, neither African nor black, but imagery of blackness bolsters Anne's characterization of Richard's body as ugly, bestial, and infectious.

Remarkably, however, Richard's successful performance of love-sickness and penitence persuades Anne into entertaining what even he acknowledges to be a grotesquely inappropriate courtship. Once alone, Richard gleefully recounts how ill-suited as lovers he and the 'divine' 'sweet', and 'fair' Anne are (1.2.75, 124, 132). Richard's amazement that Anne could so soon forget her first husband, Prince Edward, to 'abase her eyes' on him recalls Hamlet's amazement that Gertrude could rush to marry the 'bloat' Claudius after having enjoyed the lovely King Hamlet (1.2.233; *Ham.* 3.4.1.66). There is no 'sweeter and a lovelier gentleman, / Framed in the prodigality of nature, / Young, valiant, and wise' than was Edward, Richard muses (1.2.229–231). Whereas Nature 'prodigal[ly]' (excessively) bestowed beauty and virtue on Edward, she fashioned Richard into a deformed prodigy or monster. Howsoever sardonic, Richard's mockery of Anne for mistaking him as a 'marv'lous proper' or handsome man might suggest his belief that she has suddenly developed a sexual attraction to him (1.2.241). Such a transformation would indeed be extraordinary, since Anne has volubly expressed her aversion to Richard's deformities; even if her heart has softened in response to his blandishments, she does not explicitly confess a new-found appreciation of his physical appearance.

Just as Hamlet expresses bafflement at Gertrude's desire for Claudius, and Richard expresses bafflement at Anne's desire for him, Brabanzio in *Othello* is stunned that his lovely daughter Desdemona would reject handsome, refined Venetian gentlemen only to marry the African Othello, whom he regards as coarse, ugly, and barbarous. Iago stokes Brabanzio's disgust by tormenting him with racist sexual images: at this very moment, he warns Brabanzio, 'an old black ram / Is tupping your white ewe'; consequently, 'the devil' will make him a 'grandsire' (1.1.88, 91). Horrified at the thought of his daughter enjoying sexual intimacy with Othello, Brabanzio weighs several incompatible explanations for her behaviour:

> O heaven, how got she out? O, treason of the blood!
> Fathers, from hence trust not your daughters' minds
> By what you see them act. Is there not charms
> By which the property of youth and maidenhood
> May be abused?   (1.1.170–174)

Accusing Desdemona of 'treason of the blood', Brabanzio implies that it was in her nature to betray her kin or family 'race'.[33] At the same time, in his advice to other fathers he portrays daughters as expertly 'act[ing]' obedience only in order to achieve their secret desires. Finally, Brabanzio considers that Othello might have used potions or spells to enforce Desdemona to yield her 'maidenhead'—a real-life version of

Oberon's irresistible love juice in *A Midsummer Night's Dream*. In Brabanzio's eyes, such an external compulsion would presumably exonerate Desdemona of responsibility for having betrayed him. Brabanzio settles on compulsion as the most plausible explanation not only because he believes that an African would be likely to use exotic charms or drugs to commit rape, but also because he believes his daughter to be innocent of sexual inclinations. Desdemona, he insists, was '[s]o opposite to marriage that she shunned / The wealthy curlèd darlings of our nation' (1.2.68–69). Brabanzio evidently takes Desdemona's rejection of attractive Venetian suitors as evidence that she was simply 'opposite to marriage': whether constitutionally asexual or otherwise averse to becoming a wife. He seems not to have considered that Desdemona might not have been attracted to men who resembled her in complexion, status, nationality, age, or lifestyle. For Brabanzio, the stark differences obtaining between a fair Venetian noblewoman and an African general with a 'sooty bosom' makes their union not just socially transgressive but unnatural (1.2.71). How, he asks of his daughter's choice of spouse, could 'perfection so...err / Against all rules of nature' (1.3.100–101)? In this way, he describes an interracial marriage as tantamount to one of the 'unnatural commixtions' decried by Gouge such as sodomy, bestiality, or incest. Aside from medical or magical compulsion, Brabanzio posits that Desdemona's marriage to a black African could only be explained as a result of mental or physical disability: being 'deficient, blind, or lame of sense' (1.3.63). Brabanzio's distress thus becomes another iteration—in an explicitly racist register—of Hamlet's and Richard's amazement that a woman would marry and enjoy sex with a foul, bestial man instead of a suitably lovely and refined man.

When Desdemona publicly testifies to her uncompelled love for Othello, the Duke of Venice attempts to comfort Brabanzio by assuring him of Othello's goodness. Delivering a rhymed couplet that underscores the sententious tenor of his words, the Duke observes: 'If virtue no delighted beauty lack, / Your son-in-law is far more fair than black' (1.3.288–289). This assessment has garnered much commentary for the way in which it reinscribes common racist beliefs even as it aims to praise Othello as an exceptionally virtuous Moor.[34] Essentially, the Duke avers that Othello's epidermal blackness, which he understands as a sign of physical ugliness—black skin is not 'fair' in the sense of white/beautiful—is less important than Othello's inner fairness, or 'virtue', particularly since Christian baptism 'offers the prospect of making the soul white'.[35] In the end, the Duke implies, Desdemona has married a 'fair' (morally beautiful, Christian) man, even if Othello cannot pretend to possess the outward beauty of the 'curléd' Venetian 'darlings' whom she has rejected as husbands.

Since the Duke is trying to assuage Brabanzio's disappointment at his daughter's choice of spouse, it makes sense for him to tout Othello's virtues, but why does he focus specifically on Othello's *beauty*? The Duke evidently gleans that for all of Brabanzio's objections to the incompatibilities of 'nature', 'years' (age), 'country', and 'credit' (reputation) between Desdemona and Othello, what most horrifies him is his daughter's queer sexual desire for a black man, whom she should 'look on' with 'fear', not longing (1.3.96–98). Not only does Desdemona's elopement belie Brabanzio's account of her as a desireless, passive virgin—'a maiden never bold, / Of spirit so still and quiet that her motion / Blushed at itself' (1.3.94–96)—but her elopement with a Moor suggests that her sexual desires are bestial, unconstrained, and corrupt. Iago capitalizes on this racist logic in describing Desdemona and Othello as copulating sheep. Under such circumstances, Brabanzio might find some comfort in considering the possibility that Desdemona married Othello not for his 'black' body, but for his 'fair' virtues.

In an important sense, the relationship between Desdemona and Othello is atypical of the queer heteroerotic relationships that I have explored in this chapter. By marrying the man she loves, Desdemona pursues traditionally 'monogamous and loving relations'.[36] In this regard, she does not resemble those women who masochistically pursue men who despise them, who attempt to sexually dominate men who resist them, or who engage in culturally prohibited practices such as incest. Nonetheless, the marriage of Desdemona and Othello can be considered queer because of early modern beliefs about African men's excessive sexuality as well as the social taboo against couples of mixed race and religion—views vigorously expressed in the play by Iago and Brabanzio. *Othello* counters such engrained racism by establishing the sincerity of Desdemona's and Othello's love and by having the Duke refuse Brabanzio's plea to dissolve the marriage.

Where Brabanzio fails to separate Desdemona and Othello, however, Iago spectacularly succeeds. He does so both by provoking Othello's anxieties about his incompatibility with Desdemona and by convincing him of the likelihood that she will sexually betray him with a beautiful, young, Italian man such as Cassio, who recalls the 'curlèd darlings' favoured by Brabanzio. Horribly, Othello comes to credit Brabanzio's warning about Desdemona's treachery—'She hath deceived her father, and may thee'—a warning that is bolstered by a shared male belief in women's sexual inconstancy (1.3.292). Preparing to murder Desdemona, Othello muses that 'she must die, or she'll betray more men' (5.2.6). Having lost his faith in the woman who loves him despite and because of their many differences, Othello takes refuge in the supposed wisdom of Venetian men such as Brabanzio and Iago, notwithstanding the many differences of culture, race, status, and age that also separate him from *them*, whatever their common values or experiences as men. Whereas Othello imagines a future in which Desdemona will 'betray more men', we should hear in his words an echo from the past: Brabanzio's claim that in marrying Othello, in pursuing her sexual desires in defiance of family honour and social convention, Desdemona has betrayed *him*. That Othello adopts Brabanzio's patriarchal belief in Desdemona's capacity for betrayal is a chilling sign of the vulnerabilities faced by the queerly desiring woman in Shakespeare.

Shakespeare and Queer Studies. Mario DiGangi, Oxford University Press. © Mario DiGangi 2025.
DOI: 10.1093/9780191994951.003.0006

Historical Perspectives, Present-Day Concerns

My hope is that *Shakespeare and Queer Studies* has modelled productive strategies for reading queer sexuality and gender in Shakespeare's texts. I offer here a final reflection on the book's central methods and arguments, with the aim of foregrounding aspects of this study that might further advance readers' own thinking, writing, and research. I am not the first to use these methods or make these arguments; I have built on the solid foundation of more than thirty years of lesbian, gay, and queer Shakespeare scholarship. Specific debts to this work are recorded in the endnotes to individual chapters, as well as in 'Further Reading'. If *Shakespeare and Queer Studies* has both effectively synthesized those earlier strands of scholarship and pointed to fruitful ways forward, it will have done its job.

My readings of Shakespeare's texts have been guided throughout by six central premises:

1) the *interpretive possibilities* made available by a historical understanding of early modern languages of gender and sexuality;

2) the *analytical complexity* gained from an intersectional approach, in which sexual meaning is interpreted in conjunction with gender, race, status, nationality, ability, age, or other categories of cultural significance;

3) the *conceptual portability* to early modern literary texts of guiding ideas in queer studies, such as queer temporality;

4) the *historical perspective* imparted by understanding early modern male-female sexual/marital relations in terms drawn from that culture, not from the modern ideology of heterosexuality;

5) the *political recognition* of the ways in which queer gender and sexual practices might not be socially transgressive or inclusive of other forms of difference, such as race or religion; and

6) the *intellectual and ethical urgency* of centring the insights of scholars of asexuality and transgender, fields that have historically been marginalized in early modern queer studies.

Below, I will briefly elaborate on each of these six premises. By citing examples from across different chapters, I aim to demonstrate some additional ways of putting Shakespeare's explorations of queer gender and sexuality into conversation with each other.

1. Interpretative Possibilities

Before the modern notion of binary sexuality had imparted to hetero-sexuality the status of a naturalized, incontestable norm, sexual language evinced a remarkable transitivity across same-sex and male-female rela-tionships. This means that we cannot determine what a Shakespearean character might mean by the word 'love', for instance, by appealing only to the genders of the persons involved. What Romeo (*Romeo and Juliet*; Chapter 1) feels for both Rosaline and Benvolio is 'love'. The gendered difference between Rosaline and Benvolio does not mean that 'love' is erotic or sexual only in the former case. Rather, an inter-pretation of the nature of Romeo's love for Benvolio must consider the possibilities suggested by attention to the specific circumstances, histories, motives, and temperaments of these characters—as well as the words used to represent all those aspects of their experience. Similarly, we need to hear the erotic as well as political connotations of the claim that King Harry (*Henry V*, Chapter 2) 'dulled and cloyed' his 'bedfellow' Scrope with 'favours'. In short, when intimate relations are under discussion, we cannot assume that heteroeroticism is the default norm or that same-sex bonds are less likely to be erotic than male-female relations.

2. Analytical Complexity

Interpreting sexual language often requires us to understand how the bonds between characters are informed by similarities or differences of gender, status, race, age, and so on. An intersectional approach, which was developed in the late twentieth century by critical race and legal scholar Kimberlé Crenshaw, begins from the premise that we embody a multiplicity of identity categories, and that the interplay among these categories affects how we are treated within and navigate our social worlds. Foregrounding the intersections of sexuality, gender, and race, for example, can reveal how Shakespeare uses the language of black/white complexions to convey the erotic appeal of feminine beauty. When Rosalind and Viola (*As You Like It*, *Twelfth Night*; Chapter 3) attempt to pass as men, their male personas' fair/white femininity draws male and female suitors alike. At the same time, Rosalind insults Phoebe in racial terms ('inky brows', 'Ethiop words'), and Viola expresses her self-alienation through figures of blackness, namely the eunuch and the devil. The fairness of asexual young men and women such as Adonis and Diana (*Venus and Adonis*, *All's Well That Ends Well*; Chapter 4) provokes their suitors' critiques of the refusal of (potentially) reproductive sex acts. The intersection of embodied differences can also provoke sexual disgust, as when Dromio (*The Comedy of Errors*; Chapter 5) demeans the fat, low-status kitchen drudge Nell by comparing her body parts to racialized foreign lands such as Ireland, Spain, and the Americas.

3. Conceptual Portability

As with the late twentieth-century theory of intersectionality, recent ways of identifying and conceptualizing queer fantasies, acts, and relationships can illuminate understudied kinds of sexual experience in Shakespeare's texts. Through terms such as thruple (Chapter 2), fluffer (Chapter 2), and angry sex (Chapter 5), I have posited structural or functional similarities between early modern and contemporary sexual arrangements, roles, and practices. To propose that Bassanio (*The Merchant of Venice*; Chapter 2) might fantasize about being cuckolded or that Helena (*A Midsummer Night's Dream*; Chapter 5) might enjoy being sexually humiliated prompts us to consider how certain sexual idiosyncrasies were just as available to early moderns as to us, even if they might have understood their causes and effects in different terms. Moreover, concepts formulated within contemporary queer studies— such as queer temporality, queer failure, reproductive futurism, and homonormativity—can illuminate the phenomenological, ideological, and political aspects of sex in Shakespeare. Some characters, for instance, find themselves dislocated from a culturally privileged timeline of adulthood, marriage, and reproduction. Arcite (*The Two Noble Kinsmen*; Chapter 1) laments that perpetual imprisonment will freeze time, forestalling the possibility of sexual reproduction and generational continuity. Also childless, Macbeth (*Macbeth*; Chapter 2) is tormented by his inability to bequeath his throne to an heir, and by the barren-ness that such a future represents. Nonetheless, the queer failure to fulfil the imperative of reproductive futurism offers other characters, such as the celibate nun Isabella (*Measure for Measure*; Chapter 4), the prospect of a life conducted on their own terms.

4. Historical Perspective

Queer temporality offers one strategy among many for understanding the dynamics of queer heteroeroticism: male-female sexual relations that violate social, cultural, or religious prescriptions. For instance, having taken sexual possession of his daughter's body before she had the opportunity to find an appropriate husband, Antiochus (*Pericles*; Chapter 5) perverts the culturally valorized process through which a daughter moves from one patriarchal household, as a virgin, to another, as wife and mother. Although Desdemona (*Othello*; Chapter 5) accomplishes precisely that movement, her choice of an African husband horrifies her father, who reads her agency as a sign of the unnatural sexual inclinations that have shifted her loyalties from her own kin to a stranger. Even licit marriages such as that between King Harry and Katherine (*Henry V*; Chapter 5), Oberon and Titania (*A Midsummer Night's Dream*; Chapter 5), Henry VI and Margaret (*Henry VI*; Chapter 2), and Macbeth and Lady Macbeth (*Macbeth*, Chapter 2) can be tainted with sexual irregularity through unchaste rhetorics, fantasies, or practices involving anal eroticism, bestiality, female masculinity, adultery, and debilitating lust. Without the natur-alized concept of heterosexuality to regulate the alignment among biological sex, gender identity, sexual practice, and sexual desire, early moderns experienced heteroerotic desire as a volatile, sometimes dan-gerous, force that could queerly subvert the orderly government of the self, the household, and even the nation.

5. Political Recognition

If male-female sexual relations do not always conform to social or religious orthodoxies, same-sex relations do not always challenge dominant sexual, gender, racial, or other cultural ideologies; nor do all gender transformations carry a socially radical agenda. For instance, the homonormative Venetian camaraderie that subtends the loving friendship between Antonio and Bassanio (*The Merchant of Venice*; Chapter 1) excludes Shylock on the grounds of race, religion, and profession. Urging Achilles to embody military masculinity, Patroclus (*Troilus and Cressida*; Chapter 2) denigrates manly women and effeminate men; urging Romeo to be a more affectionate and available friend, Mercutio (*Romeo and Juliet*; Chapter 1) denigrates women's sexual inconstancy. When Julia (*The Two Gentlemen of Verona*; Chapter 3) takes on a male persona at the risk of her sexual reputation, her ultimate aim is not to unsettle patriarchal values but to uphold them by becoming a legitimate wife. Even Joan la Pucelle (*1 Henry VI*; Chapter 3), who more radically violates patriarchal prescriptions against women combatants, authorizes her transgression by claiming to have been racially whitened by the Virgin Mary's clarifying light.

6. Intellectual and Ethical Urgency

Since the 1980s, a large body of feminist and sexuality Shakespeare scholarship has addressed gender performance in comedies such as *As You Like It* and *Twelfth Night* and the politics of celibacy in plays such as *Measure for Measure*. On these subjects, I have taken my cues instead from recent transgender and asexuality scholarship, with two primary goals: contributing to the advancement of these relatively new approaches in early modern studies; and making space for perspectives that have been historically marginalized within queer studies. Because queer studies has understandably foregrounded the importance of sexual desires and practices, it has not always been able to recognize that sexuality, no less than heterosexuality, can be compulsory. In cultures that place a high value on sexual or marital coupledom, a lack of sexual desire or a desire to remain single can seem queer. When characters such as Adonis, Rosaline, or Angelo (*Venus and Adonis*, *Romeo and Juliet*, *Measure for Measure*; Chapter 4) express aversion to sex, courtship, or marriage, we should not assume that they really want a same-sex union, that they are simply experiencing a pre-sexual phase of youth, or that they are behaving pathologically. Likewise, the specific kind of queerness valued by queer studies has sometimes marginalized transgender. Whereas queer theorists tend to define all gender/sexuality identities as phantasmatic, contingent, and performative instead of grounded in the body, transgender scholars have stressed the importance of achieving an authentic gender identity, which might require bodily intervention such as surgery or hormone treatment. Analyses of characters such as Rosalind and Viola (*As You Like It*, *Twelfth Night*, Chapter 3) that regard clothing as the essence of gender transformation can seem dismissive of the deeply felt, embodied experiences of those who live the complexities of gender dysphoria and transition.

Characters in a Shakespeare play, of course, are not real people. Still, a book like this one can exist only because feminist, LGBTQAI+, critical race, and other identity-adjacent approaches have taught us the value of bringing our own urgent questions and embodied perspectives to bear on our readings of literary texts, even ones as entrenched in history and tradition as Shakespeare's. As this book has demonstrated and as these concluding reflections have reiterated, a historical approach to reading Shakespeare does not require us to ignore the theoretical, political, and ethical concerns of our own time.

Shakespeare and Queer Studies. Mario DiGangi, Oxford University Press. © Mario DiGangi 2025.
DOI: 10.1093/9780191994951.003.0007

All quotations of Shakespeare are taken from *The Norton Shakespeare*, 2nd ed., ed. Stephen Greenblatt et al. (New York: Norton, 2008).

QUEER THEORIES, QUEER HISTORIES, AND SHAKESPEARE STUDIES

1. On the 'de-queer[ing]' of queerness in 'Queer Eye for the Straight Guy', see Jennifer Drouin, 'Queer Eye for the Not So Straight Guy: Ocular Excesses and Erotic Gazes in *The Two Noble Kinsmen*', *Shakespeare/Sex: Contemporary Readings in Gender and Sexuality*, ed. Jennifer Drouin (London: Arden Shakespeare-Bloomsbury, 2020), 212–240, p. 213.

2. *Oxford English Dictionary* [*OED*], queer *adj*1,1a; *adj*2, 1.

3. *OED*, queer *adj*1, 3a; queer *n*., 2a.

4. Teresa de Lauretis, ed., 'Queer Theory: Lesbian and Gay Sexualities', *differences* 3.2 (1991). A few years later, however, de Lauretis ('Habit Changes', 'More Gender Trouble: Feminism Meets Queer Theory', *differences* 6.2–3 [1994]: 296–313), called queer theory 'a conceptually vacuous creature of the publishing industry' (297). Some scholars have argued that academic elitism and racism are responsible for the often overlooked fact that creative writer and cultural theorist Gloria Anzaldua used the word 'queer' much earlier than 1991 to refer to her own experience as a Chicana lesbian in 'La Prieta', *This Bridge Called My Back: Writings by Radical Women of Color*, ed. Cherríe Moraga and Gloria Anzaldúa (Watertown: Persephone, 1981). See Kadji Amin, 'Genealogies of Queer Theory', *The Cambridge Companion to Queer Studies*, ed. Siobhan B. Somerville (Cambridge: Cambridge University Press, 2020), 17–29, p. 25.

5. Amin, 'Genealogies', 18.

6. Judith Butler, *Gender Trouble: Feminism and the Subversion of Identity* (New York: Routledge, 1990), 16.

7. Butler, *Trouble*, 17.

8. Butler, *Trouble*, 21.

9. Judith Butler, *Undoing Gender* (New York: Routledge, 2004), 1.

10. Eve Kosofsky Sedgwick, *The Epistemology of the Closet* (Berkeley: University of California Press, 1990), 2.

11. Butler, *Trouble*, xiii, 137.

12. One can identify as lesbian or gay and still endorse queer theory's stance on the incoherence of gender and sexual identities. As Sharon Marcus writes, 'While *queer* foregrounds the belief that sexual identity is flexible and unstable, *gay* and *lesbian* do not assert the contrary'. See 'Queer Theory for Everybody: A Review Essay', *Signs* 13.1 (2005): 191–218, p. 196. Despite its often imprecise definition, 'identity' carries a lot of weight in queer theory as one of the primary targets of critique.

13. Something of an exception is Joseph Pequigney's *Such is My Love: A Study of Shakespeare's Sonnets* (Chicago: University of Chicago Press, 1985), which argues that the speaker of Shakespeare's *Sonnets* is bisexual.

14. On the epistemological challenge that trans and asexuality studies pose to early modern queer studies, see Joseph Gamble, *Sex Lives: Intimate Infrastructures in Early Modernity* (Philadelphia: University of Pennsylvania Press, 2023), 101.

15. Eve Kosofsky Sedgwick, *Tendencies* (Durham: Duke University Press, 1993), 8. For a critique of this passage's erasure of racialized queer identities, see Omise'eke Natasha Tinsley, 'Black Atlantic, Queer Atlantic: Queer Imaginings of the Middle Passage', *GLQ* 14:2–3 (2008): 191–214, p. 204.

16. 'Early modern' is a term used by historians, and adopted by literary scholars, to describe the period from roughly 1500–1800 in Europe, which is also known as the 'Renaissance'. In this book, my usage of 'early modern' tends to refer more narrowly to Shakespeare's era: late sixteenth-century through early seventeenth-century England.

17. Gregory W. Bredbeck, *Sodomy and Interpretation, Marlowe to Milton* (Ithaca: Cornell University Press, 1991), 21.

18. Jonathan Goldberg, *Sodometries: Renaissance Texts, Modern Sexualities* (Stanford: Stanford University Press, 1992), xv.

19. Madhavi Menon, *Shakesqueer: A Queer Companion to the Complete Works of Shakespeare* (Durham: Duke University Press, 2011), 7.

20. Menon, *Shakesqueer*, 2, 4, 15–16.

21. Sedgwick, *Tendencies*, 8; Menon, *Shakesqueer*, 9; emphasis added.

22. Elizabeth Freeman, *Time Binds: Queer Temporalities, Queer Histories* (Durham: Duke University Press, 2010), xxi.

23. Benjamin Kahan, *Celibacies: American Modernism and Sexual Life* (Durham: Duke University Press, 2013), 2.

24. Karma Lochrie, *Heterosyncrasies: Female Sexuality When Normal Wasn't* (Minneapolis: University of Minnesota Press, 2005), 2.

25. Laurie Shannon, 'Likenings: Rhetorical Husbandries and Portia's "True Conceit" of Friendship', *Renaissance Drama* n.s. 31 (2002): 3–26, p. 5; Julie Crawford, 'The Homoerotics of Shakespeare's Elizabethan Comedies', *A Companion to Shakespeare's Works, Volume III*, ed. Richard Dutton and Jean E. Howard (Oxford: Blackwell, 2003), 137–159, p. 139.

26. Butler, *Undoing*, 8.

27. Ian Frederick Moulton, 'As You Like It or What You Will: Shakespeare's Sonnets and Beccadelli's *Hermaphroditus*', *Queer Shakespeare: Desire and Sexuality*, ed. Goran Stanivukovic (London: Arden Shakespeare-Bloomsbury, 2017), 87–103, pp. 94–95.

28. Moulton, 'As', 98.

29. Moulton, 'As', 103.

30. Michel Foucault, *The History of Sexuality: An Introduction*, trans. Robert Hurley [1978] (New York: Random House-Vintage, 1990), 68. The terms 'Homosexual' and 'Heterosexual' were coined by Karl Maria Kertbeny in a letter (written in German) of 1868. See Jonathan Ned Katz, *The Invention of Heterosexuality* (New York: Penguin-Plume, 1996), 51. The *OED* dates the first English appearances of those words to 1891–1892.

31. Foucault, *History*, 47.

32. Peter Coviello, *Tomorrow's Parties: Sex and the Untimely in Nineteenth-Century America* (New York: New York University Press, 2013), 24.

33. Coviello, *Parties*, 24.

34. Foucault, *History*, 43.

35. The English translation of this passage contains several misleading inaccuracies, as meticulously analysed by Lynne Huffer, *Mad for Foucault: Rethinking the Foundations of Queer Theory* (New York: Columbia University Press, 2009), 67–80. Huffer understands Foucault's primary point as a contrast between the resistant sexual agency of the premodern sodomite and the medical objectification and subjugation of the modern homosexual.

36. David M. Halperin, *How to Do the History of Sexuality* (Chicago: University of Chicago Press, 2004), 31–32.

37. In an important argument, Benjamin Kahan shows that the 'congenital' or inherent theory of male homosexuality did not significantly displace what had been a more prominent 'acquired' theory of male homosexuality until the 1930s: '[w]hile the species of the congenital homosexual exists by 1870, he is only recognizable as such for a handful of specialists and is not understood in those terms even by many within the sexological community until much later.' See *The Book of Minor Perverts* (Chicago: University of Chicago Press, 2017), 16. On the definitional incoherence of homosexual identity in early twentieth-century scientific texts, see also, Dana Seitler, 'Queer Physiognomies: Or, How Many Ways Can We Do the History of Sexuality?' *Criticism* 46.1 (2004), 71–102.

38. Sarah Salih, 'Sexual Identities: A Medieval Perspective', *Sodomy in Early Modern Europe*, ed. Tom Betteridge (Manchester: Manchester University Press, 2002), 117.

39. Salih, 'Sexual', 126.

40. Melissa E. Sanchez, *Queer Faith: Reading Promiscuity and Race in the Secular Love Tradition* (New York: New York University Press, 2019), 113.

41. Ruth Mazo Karras, *Common Women: Prostitution and Sexuality in Medieval England* (Oxford: Oxford University Press, 1996), 12. See also Carla Freccero, *Queer/Early/Modern* (Durham: Duke University Press, 2006), 31–50.

42. See Mario DiGangi, *Sexual Types: Embodiment, Agency, and Dramatic Character from Shakespeare to Shirley* (Philadelphia: University of Pennsylvania Press, 2011), and 'Rethinking Sexual Acts and Identities', *Shakespeare in Our Time: A Shakespeare Association of America Companion*, ed. Suzanne Gossett and Dympna Callaghan (London: Bloomsbury-Arden Shakespeare, 2016), 31–35.

43. Jennifer Panek, '"This Base Stallion Trade": He-Whores and Male Sexuality on the Early Modern Stage', *English Literary Renaissance* 40.3 (2010): 357–392.

44. Ari Friedlander, *Rogue Sexuality in Early Modern English Literature: Desire, Status, Biopolitics* (Oxford: Oxford University Press, 2022), 3.

45. For a similar argument, see Kim M. Phillips and Barry Reay, *Sex before Sexuality: A Premodern History* (Cambridge: Polity Press, 2011), 40–41.

46. Katz, *Invention*, 88.

47. To use Eve Sedgwick's terms explained above (p. 5), a universalizing theory of sexuality obtained in the early modern period because it was thought that anyone could experience same-sex desires.

48. James A. Schultz, *Courtly Love, the Love of Courtliness, and the History of Sexuality* (Chicago: University of Chicago Press, 2016), 53.

49. Thomas Laqueur's *Making Sex: Body and Gender from the Greeks to Freud* (Cambridge, MA: Harvard University Press, 1990) widely brought the 'one-sex' model to the attention of Shakespeareans. Many scholars have critiqued Laqueur for misrepresenting how hotly contested the theory of genital homology was in the sixteenth century; by the early seventeenth century, many European physicians, largely influenced by new anatomical research, regarded that theory as incorrect.

50. Schultz, *Courtly Love*, 54–55.

51. Katz, *Invention*, 38.

52. Richard Godbeer, *Sexual Revolution in Early America* (Baltimore: Johns Hopkins University Press, 2002), 84.

53. Ann Rosalind Jones, 'Heterosexuality: A Beast with Many Backs', *A Cultural History of Sexuality in the Renaissance*, ed. Bette Talvacchia (London: Bloomsbury, 2013), 35–50, 38.

54. Will Stockton, *Members of His Body: Shakespeare, Paul, and a Theology of Nonmonogamy* (New York: Fordham University Press, 2017), 5, 11.

55. Sanchez, *Faith*, 76.

56. William Gouge, *Of Domestical Duties* (1622), 225.

57. Stephen Orgel, *Impersonations: The Performance of Gender in Shakespeare's England* (Cambridge: Cambridge University Press, 1996), 26. For the belief in women's sexual 'voraciousness', see Valerie Traub, *The Renaissance of Lesbianism in Early Modern England* (Cambridge: Cambridge University Press, 2002), 266–268.

58. Margaret Ferguson, 'Hymeneal Instruction', *Masculinities, Violence, Childhood: Attending to Early Modern Women—and Men*, ed. Amy E. Leonard and Karen L. Nelson (Newark: University of Delaware Press, 2010), 97–129, p. 110.

59. Ferguson, 'Hymeneal', 111.

60. Rebecca Ann Bach, *Shakespeare and Renaissance Literature before Heterosexuality* (New York: Palgrave Macmillan, 2007), 5, 2.

61. Carmen Nocentelli, *Empires of Love: Europe, Asia, and the Making of Early Modern Identity* (Philadelphia: University of Pennsylvania Press, 2013), 131–132.

62. William Whately, *A Bride-Bush, or, A Direction for Married Persons* (1623), 18.

63. Traub, *Renaissance*, 269.

64. Nocentelli, *Empires*, 118.

65. Lisa Jardine, *Reading Shakespeare Historically* (London: Routledge, 1996), 77.

66. Coviello, *Parties*, 24.

67. Foucault, *History*, 103.

68. Lochrie, *Heterosyncrasies*, xi–xxviii.

69. Acknowledging that transgender and queer studies 'share a foundational critique of disciplinary power that undergirds their resistance to fixed methods and proper objects', Cáel M. Keegan also observes that 'unlike queer studies' more deconstructionist stance toward identity, transgender studies places high value on the embodied, speaking transgender subject as the producer of constative self-knowledge' (67).

CHAPTER 1

1. See Alan Sinfield, *Shakespeare, Authority, Sexuality: Unfinished Business in Cultural Materialism* (London: Routledge, 2006), 84.

2. Laurie Shannon, 'Nature's Bias: Renaissance Homonormativity and Elizabethan Comic Likeness', *Modern Philology* 98.2 (2000): 183–210.

3. Qtd. M. Lindsay Kaplan, *The Merchant of Venice: Texts and Contexts* (New York: Palgrave, 2002), 344.

4. Qtd. Laurie Shannon, 'Likenings: Rhetorical Husbandries and Portia's "True Conceit" of Friendship', *Renaissance Drama* n.s. 31 (2002): 3–26, pp. 6–7.

5. Jeffrey Masten, *Textual Intercourse: Collaboration, Authorship, and Sexualities in Renaissance Drama* (Cambridge: Cambridge University Press, 1997), 35.

6. Misha Teramura, 'Against Friendship: An Essay by the "Wizard" Earl of Northumberland', *English Literary Renaissance* 47.3 (2017): 380–411, p. 380. Teramura focuses on a previously unpublished essay by the ninth Earl of Northumberland complaining that the ideal of true friendship promoted by philosophers and poets was impossible to achieve.

7. Qtd. Masten, *Textual Intercourse*, 35.

8. Masten, *Textual Intercourse*, 35.

9. Qtd. Will Tosh, *Male Friendship and Testimonies of Love in Shakespeare's England* (Palgrave Macmillan: 2016), 45.

10. Lisa Duggan, *The Twilight of Equality? Neoliberalism, Cultural Politics, and the Attack on Democracy* (Boston: Beacon Press, 2003), 50.

11. Duggan, *Twilight*, 45.

12. Masten, *Textual Intercourse*, 35.

13. Julie Crawford, 'The Place of a Cousin in *As You Like It*', *Shakespeare Quarterly* 69.2 (2018): 101–127, p. 106.

14. Joseph Porter observes that the 'most highly charged pair-bond' in the play, e.g., Romeo and Mercutio, 'never appear alone together, while each does appear alone with Benvolio'. Joseph A. Porter, *Shakespeare's Mercutio: His History and Drama* (Chapel Hill: University of North Carolina Press, 1989), 102.

15. Porter, *Shakespeare's Mercutio*, 157.

16. The term 'open-arse' does not appear in any early editions of *Romeo and Juliet*, which have 'open, or' or 'open *Et cetera*' (Porter, *Shakespeare's Mercutio*, 161). That the slang term for medlar was 'open-arse' suggests that it is the correct reading.

17. *OED*, butt *n.6*, 8.a.

18. *OED*, butt *n.6*, 8.b.

19. *OED*, hair *n.*, P1.

20. *OED*, consort *v.*, 2.

21. Nicholas F. Radel, 'Queer Romeo and Juliet: Teaching Early Modern "Sexuality" in Shakespeare's "Heterosexual" Tragedy', *Approaches to Teaching Shakespeare's Romeo and Juliet*, ed. Maurice Hunt (New York: Modern Language Association, 2000), 91–97, p. 93.

22. Will Stockton, *Members of His Body: Shakespeare, Paul, and a Theology of Nonmonogamy* (New York: Fordham University Press, 2017), 56.

23. On friendship in 'group formations', see John S. Garrison, *Friendship and Queer Theory in the Renaissance: Gender and Sexuality in Early Modern England* (New York: Routledge, 2014), xii.

24. Bruce Smith, *Homosexual Desire*, 67.

25. On the queerness of 'strange' in Shakespeare, see Urvashi Chakravarty, 'More Than Kin, Less Than Kind: Similitude, Strangeness, and Early Modern English Homonationalisms', *Shakespeare Quarterly* 67.1 (2016): 14–29, pp. 18–20.

26. Geraldine Heng, *The Invention of Race in the European Middle Ages* (Cambridge: Cambridge University Press, 2018), 55–109.

27. Shannon, 'Likenings', 14.

28. James Shapiro, *Shakespeare and the Jews* (New York: Columbia University Press, 1995), 117–130.

29. Ian Smith, *Black Shakespeare: Reading and Misreading Race* (Cambridge: Cambridge University Press, 2022), 82.

30. Among the many queer readings of Falstaff and his relationship with Hal, see Valerie Traub, 'Prince Hal's Falstaff: Positioning Psychoanalysis and the Female Reproductive Body', *Shakespeare Quarterly* 40 (1989): 456–474; Vin Nardizzi, 'Grafted to Falstaff and Compounded with Catherine: Mingling Hal in the Second Tetralogy', *Queer Renaissance Historiography: Backward Gaze*, ed. Vin Nardizzi, Stephen Guy-Bray, and Will Stockton (Farnham, Surrey: Ashgate, 2009), 149–169; and Simone Chess, *Male-to-Female Crossdressing in Early Modern English Literature: Gender, Performance, and Queer Relations* (London: Routledge, 2016), 23 n.2, 4.

31. Shannon, 'Likenings', 17–18.

32. Shannon', Likenings', 18.

33. *OED*, spirit *n.*, 17a.

34. *OED*, fair *adj.* and *n1.*, 6. See Kim F. Hall, '"These bastard signs of fair": Literary Whiteness in Shakespeare's Sonnets', *Post-Colonial Shakespeares*, ed. Ania Loomba and Martin Orkin (London: Routledge, 1998): 64–83.

35. Garrison, *Friendship*, 26.

36. Karen Newman, *Fashioning Femininity and English Renaissance Drama* (Chicago: University of Chicago Press, 1991), 31.

37. Shannon, 'Likenings', 19.

38. Garrison, *Friendship*, 23.

39. Newman, *Fashioning*, 31.

40. Shannon, 'Likenings', 20.

41. Stockton, *Members*, 55.

42. Julie Crawford, 'The Homoerotics of Shakespeare's Elizabethan Comedies', *A Companion to Shakespeare's Works, Volume III*, ed. Richard Dutton and Jean E. Howard (Oxford: Blackwell, 2003), 137–159.

43. Anal sex was commonly associated in early modern Europe with physical injury. According to Paolo Zacchia's 1630 treatise on forensic medicine, tearing or inflammation of the anus could provide legal evidence of anal sex. See George Rousseau, 'Policing the Anus: Stuprum and Sodomy

According to Paolo Zacchia's Forensic Medicine', *The Sciences of Homosexuality in Early Modern Europe*, ed. Kenneth Borris and George Rousseau (London: Routledge, 2008), 75–91, pp. 78–79.

44. Bruce R. Smith, *Homosexual Desire in Shakespeare's England: A Cultural Poetics* (Chicago: University of Chicago Press, 1991), 70.

45. J. Jack Halberstam, *In a Queer Time and Place: Transgender Bodies, Subcultural Lives* (New York: New York University Press, 2005), 2.

46. Halberstam, *Queer Time*, 2.

47. Julie Crawford, 'All's Well That Ends Well, Or, Is Marriage Always Already Heterosexual?' *Shakesqueer: A Queer Companion to the Complete Works of Shakespeare*, ed. Madhavi Menon (Durham: Duke University Press, 2011), 39–47, p. 39; Kathryn Bond Stockton, *The Queer Child, or Growing Sideways in the Twentieth Century* (Durham: Duke University Press: 2009), 425.

48. *OED*, grace *n.*, 14.a.

49. *OED*, conversation *n.*, 3.

50. Stephen Guy-Bray argues that the 'endless mine' is an anal image pointing to the cousins' sexual practices. See *Against Reproduction: Where Renaissance Texts Come From* (New York: Routledge, 2021), 85. Jeffrey Masten more precisely observes that to be 'one another's wife' in this context 'does not register "homosexuality" in the modern sense so much as it figures each kinsman, reciprocally, in the position of wife in order to further the continuous reproduction of male heirs' (*Textual Intercourse*, 53).

51. Robert Stretter, 'Flowers of Friendship: Amity and Tragic Desire in *The Two Noble Kinsmen*', *English Literary Renaissance* 47.2 (2017): 270–300, p. 271.

52. Laurie Shannon, *Sovereign Amity: Figures of Friendship in Shakespearean Contexts* (Chicago: University of Chicago Press, 2002), 106. Alan Stewart ('"Near Akin": The Trials of Friendship in *The Two Noble Kinsmen*', *Shakespeare's Late Plays: New Readings*, ed. Jennifer Richards and James Knowles [Edinburgh: Edinburgh University Press, 1999], 57–71) argues that the structural weakness of a kinship relationship between *maternal* cousins, who might not share the same social and familial interests, is responsible for the rapid demise of their friendship.

53. Stretter, 'Flowers', 291.

54. Masten, *Textual Intercourse*, 50. On the gendered and sexual meaning of knots, see also Margaret Ferguson, 'Hymeneal Instruction', *Masculinities, Childhood, Violence: Attending to Early Modern Women—and Men: Proceedings of the 2006 Symposium,* ed. Amy E. Leonard and Karen L. Nelson (Newark: University of Delaware Press, 2011), 97–129, p. 108. Writing to Anthony Bacon in 1582, Nicholas Faunt refers to the 'principall knott of our amitie' (qtd. Tosh, *Male Friendship*, 45).

55. Melissa Sanchez, 'Colonial Cacaphony and Early Modern Trans Studies: Spenser with Julia Serano', *Spenser Studies* 37 (2023): 317–344, p. 334.

56. Valerie Traub, *The Renaissance of Lesbian in Early Modern England* (Cambridge: Cambridge University Press, 2002), 66.
57. Bruster, 'Female-Female', 5; Traub, *Renaissance*, 67.
58. Shannon, *Sovereign Amity*, 108.
59. Shannon, *Sovereign Amity*, 108.
60. Shannon, *Sovereign Amity*, 114.
61. Traub, *Renaissance*, 330.
62. Bruster, 'Female-Female', 12.
63. Thomas Heywood, *The Golden Age* (1641), sig. D3v.
64. Bruster, 'Female-Female', 14.
65. Crawford, 'Place', 106.
66. For an excellent account of affective pedagogy here and elsewhere in *As You Like It*, see Joseph Gamble, *Sex Lives: Intimate Infrastructures in Early Modernity* (Philadelphia: University of Pennsylvania Press, 2023), 104–109.
67. *OED* truth *n.* 1., 2.b.
68. Traub, *Renaissance*, 171; Mario DiGangi, *The Homoerotics of Early Modern Drama* (Cambridge: Cambridge University Press, 1997), 52–53.
69. DiGangi, *Homoerotics*, 53. See also Joseph Gamble, *Sex Lives: Intimate Infrastructures in Early Modernity* (Philadelphia: University of Pennsylvania Press, 2023), 106–109.
70. Traub, *Renaissance*, 174.
71. Traub, *Renaissance*, 174.
72. Qtd. Sarah Carter, *Ovidian Myth and Sexual Deviance in Early Modern English Literature* (New York: Palgrave Macmillan, 2011), 92.
73. Carter, *Ovidian*, 88.
74. Crawford, 'Place', 119.
75. Crawford, 'Place', 121.

CHAPTER 2

1. Jean Calvin, *Commentary upon the First Book of Moses Called Genesis*, qtd. Kenneth Borris, ed., *Same-Sex Desire in the English Renaissance: A Sourcebook of Texts, 1470–1650* (London: Routledge, 2004), 52.
2. Alan Bray, *Homosexuality in Renaissance England* (London: Gay Men's Press, 1982), 21. There were only a handful of sodomy trials in sixteenth- and seventeenth-century England. Nonetheless, men were regularly punished for sodomy in early modern European nations such as Spain and Italy. The account of a Moorish slave executed for sodomy in Portugal is full of everyday detail: 'And they both dined and went to bed, and the said António Luís began to embrace and to kiss him calling him brother and saying other sweet words and putting his hand on his shameful parts. And then António Luís put himself on top of the confessant and slept with

him carnally like a man with a woman, putting his nature in the back passage.' See David Higgs, 'The Historiography of Male-Male Love in Portugal, 1550–1800', *Queer Masculinities, 1550–1800: Siting Same-Sex Desire in the Early Modern World*, ed. Katherine O'Donnell and Michael O'Rourke (London: Palgrave Macmillan, 2006), 38–39. Female-female sexual transgressions were less frequently remarked and punished than male-male transgressions.

3. *OED*, mooncalf *n*, 2a, 3.

4. *The Works of Michael Drayton* (London, 1748), 171.

5. Patricia Parker, 'Preposterous Events', *Shakespeare Quarterly* 43 (1992): 186–213.

6. Cynthia B. Herrup, *A House in Gross Disorder: Sex, Law, and the 2nd Earl of Castlehaven* (Oxford: Oxford University Press, 1999), 26; H. G. Cocks, *Visions of Sodom: Religion, Homoerotic Desire, and the End of the World in England, c. 1550–1850* (Chicago: University of Chicago, 2017), 5.

7. *OED*, cloy *v.1*, 8a.

8. Shakespeare's source, Holinshed's *Chronicles*, reports that Scrope 'was in such favour with the king, that he admitted him sometime to be his bedfellow...' Qtd. T. W. Craik, ed., *King Henry V*, by William Shakespeare (London: Arden Shakespeare-Cengage, 1995), 2.2.8, n.8–11.

9. *OED*, favor *n.*, 7a.

10. Herrup, *House*, 19.

11. Eliza Greenstadt, 'Strange Insertions in *The Merchant of Venice*', *Queer Shakespeare: Desire and Sexuality*, ed. Goran Stanivukovic (London: Arden Shakespeare-Bloomsbury, 2017), 197–225, p. 198.

12. 2.2.147; *OED* rape *n3*, 3. Early modern English law criminalized both sodomy and rape.

13. Herrup, *House*, 31.

14. Daniel Juan Gil, *Before Intimacy: Asocial Sexuality in Early Modern England* (Minneapolis: University of Minnesota Press, 2006), 96.

15. Gary Spear, 'Shakespeare's "Manly" Parts: Masculinity and Effeminacy in *Troilus and Cressida*', *Shakespeare Quarterly* 44.4 (1993): 409–422, p. 417.

16. Qtd. M. Lindsay Kaplan, ed., *The Merchant of Venice: Texts and Contexts* (New York: Palgrave, 2002), 351.

17. On racial genealogies in the Henriad, see Andrew Clark Wagner, '"Pales in the Flood": Blood, Soil, and Whiteness in Shakespeare's Henriad', *White People in Shakespeare: Essays on Race, Culture and the Elite*, ed. Arthur L. Little, Jr (London: Arden Shakespeare-Bloomsbury, 2023), 121–134.

18. Jennifer C. Vaught, *Masculinity and Emotion in Early Modern English Literature* (Aldershot: Ashgate, 2008).

19. Jean E. Howard and Phyllis Rackin, *Engendering a Nation: A Feminist Account of Shakespeare's English Histories* (London: Routledge, 1997), 67.
20. Howard and Rackin, *Engendering*, 59.
21. Qtd. Howard and Rackin, *Engendering*, 62.
22. Theodora A. Jankowski, *Women in Power in the Early Modern Drama* (Urbana: University of Illinois Press, 1992), 101.
23. Kathryn Schwarz, *Tough Love: Amazon Encounters in the English Renaissance* (Durham: Duke University Press, 2000), 101.
24. Heather Love, 'Milk', *Shakesqueer: A Queer Companion to the Complete Works of Shakespeare*, ed. Madhavi Menon (Durham: Duke University Press, 2011), 201.
25. On the weather as manifestation of the queerness of nature, see Christine Varnado, 'Queer Nature, or the Weather in *Macbeth*', *Queer Shakespeare*, 177–195.
26. On reproductive futurism in *Macbeth*, see Love, *Shakesqueer*, 202–203.
27. Francesca T. Royster, '"White-Limed Walls": Whiteness and Gothic Extremism in Shakespeare's *Titus Andronicus*', *Shakespeare Quarterly* 51 (2000): 432–455.
28. *OED* stately *adj.* and *n.*, 1.a.
29. 'Gyspy' is a derogatory term used for Roma people in Europe, who were believed to have originated in Egypt. Carol Mejia LaPerle explores how the designation of Cleopatra as a gypsy degrades her by associating her with trickery, etc. See 'An Unlawful Race: Shakespeare's Cleopatra and the Crimes of Early Modern Gypsies', *Shakespeare* 13.3 (2017): 226–238.

CHAPTER 3

1. Robert Mills, 'Visibly Trans? Picturing Saint Eugenia in Medieval Art', *TSQ: Transgender Studies Quarterly* 5.4 (2018): 540–564, p. 542. Susan Stryker uses 'transgender' broadly to refer to 'people who move away from the gender they were assigned at birth, people who cross over (trans-) the boundaries constructed by their culture to define and contain that gender'. See *Transgender History* (Berkeley: Seal, 2008), 1.
2. According to Kathleen Perry Long, the French physician Jacques Duval acknowledged in his book *On Hermaphrodites* (1612) the wide diversity of gendered anatomical features 'not only among intersex individuals but also among all men and women', thus suggesting that 'the constraining categories of male and female need to be rethought'. See 'The Case of Marin le Marcis', *Trans Historical: Gender Plurality before the Modern*, ed. Anna Klosowska, Greta LaFleur, and Masha Raskolnikov (Ithaca: Cornell University Press, 2021), 68–94, p. 87.

3. Donald Beecher, 'Concerning Sex Changes: The Cultural Significance of a Renaissance Medical Polemic', *The Sixteenth-Century Journal* 36.4 (2005): 991–1016, p. 998.
4. Jean E. Howard, *The Stage and Social Struggle in Early Modern England* (London: Routledge, 1994), 98.
5. See also Ian Maclean, *The Renaissance Notion of Woman: A Study in the Fortunes of Scholasticism and Medical Science in European Intellectual Life* (Cambridge: Cambridge University Press, 1980), 20. Sara Gorman observes that 'for gender transformative gestures to be theatrical, and hence titillating in part due to their invocation of *imagination*, there must have existed a sense of the two sexes as in some ways very much distinct'. See 'The Theatricality of Transformation: Cross-Dressing, Sexual Misdemeanour, and Gender/Sexuality Spectra on the Elizabethan Stage, Bridewell Hospital Court Records, and the Repertories of the Court of the Aldermen, 1574–1607', *Early Modern Literary Studies* 13.3 (2008): 1–37, para. 36. http://purl.oclc.org/emls/13-3/theatran.htm.
6. Kathleen E. McLuskie, '"Bless thee Bottom, bless thee! Thou art translated": Gender Identity and Transformation in Shakespeare', *Shakespeare/ Sex: Contemporary Readings in Gender and Sexuality*, ed. Jennifer Drouin (London: Arden Shakespeare-Bloomsbury, 2020), 243–267, p. 252.
7. Sawyer Kemp, '"In That Dimension Grossly Clad": Transgender Rhetoric and Shakespeare', *Shakespeare Studies* 47 (2019): 120–126, p. 123.
8. Kemp, 'Dimension', 124. Body or gender dysphoria refers to feelings of distress and discomfort caused by the misfit between one's assigned birth gender (usually based on genitalia) and authentic gender identity. Transitioning is often, but not always, an attempt to resolve gender dysphoria by aligning one's authentic gender identity with one's public gender presentation. Alignment strategies are usually categorized as *social* (changing one's pronouns, name, hair, clothes, speech, manner, activities and/or bodily appearance); *legal* (changing one's name and gender on official documents); and *medical* (altering one's body through surgery and/or hormone therapy).
9. Lorna Hutson, 'On Not Being Deceived: Rhetoric and the Body in *Twelfth Night*', *Texas Studies in Literature and Language* 38.2 (1996): 140–174, p. 146.
10. Masha Raskolnikov, 'Without Magic or Miracle: The Romance of Silence and the Prehistory of Genderqueerness', *Trans Historical*, 178–206, p. 186.
11. Kimberly Poitevin, 'Inventing Whiteness: Cosmetics, Race, and Women in Early Modern England', *Journal for Early Modern Cultural Studies* 11.1 (2011): 59–89, p. 62.
12. Kim F. Hall, '"These bastard signs of fair": Literary Whiteness in Shakespeare's Sonnets', *Post-Colonial Shakespeares*, ed. Ania Loomba and Martin Orkin (London: Routledge, 1998): 64–83, p. 67.

13. Qtd. Laura Levine, *Men in Women's Clothing: Anti-theatricality and Effeminization 1579–1642* (Cambridge: Cambridge University Press, 1994), 19.
14. Qtd. Levine, *Men*, 22.
15. Qtd. Tanya Pollard, *Shakespeare's Theater: A Sourcebook* (Oxford, Blackwell, 2004), 176.
16. Levine, *Men*, 19.
17. Roberta Barker, 'Acting against the Rules: Remembering the Eroticism of the Shakespearean Boy Actress', *Shakespeare Re-Dressed: Cross-Gender Casting in Contemporary Performance*, ed. James C. Bulman (Madison, NJ: Fairleigh Dickinson University Press, 2008), 57–78, p. 57.
18. Bruce R. Smith, 'Making a Difference: Male/Male Desire in Comedy, Tragedy, and Tragi-comedy', *Erotic Politics: The Dynamics of Desire on the English Renaissance Stage*, ed. Susan Zimmerman (London: Routledge, 1992), 127–149, p. 137.
19. Bruce Smith, 'Making', 129.
20. Simone Chess, 'Queer Residue: Boy Actors' Adult Careers in Early Modern England', *Journal for Early Modern Cultural Studies* 19.4 (2019): 242–264, p. 258.
21. *OED*, outface *v.*, 1a, 3a.
22. *OED*, heart *n.*, 11a, 11b, 8, II.
23. Jennifer Drouin, 'Cross-Dressing, Drag, and Passing: Slippages in Shakespearean Comedy', *Shakespeare Re-Dressed*, 23–56, p. 34.
24. Poitevin, 'Inventing', 80–81.
25. On the racial implications of Aliena's brownface, see Ruben Espinosa, *Shakespeare on the Shades of Racism* (New York: Routledge, 2021), 79–81.
26. See Arthur L. Little, Jr, 'Is it Possible to Read Shakespeare through Critical White Studies?' *The Cambridge Companion to Shakespeare and Race*, ed. Ayanna Thompson (Cambridge: Cambridge University Press, 2020), 268–280, p. 276.
27. Drouin, 'Cross-Dressing', 48.
28. Jeffrey Masten, *Queer Philologies: Sex, Language, and Affect in Shakespeare's Time* (Philadelphia: University of Pennsylvania Press, 2016), 62–63. Stephen Orgel argues that Rosalind is still dressed as Ganymede, and hence is 'correctly gendered male'. See *Impersonations: The Performance of Gender in Shakespeare's England* (Cambridge: Cambridge University Press, 1996), 33. Many commentators discuss the play's genderqueer Epilogue, in which Rosalind speaks both as herself and as the boy actor playing the role.
29. Margaret Ferguson, 'Hymeneal Instruction', *Masculinities, Childhood, Violence: Attending to Early Modern Women—and Men: Proceedings of the 2006 Symposium,* ed. Amy E. Leonard and Karen L. Nelson (Newark: University of Delaware Press, 2011), 97–129, p. 107, 125n.40.

30. Because Rosalind's lines are not explicitly addressed to particular characters, it's also possible to imagine that she is giving herself not to Orlando and her father, but to Orlando and Celia, for instance.

31. Drouin ('Cross-Dressing', 41) observes that Julia never mentions her breasts as a possible obstacle to her male disguise. Of course, readers then and now might imagine Julia as a young woman with small breasts, and original audiences would have seen a teenage boy portraying Julia.

32. *OED*, ill-favored *adj.*, a., b.

33. Will Fisher, '"Had it a codpiece, 'twere a man indeed": The Codpiece as Constitutive Accessory in Early Modern English Culture', *Ornamentalism: The Art of Renaissance Accessories*, ed. Bella Mirabella (University of Michigan Press, 2011), 102–129, pp. 102, 122.

34. Susan Stryker, 'My Words to Victor Frankenstein Above the Village of Chamounix: Performing Transgender Rage', *The Transgender Studies Reader Remix*, ed. Susan Stryker and Dylan McCarthy Blackston (London: Routledge, 2023), 68–79, p. 68.

35. Marjorie B. Garber, *Vested Interests: Cross-dressing and Cultural Anxiety* (London: Routledge, 1992), 77. Colby Gordon addresses the transphobia of Garber's influential study (*Glorious Bodies: Trans Theologies and Renaissance Literature* [Chicago: University of Chicago Press, 2024], 29–30).

36. On race and beauty in this passage, see Kim F. Hall, *Things of Darkness: Economies of Race and Gender in Early Modern England* (Ithaca: Cornell University Press, 1995), 181.

37. Pamela Allen Brown, *The Diva's Gift to the Shakespearean Stage: Agency, Theatricality, and the Innamorata* (Oxford: Oxford University Press, 2021), 145; Sophie Tomlinson, 'The Actress and Baroque Aesthetic Affects in Renaissance Drama', *Shakespeare Bulletin* 33.1 (2015): 67–82, p. 71.

38. Tomlinson, 'Actress', 71.

39. Michael Shapiro, *Gender in Play on the Shakespearean Stage: Boy Heroines and Female Pages* (Ann Arbor: University of Michigan Press, 1994), 65.

40. Jason Demeter, 'Pearls in Beauteous Ladies' Eyes: Shakespeare, Race, and Riots in the American Metropolis', *Journal of Narrative Theory* 41.3 (2011): 378–400, pp. 385–386.

41. Ambereen Dadabhoy (*Shakespeare through Islamic Worlds* [New York: Routledge, 2024], 176–217) details *Twelfth Night*'s evocation of the sex-segregated, homoerotic, spaces of Ottoman society. See also Su Fang Ng, 'The Frontiers of *Twelfth Night*', *Early Modern England and Islamic Worlds*, ed. Bernadette Andrea and Linda McJannet (New York: Palgrave Macmillan, 2011), 173–196.

42. Abdulhamit Arvas, 'Early Modern Eunuchs and the Transing of Gender and Race', *Journal for Early Modern Cultural Studies* 19.4 (2019): 116–136, p. 117.

43. Arvas, 'Eunuchs', 126.

44. Arvas, 'Eunuchs', 128.

45. Keir Elam, 'The Fertile Eunuch: *Twelfth Night*, Early Modern Intercourse, and the Fruits of Castration', *Shakespeare Quarterly* 47.1 (1996): 1–36, p. 4.

46. Arvas, 'Eunuchs', 119–120.

47. Katherine Crawford, 'Desiring Castrates, or How to Create Disabled Social Subjects', *Journal for Early Modern Cultural Studies* 16.2 (2016): 59–90, p. 61.

48. Simone Chess, 'Queer Gender Informants in Ovid and Shakespeare', *Ovid and Adaptation in Early Modern English Theatre*, ed. Lisa S. Starks (Edinburgh: Edinburgh University Press, 2020), 21–38, 23; Simone Chess, *Male-to-Female Cross-dressing in Early Modern English Literature: Gender, Performance, and Queer Relations* (London: Routledge, 2016), 104.

49. Chess, 'Queer Gender', 33.

50. Masten, *Queer*, 113, 110–111. As Will Fisher argues, early modern culture recognized a gender distinction between boys and adult men. See *Materializing Gender in Early Modern English Literature and Culture* (Cambridge: Cambridge University Press, 2006), 87–93.

51. Adam Shepherd, Benjamin Hanckel, and Andy Guise, 'Trans Health and the Risks of Inappropriate Curiosity', *BMJ Opinion* (2019). https://blogs.bmj.com/bmj/2019/09/09/trans-health-and-the-risks-of-inappropriate-curiosity/.

52. The *OED* cites a 1611 reference to the labia, or 'the lips of a womans Priuities' (*OED*, lip *n.*, II.5.b). 'Cod' and 'codling' refer to the scrotum, or to the scrotum and testicles (*OED* cod *n.1*, 3.a; codling *n.3*, 1).

53. Masten, *Queer*, 112.

54. Patricia Parker, 'Fantasies of "Race" and Gender: Africa, *Othello*, and Bringing to Light', *Women, 'Race', and Writing in the Early Modern Period*, ed. Margo Hendricks and Patricia Parker (New York: Routledge, 1994), 84–100.

55. *OED*, disguise *n.*, 3.a, 4. Although the first citation the *OED* gives for this second meaning is from 1632, I would argue that it is available in *Twelfth Night*. The play clearly opens up room for interpreting 'disguise' either narrowly as clothing or more broadly as an embodied performance of false identity.

56. See *OED*, favour, *n.*: 'appearance, aspect, look' (9.a); 'countenance, face' (9.b).

57. On the 'diabolical script of blackness' in early modern English theatre, see Noémie Ndiaye, *Scripts of Blackness: Early Modern Performance Culture and the Making of Race* (Philadelphia: University of Pennsylvania Press, 2022), 40–45. In an argument relevant to my reading of Cesario, Ndiaye argues

that in *Othello* Iago represents Desdemona's 'whiteface' as diabolical, that is, as a sign of deceitfulness (57). On the premodern representation of devils as black, see Robert Hornback, *Racism and Early Blackface Comic Traditions: From the Old World to the New* (Cham, Switzerland: Palgrave MacMillan, 2018), 74–84.

58. On the invasive demand for transgender confession, see Colby Gordon, 'The Sign You Must Not Touch: Lyric Obscurity and Trans Confession', *postmedieval: a journal of medieval cultural studies* 11 (2020): 195–203.

59. Valerie Traub, *The Renaissance of Lesbianism in Early Modern England* (Cambridge: Cambridge University Press, 2002), 56. 'Tribade' was a derogatory early modern term for a masculine woman who had sex with women. English writers often identified tribades as foreign, racialized, figures.

60. Susan Stryker, 'My Words', 71.

61. Phyllis Rackin, 'Shakespeare's Cross-dressing Comedies', *A Companion to Shakespeare's Works. Vol III: The Comedies*, ed. Richard Dutton and Jean E. Howard (Oxford: Blackwell, 2003), 114–136, p. 123. I avoid using language like 'true sex' because it assumes a stability of biological or natural sex that the plays call into question. For a similar scepticism about the existence of a 'real' sex in *Twelfth Night*, see Ezra Horbury, 'Transgender Reassessments of the Cross-Dressed Page in Shakespeare, *Philaster*, and *The Honest Man's Fortune*', *Shakespeare Quarterly* 73.1–2 (2020): 100–120, pp. 102–107.

62. In early modern England, 'pucelle' might refer to a girl or virgin (*pusel, puzel, pucell, pusil*), whore (*puzzle, pussle*), state of perplexity (*puzzle*), or bull's penis (*pizzle, pissell, peezel*). *OED*, pucelle *n.*, 1b, 2; puzzle, *n.*, 1; pizzle, *n.*, 1. See also Marjorie Garber, *Shakespeare After All* (New York: Pantheon, 2004), 95–96; Leslie Feinberg, *Transgender Warriors: Making History from Joan of Arc to Dennis Rodman* (Boston: Beacon Press, 1996), 31–37.

63. See Stephen Spiess, 'Puzzling Embodiment: Proclamation, La Pucelle, and *The First Part of Henry VI*', *The Oxford Handbook of Shakespeare and Embodiment: Gender, Sexuality, and Race*, ed. Valerie Traub (Oxford: Oxford University Press, 2016): 93–111, p. 103.

64. *OED* clear *adj.*, 1a, 4c, 4d.

65. Although *1 Henry VI* does not provide much detail on how Joan dresses (aside from 'in armour'), contemporary accounts of Joan stress that she consistently dressed as a knight both on and off the battlefield: 'The said Jeanne put off and entirely abandoned woman's clothes, with her hair cropped short and round in the fashion of young men, she wore shirt, breeches, doublet, with hose joined together', etc. Qtd. Lisa Jardine, *Still*

Harping on Daughters: Women and Drama in the Age of Shakespeare (New York: Columbia University Press, 1989), 157.

66. Spiess, 'Puzzling', 103.

67. For instance, John Marston's satire *The Scourge of Villainy* asks 'what Ganymede is that doth grace / The gallant's heels? One who for two days' space / Is closely hired'. Qtd. Mario DiGangi, *The Homoerotics of Early Modern Drama* (Cambridge: Cambridge University Press, 1997), 70.

68. See Horbury, 'Transgender', 107: '"Class drag" or "class cross-dressing" enables gender passing by translating gender difference into class difference.' Since Rosalind, Julia, and Viola are all gentlewomen, however, they are not appropriating a higher status through their male disguises. Arguably, as a Duke's daughter, Rosalind in particular is dressing 'down' as Ganymede.

69. Spiess, 'Puzzling', 107.

70. Early moderns regarded dolphins as 'near-humans' who queerly 'span the indistinct boundaries between land and sea, human and animal'. See Steve Mentz '"Half-Fish, Half-Flesh": Dolphins, the Ocean, and Early Modern Humans', *The Indistinct Human in Renaissance Literature*, ed. Jean E. Feerick and Vin Nardizzi (Palgrave Macmillan, 2012), 29–46, p. 31.

71. *OED* juggle, *v.*, 2, 3; ingle, *v.*, 1a, 1b.

72. In a previous scene Joan is shown asking devils to assist her, justifying English suspicions that her military success is based on witchcraft.

73. Gary Ferguson, *Same-Sex Marriage in Renaissance Rome: Sexuality, Identity, and Community in Early Modern Europe* (Ithaca: Cornell University Press, 2016), 85.

74. Stryker, *Transgender*, 1.

CHAPTER 4

1. J. Jack Halberstam, *The Queer Art of Failure* (Durham: Duke University Press, 2011), 2.

2. Single women living alone, for instance, might be accused of being prostitutes. Amy M. Froide, *Never Married: Singlewomen in Early Modern England* (Oxford: Oxford University Press, 2007), 1–4, 20–22.

3. Ela Przybylo and Danielle Cooper, 'Asexual Resonances: Tracing a Queerly Asexual Archive', *GLQ* 20.3 (2014): 297–318, p. 298.

4. Przybylo and Cooper, 'Asexual', 298–299.

5. Kristina Gupta, 'Compulsory Sexuality: Evaluating an Emergent Concept', *Signs* 41.1 (2015): 131–154, p. 132.

6. Simone Chess, 'Asexuality, Queer Chastity, and Adolescence in Early Modern Literature', *Queering Childhood in Early Modern English Drama*

and Culture, ed. Jennifer Higginbotham and Mark Albert Johnston (Detroit: Wayne State University Press, 2018): 31–55, p. 31.

7. *OED*, appetite *n.*, 4a, 3.

8. *OED*, leaden *adj.*, 2c, 1a.

9. 'Unapt' means 'unfitted or unfit to do something' (*OED*, unapt *adj.*, 1). A modern English translation of the Chaucer might be: 'Never yet was a man or woman born who was unfit to suffer love's celestial heat.'

10. *OED*, obdurate *adj.*, 1a.

11. Lee Edelman, *No Future: Queer Theory and the Death Drive* (Durham: Duke University Press, 2004), 30, 21.

12. Subha Mukherji, 'Outgrowing Adonis, Outgrowing Ovid: The Disorienting Narrative of *Venus and Adonis*', *The Oxford Handbook of Shakespeare's Poetry*, ed. Jonathan Post (Oxford: Oxford University Press, 2013), 396–412, p. 400. See also Jonathan Bate, *Shakespeare and Ovid* (Oxford: Oxford University Press, 1993), 51–55.

13. Mukherji, 'Outgrowing', 397.

14. *OED*, tempering, *v.*, 13.

15. Margreta DeGrazia, 'Imprints: Shakespeare, Gutenberg, Descartes', *Alternative Shakespeares* vol. 2, ed. Terence Hawkes (London: Routledge, 1996), 63–94, p. 69.

16. Qtd. Theodora A. Jankowski, *Pure Resistance: Queer Virginity in Early Modern English Drama* (Philadelphia: University of Pennsylvania Press, 2000), 94.

17. *OED*, list *n.*3, II.9a.

18. This does not mean, of course, that 'a woman can't rape a man', as Bate (*Shakespeare and Ovid*, 65) asserts.

19. Goran V. Stanivukovic argues that Adonis' death is a punishment for his sodomitical refusal of heterosexual desire. See '"Kissing the Boar": Queer Adonis and Critical Practice', *Straight with a Twist: Queer Theory and the Subject of Heterosexuality*, ed. Calvin Thomas (Urbana: University of Illinois Press, 2000), 87–108.

20. *OED*, mew, *n.*2, 2, 3.

21. Alison Findlay, *A Feminist Perspective on Renaissance Drama* (Oxford: Wiley-Blackwell, 1999), 32.

22. *OED*, blood *n.*, 11, 12, 13.

23. Qtd. Jankowski, *Pure*, 88.

24. Qtd. Jankowski, *Pure*, 88.

25. Qtd. Jankowski, *Pure*, 88. The Latin reads: 'sed quid iuxta naturam prodigiosius anu virgine?' or 'but what is more prodigious according to nature than an old virgin?'

26. Valerie Traub, *The Renaissance of Lesbianism in Early Modern England* (Cambridge: Cambridge University Press, 2002), 65.

27. Jankowski, *Pure*, 177.
28. Andrew Marvell, *Miscellaneous Poems by Andrew Marvell* (1681), 82.
29. James M. Bromley, *Intimacy and Sexuality in the Age of Shakespeare* (Cambridge: Cambridge University Press, 2012), 140.
30. See especially Carolyn E. Brown, 'Erotic Religious Flagellation and Shakespeare's *Measure for Measure*', *English Literary Renaissance* 16.1 (1986): 139–165, pp. 164–165. Dennis Austin Britton instead finds in the passage Isabella's representation of herself as a bloodied virgin martyr whose white body signifies sanctity. See 'Red Blood on White Saints: Affective Piety, Racial Violence, and *Measure for Measure*', *White People in Shakespeare: Essays on Race, Culture and the Elite*, ed. Arthur L. Little, Jr (London: Arden Shakespeare-Bloomsbury, 2023), 65–76, p. 73.
31. Benjamin Kahan, *Celibacies: American Modernism and Sexual Life* (Durham: Duke University Press, 2013), 5. See also Liza Blake, 'Teaching Premodern Asexualities and Aromanticisms', *Medium* (https://medium.com/the-sundial-acmrs/teaching-premodern-asexualities-and-aromanticisms-908cc375af12).
32. Jankowski, *Pure*, 171.
33. Jankowski, *Pure*, 173.
34. Melissa E. Sanchez, 'Protestantism, Marriage and Asexuality in Shakespeare', *Shakespeare/Sex: Contemporary Readings in Gender and Sexuality*, ed. Jennifer Drouin (London: Arden Shakespeare-Bloomsbury, 2020), 98–122, pp. 115–116.
35. Sanchez, 'Protestantism', 110.
36. Jankowski, *Pure*, 171.
37. Qtd. Jankowski, *Pure*, 93.
38. Qtd. Jankowski, *Pure*, 94.
39. Sanchez, 'Protestantism', 100.
40. *OED*, wonder *adj.*, 7a.
41. Paul Morrison, 'Same-Saint Desire', *Shakesqueer: A Queer Companion to the Complete Works of Shakespeare*, ed. Madhavi Menon (Durham: Duke University Press, 2011), 209–215, 211.
42. Sanchez, 'Protestantism', 111.
43. In practice, it seems, the Viennese law against fornication (like early modern European law generally) stops short of enacting literal abortion. Whereas Claudio is to be executed immediately, Juliet presumably cannot be executed because she is pregnant. She will wait out childbirth in jail; the play never makes clear if she would have suffered further punishment once her child had been born.
44. Bruce R. Smith, *Homosexual Desire in Shakespeare's England: A Cultural Poetics* (Chicago: University of Chicago Press, 1991), 66.

45. Qtd. Melissa E. Sanchez, *Queer Faith: Reading Promiscuity and Race in the Secular Love Tradition* (New York: New York University Press, 2019), 129.
46. Jordan Windholz, 'The Queer Testimonies of Male Chastity in *All's Well That Ends Well*', *Modern Philology* 116.4 (2019): 322–349, p. 329.
47. *OED*, box *n*.2, 12.
48. *OED*, spend *v*.1, 5a.
49. *OED*, marrow *n*.1, 3c.
50. Windholz, 'Queer', 335.
51. *OED*, jade *n*.1, 2a.
52. *OED*, cold *adj*, 7a, 7c, 8.
53. *OED*, cold *adj*, 6a.
54. Kahan objects that queer critics sometimes interpret sexual absences or silences as evidence of same-sex eroticism. In other words, when a woman doesn't express desire for a man, we might wrongly assume that she is a 'closeted' lesbian who cannot or will not articulate her desire for a woman. The 'least queer aspect of queer theory,' Kahan writes, is 'its tendency to turn other sexualities into same-sex alloeroticism'. See *Celibacies*, 3.
55. *OED*, rude *adj*., I.4.

CHAPTER 5

1. Pierre Boaistuau, *Theatrum Mundi*, tr. J. Alday (1581), pp. 199–200.
2. Lucian, 'Affairs of the Heart', *Lucian* vol. 8, ed. M.D. Macleod (Cambridge, MA: Harvard University Press, 1967), 177.
3. Tomaso Garzoni, *The Hospital of Incurable Fools* (1600), 85.
4. William Gouge, *Of Domestical Duties* (1622), 185–186.
5. Cf. Simone Chess's use of 'queer heterosexuality' in *Male-to-Female Crossdressing in Early Modern English Literature: Gender, Performance, and Queer Relations* (London: Routledge, 2016), 103–105. Joseph Gamble also discusses the importance of queering 'heteronormative [penile-vaginal] sex' in *Sex Lives: Intimate Infrastructures in Early Modernity* (Philadelphia: University of Pennsylvania Press, 2023), 30.
6. Melissa E. Sanchez, '"Use Me But as Your Spaniel": Feminism, Queer Theory, and Early Modern Sexualities', *PMLA* 127.3 (2012): 493–511, p. 505.
7. Sanchez, '"Use"', 505.
8. James Kuzner, '*All's Well That Ends Well* and the Art of Love', *Shakespeare Quarterly* 68.3 (2018): 215–240, p. 217.
9. Kuzner, '*All's Well*', 226.
10. Kuzner, '*All's Well*', 230.
11. Kuzner, '*All's Well*', 231.
12. Gail Kern Paster, *The Body Embarrassed: Drama and the Disciplines of Shame in Early Modern England* (Ithaca: Cornell University Press, 1993), 133, 114.

13. Andrew Gurr, ed., *King Henry V*, by William Shakespeare, updated edition (Cambridge: Cambridge University Press, 2005), 5.2.280n.; T. W. Craik, ed., *King Henry V*, by William Shakespeare (London: Arden Shakespeare-Cengage, 1995), 5.2.310-311n.

14. Vin Nardizzi explains this sodomitical allusion as a sign of Harry's sexual 'mixing' with a woman of a different nationality. See 'Grafted to Falstaff and Compounded with Catherine: Mingling Hal in the Second Tetralogy', *Queer Renaissance Historiography: Backward Gaze*, ed. Vin Nardizzi, Stephen Guy-Bray, and Will Stockton (Burlington, VT: Ashgate, 2009), 149–169, p. 154.

15. Ian Smith addresses European figurations of Turkish invasion as a kind of military 'sodomy' in 'The Queer Moor: Bodies, Borders, and Barbary Inns', *A Companion to the Global Renaissance: English and Culture in the Age of Expansion*, ed. Jyotsna G. Singh (Oxford: Wiley-Blackwell, 2009), 190–204. On the relation between military invasion and sexual assault in *Henry V*, see Lance Wilcox, 'Katherine of France as Victim and Bride', *Shakespeare Studies* 17 (1985): 61–76.

16. Gordon Williams, *A Glossary of Shakespeare's Sexual Language* (London: Athlone, 1997), 300–301.

17. James M. Bromley, 'Rimming the Renaissance', *Sex Before Sex: Figuring the Act in Early Modern England*, ed. James M. Bromley and Will Stockton (Minneapolis: University of Minnesota Press, 2013), 171–194, p. 178.

18. On anger generally in the play, see Maurice Hunt, '*The Taming of the Shrew* and Anger', *The Ben Jonson Journal* 27.1 (2020): 105–125.

19. See Jonathan Goldberg, *Shakespeare's Hand* (Minneapolis: University of Minnesota Press, 2003), 181.

20. Rick Rambuss, 'Shakespeare's Ass Play', *Shakesqueer: A Queer Companion to the Complete Works of Shakespeare*, ed. Madhavi Menon (Durham: Duke University Press, 2011), 234–244, p. 243.

21. Rambuss, 'Ass', 236, 240.

22. Goldberg, *Hand*, 181.

23. Richard Hillman, 'Criminalizing the Woman's Incest: *Pericles* and Its Analogues', *Female Transgression in Early Modern Britain: Literary and Historical Explorations*, ed. Richard Hillman and Pauline Ruberry-Blanc (Burlington, VT: Ashgate, 2014), 16–28, p. 18.

24. *OED*, buxom, *adj.*, 1a, 1b, 2, 3, 4.

25. Laura Gowing, *Common Bodies: Women, Touch and Power in Seventeenth-Century England* (New Haven: Yale University Press, 2003), 109, 99.

26. Most commentators rationalize this strange implication by explaining that Antiochus is 'son' to *himself*. For instance, Charles R. Forker explains that 'Antiochus is his own son-in-law because he functions as his daughter's spouse'. See '"A Little More Than Kin, and Less Than Kind":

Incest, Intimacy, Narcissism, and Identity in Elizabethan and Stuart Drama', *Medieval and Renaissance Drama in England* 4 (1989): 13–51, p. 35.

27. *OED*, moor *n.*1, 2a; Moor *n.*2, 1.
28. The description reads, in part: 'An old man in a nightgown offers his beautiful young wife a flower. He does not notice that a young man puts two horns on his head'—the sign of being cuckolded.
29. William Whately, *A Bride-Bush, or, A Direction for Married Persons* (1623), 45.
30. Valerie Billing, 'The Queer Erotics of Size in Shakespeare's *Venus and Adonis*', *Shakespeare Studies* 65 (2017), 131–136, pp. 132–133.
31. Will Fisher, 'Stray[ing] Lower Where the Pleasant Fountains Lie: Cunnilingus in *Venus and Adonis* and in English Culture, c. 1600-1700', *The Oxford Handbook of Shakespeare and Embodiment*, ed. Valerie Traub (Oxford: Oxford University Press, 2016), 333–346, pp. 334–336.
32. Holly Dugan, 'Aping Rape: Animal Ravishment and Sexual Knowledge in Early Modern England', *Sex before Sex*, 213–232, pp. 220–221. Dugan notes Dromio's fear that Nell will use him like a 'tailless dog', an allusion to castration (222).
33. On the racial construction of family in *Othello*, see Joyce Green MacDonald, 'Black Ram, White Ewe: Shakespeare, Race, and Women', *A Feminist Companion to Shakespeare*, ed. Dympna Callaghan, 2nd ed. (Oxford: Wiley-Blackwell, 2016), 206–225.
34. See Dennis Austin Britton, *Becoming Christian: Race, Reformation, and Early Modern English Romance* (New York: Fordham University Press, 2014), 128–130; Kim F. Hall, 'Beauty and the Beast of Whiteness: Teaching Race and Gender', *Shakespeare Quarterly* 47.4 (1996): 461–475, p. 470; Sujata Iyengar, *Shades of Difference: Mythologies of Skin Color in Early Modern England* (Philadelphia: University of Pennsylvania Press, 2005), 138; Arthur J. Little, Jr, *Shakespeare Jungle Fever: National-Imperial Re-Visions of Race, Rape, and Sacrifice* (Stanford: Stanford University Press, 2000), 74–75; and Ruben Espinosa, *Shakespeare on the Shades of Racism* (New York: Routledge, 2021), 15.
35. Erickson, 'Exeunt', 283.
36. Sanchez, '"Use"', 496.

For considerations of space, the recommendations below mainly identify scholarly works not already cited in the respective chapters. Refer to the endnotes of individual chapters for more scholarship in these areas.

Queer Theories, Queer Histories, and Shakespeare Studies

Useful overviews of queer theory/studies include Annamarie Jagose, *Queer Theory: An Introduction* (New York: New York University Press, 1997); Donald E. Hall, *Queer Theories* (New York: Palgrave Macmillan, 2003); Sharon Marcus, 'Queer Theory for Everybody: A Review Essay', *Signs* 13.1 (2005): 191–218; *The Cambridge Companion to Queer Studies*, ed. Siobhan Somerville (Cambridge: Cambridge University Press, 2020); and *Keywords for Gender and Sexuality Studies*, ed. The Keywords Feminist Editorial Collective (New York: New York University Press, 2021).

For critiques of queer studies' problematic exclusions, see Roderick A. Ferguson, *Aberrations in Black: Toward a Queer of Color Critique* (Minneapolis: University of Minnesota Press, 2004); Susan Stryker, 'Transgender Studies: Queer Theory's Evil Twin', *GLQ* 10.2 (2004): 212–215; 'What's Queer about Queer Studies Now?' *Social Text* 84–85 (2005), ed. David L. Eng, Judith Halberstam, and José Estaban Muñoz; Sharon Patricia Holland, *The Erotic Life of Racism* (Durham: Duke University Press, 2012); 'GLQ at Twenty-Five', *GLQ* 25.1 (2019), ed. Jennifer DeVere Brody and Marcia Ochoa; 'Left of Queer', *Social Text* 145 (2020), ed. David L. Eng and Jasbir K. Puar; Matt Brim, *Poor Queer Studies: Confronting Elitism in the University* (Durham: Duke University Press, 2020).

Madhavi Menon, ed., *Shakesqueer: A Queer Companion to the Complete Works of Shakespeare* (Durham: Duke University Press, 2011) contains queer essays on all of Shakespeare's texts. Four other anthologies offer a wealth of material related to gender and sexuality in Shakespeare: *Presentism, Gender, and Sexuality in Shakespeare*, ed. Evelyn Gajowski (New York: Palgrave Macmillan, 2009); *The Oxford Handbook of Shakespeare and Embodiment: Gender, Sexuality, and Race*, ed. Valerie Traub (Oxford: Oxford University Press, 2016); *Queer Shakespeare: Desire and Sexuality*, ed. Goran Stanivukovic (London: Arden Shakespeare-Bloomsbury, 2017); and *Shakespeare/Sex: Contemporary Readings in Gender and Sexuality*, ed. Jennifer Drouin (London: Arden Shakespeare-Bloomsbury, 2020).

Although largely focused on writers other than Shakespeare, three excellent recent studies of queer sexuality in early modern literature are Christine Varnado, *The Shapes of Fancy: Reading for Queer Desire in Early Modern Literature* (Minneapolis: University of Minnesota Press, 2020); James M. Bromley, *Clothing and Queer Style in Early Modern English Drama* (Oxford: Oxford University Press, 2021); and Joseph Gamble, *Sex Lives: Intimate Infrastructures in Early Modernity* (Philadelphia: University of Pennsylvania Press, 2023).

Chapter 1: Queer(ing) Couples

On bisexuality in Shakespeare, see Kate Chedgzoy, '"Two loves I have": Shakespeare and Bisexuality', *The Bisexual Imaginary: Representation, Identity, and Desire*, ed. Phoebe Davidson (London: Cassell, 1997); Marjorie Garber, *Vice Versa: Bisexuality and the Eroticism of Everyday Life* (New York: Simon and Schuster, 1995); and Joseph Pequigney, 'The Two Antonios and Same-Sex Love in *Twelfth Night* and *The Merchant of Venice*', *English Literary Renaissance* 22 (1992): 201–221.

Among the many excellent accounts of race in *The Merchant of Venice*, I would recommend starting with Kim F. Hall, '"Guess Who's Coming to Dinner?" Colonization and Miscegenation in *The Merchant of Venice*', *Renaissance Drama* ns 23 (1992): 87–111; Janet Adelman, 'Her Father's Blood: Race, Conversion, and Nation in *The Merchant of Venice*', *Representations* 81 (2003): 4–30; M. Lindsay Kaplan, 'Jessica's Mother: Medieval Constructions of Jewish Race and Gender in *The Merchant of Venice*', *Shakespeare Quarterly* 58 (2007): 1–30; and Patricia Akhimie, '"Qualities of breeding": Race, Class, and Conduct in *The Merchant of Venice*', *The Merchant of Venice: The State of Play*, ed. M. Lindsay Kaplan (London: Arden Shakespeare-Bloomsbury, 2020). Notable queer scholarship on *Merchant* includes Edward J. Geisweidt, 'Antonio's Claim: Triangulated Desire and Queer Kinship in Shakespeare's *The Merchant of Venice*', *Shakespeare* 5.4 (2009): 338–354; Amy Greenstadt, 'The Kindest Cut: Circumcision and Queer Kinship in *The Merchant of Venice*', *ELH* 80.4 (2013): 946–980; and Allison P. Hobgood, 'Prosthetic Encounter and Queer Intersubjectivity in *The Merchant of Venice*', *Textual Practice* 30.7 (2016): 1291–1308.

Queer desire in *The Two Noble Kinsmen* is discussed in Alan Sinfield, *Shakespeare, Authority, Sexuality: Unfinished Business in Cultural Materialism* (London: Routledge, 2006); and Hilary Ball, '"A Fair Boy, Certain, but a Fool to Love Himself": Queer Reflections of the Myth of Narcissus in Shakespeare and Fletcher's *The Two Noble Kinsmen*', *Shakespeare* 16.1 (2020): 1–13.

Readers interested in female homoeroticism should consult Valerie Traub, *Desire and Anxiety: Circulations of Sexuality in Shakespearean Drama* (London: Routledge, 1992); Denise A. Walen, *Constructions of Female Homoeroticism in Early Modern Drama* (New York: Palgrave Macmillan, 2005); Will Fisher,

'Home Alone: The Place of Women's Homoerotic Desire in Shakespeare's *As You Like It*', *Feminisms and Early Modern Texts: Essays for Phyllis Rackin*, ed. Rebecca Ann Bach and Gwynne Kennedy (Selinsgrove: Susquehanna University Press, 2010); and Mario DiGangi, *Sexual Types: Embodiment, Agency, and Dramatic Character from Shakespeare to Shirley* (Philadelphia: University of Pennsylvania Press, 2011).

Although Chapter 1's discussion of same-sex relationships omits *Coriolanus*, see James Kuzner, 'Unbuilding the City: *Coriolanus* and the Birth of Republican Rome', *Shakespeare Quarterly* 58 (2007): 174–199; and Michael Friedman, '"Let me twine / Mine arms about that body": The Queerness of *Coriolanus* and Recent British Stage Productions', *Shakespeare Bulletin* 33.3 (2015): 395–419.

Chapter 2: (Queer) Desire and Disorder

In addition to the plays discussed in Chapter 2, *Richard II*, *King John*, and *King Lear* also connect sexual transgression to political disorder. Homoerotic favouritism in *Richard II* is analysed in Mario DiGangi, *The Homoerotics of Early Modern Drama* (Cambridge: Cambridge University Press, 1997); Madhavi Menon, *Wanton Words: Rhetoric and Sexuality in English Renaissance Drama* (Toronto: University of Toronto Press, 2004); Corey McEleney, *Futile Pleasures: Early Modern Literature and the Limits of Utility* (New York: Fordham University Press, 2017); and Derrick Higginbotham, 'The Construction of a King: Waste, Effeminacy and Queerness in Shakespeare's *Richard II*', *Shakespeare in Southern Africa* 26 (2014): 59–73. On bastardy in *King Lear*, see Mario DiGangi, 'Branded with Baseness: Bastardy and Race in *King Lear*', *Race and/ as Affect in Early Modern English Literature*, ed. Carol Mejia LaPerle (Tempe, AZ: ACMRS Press, 2022). Elizabeth Harper applies Lee Edelman's concept of reproductive futurism to Shakespearean tragedy in '"A Disease That's in My Flesh Which I Must Needs Call Mine": *Lear*, *Macbeth*, and the Fear of Futurity', *English Studies* 100.6 (2019): 604–626.

On Europeans' attribution of sodomy to non-Europeans, two good places to start are Jonathan Goldberg, *Sodometries: Renaissance Texts, Modern Sexualities* (Stanford: Stanford University Press, 1992); and Nabil Matar, *Turks, Moors, and Englishmen in the Age of Discovery* (New York: Columbia University Press, 1999).

Chapter 3: Queer Gender Transformations

Broader accounts of queer cross-dressing in Shakespeare include David L. Orvis, 'Cross-Dressing, Queerness, and the Early Modern Stage', *The Cambridge History of Gay and Lesbian Literature*, ed. E. L. McCallum and Mikko Tuhkanen (New York: Cambridge University Press, 2014); and Valerie Billing, 'Sexuality and Queerness on the Early Modern Stage', *A New Companion to Renaissance Drama*, ed. Arthur F. Kinney and Thomas Warren

Hopper (Oxford: Wiley-Blackwell, 2017). One cross-dressing female character not discussed in Chapter 3 is Innogen from *Cymbeline*, on whom see Michael Shapiro, *Gender in Play on the Shakespearean Stage: Boy Heroines and Female Pages* (Ann Arbor: University of Michigan Press, 1994); and Tracey Miller-Tomlinson, 'Queer History in *Cymbeline*', *Shakespeare* 12.3 (2016): 225–240.

Eunuchs in Shakespeare are discussed in Anston Bosnan, '"Best play with Mardian": Eunuch and Blackamoor as Imperial Culturegram', *Shakespeare Studies* 34 (2006): 123–157; and Mark Albert Johnston, 'Shakespeare's *Twelfth Night* and the Fertile Infertility of Eroticized Early Modern Boys', *Modern Philology* 114.3 (2017): 573–600. A theoretically oriented approach is provided by Howard Chiang, 'Trans without Borders: Resisting the Telos of Transgender Knowledge', *Journal of the History of Sexuality*, 32.1 (2023): 56–65.

On Ovidian myths of gender transformation and their use by premodern writers, see Gary Ferguson, *Queer (Re)Readings in the French Renaissance: Homosexuality, Gender, Culture* (Aldershot: Ashgate, 2008); Sarah Carter, *Ovidian Myth and Sexual Deviance in Early Modern English Literature* (New York: Palgrave Macmillan, 2011); *Ovidian Transversions: 'Iphis and Ianthe', 1300–1650*, ed. Valerie Traub, Patricia Badir, and Peggy McCracken (Edinburgh: Edinburgh University Press, 2019); and *Ovid and Adaptation in Early Modern English Theatre*, ed. Lisa S. Starks (Edinburgh: Edinburgh University Press, 2020).

Chapter 4: Queer Asexuality

Good resources for and studies of asexuality include *Aven: The Asexual Visibility and Education Network* (https://www.asexuality.org/); Michael Cobb, *Single: Arguments for the Uncoupled* (New York: New York University Press, 2012); *Asexualities: Feminist and Queer Perspectives*, ed. Karli June Cerankowski and Megan Milks (New York: Routledge, 2014); Ela Przybylo, *Asexual Erotics: Intimate Readings of Compulsory Sexuality* (Columbus: Ohio State University Press, 2019); and *The Asexuality and Aromanticism Bibliography* (https://acearobiblio.com/).

Chapter 5: Queer Heteroeroticism

Melissa E. Sanchez's *Shakespeare and Queer Theory* (London: Arden Shakespeare-Bloomsbury, 2019) addresses heteroeroticism in a chapter on 'Queerness beyond Homoeroticism'. On love for inanimate objects, or for women imagined as jewels, statues, and corpses, see Traub, *Desire and Anxiety*; Abbe Blum, '"Strike all that look upon with mar[b]le": Monumentalizing Women in Shakespeare's Plays', *The Renaissance Englishwoman in Print: Counterbalancing the Canon*, ed. Anne M. Haselkorn and Betty S. Travitsky (Amherst: University of Massachusetts Press, 1990); Lynn Enterline, *The Rhetoric of the*

Body from Ovid to Shakespeare (Cambridge: Cambridge University Press, 2000); and Karma Lochrie, *Heterosyncrasies: Female Sexuality When Normal Wasn't* (Minneapolis: University of Minnesota Press, 2005).

For more on female masochism, see Gillian Knoll, '*Coitus Magneticus*: Erotic Attraction in *A Midsummer Night's Dream*', *Modern Philology* 117.3 (2020): 301–322. Male masochism is discussed by Lisa S. Starks, '"Like the lover's pinch, which hurts and is desired": The narrative of male masochism and Shakespeare's *Antony and Cleopatra*', *Literature and Psychology* 45.4 (1999): 58–73. Figurations of sexual desire and activity in terms of plants and animals are analysed by Bruce Thomas Boehrer, 'Bestial Buggery in *A Midsummer Night's Dream*', *The Production of English Renaissance Culture*, ed. David Lee Miller, Sharon O'Dair, and Harold Weber (Ithaca: Cornell University Press, 1994); Dympna C. Callaghan, '(Un)natural Loving: Swine, Pets, and Flowers in *Venus and Adonis*', *Textures of Renaissance Knowledge*, ed. Phillippa Berry and Margaret Tudeau-Clayton (Manchester: Manchester University Press, 2003); Vin Nardizzi, 'Shakespeare's Penknife: Grafting and Seedless Generation in the Procreation Sonnets', *Renaissance and Reformation/Renaissance et Réforme* 32.1 (2009): 83–106; Karen Raber, *Animal Bodies, Renaissance Culture* (Philadelphia: University of Pennsylvania Press, 2013); and Natália Pikli, 'Hybrid Creatures in Context: Centaurs, Hobby-horses and Sexualized Women (*Hamlet, King Lear, The Two Noble Kinsmen*)', *Actes des congrès de la Société française Shakespeare* 38 (2020): 1–18.

Incest is an important topic in *Henry VIII*, on which see Bruce Thomas Boehrer, *Monarchy and Incest in Renaissance England: Literature, Culture, Kinship, and Kingship* (Philadelphia: University of Pennsylvania Press, 1992); and Menon, *Wanton Words*. On incest in *The Winter's Tale* see Diane Purkiss, '"As like Hermione as is her picture": The Shadow of Incest in *The Winter's Tale*', *Maternity and Romance Narratives in Early Modern England*, ed. Karen Bamford and Naomi J. Miller (Burlington, VT: Ashgate, 2015).

There is much excellent work on interracial desire in *Othello*, including Karen Newman, '"And Wash the Ethiope White": Femininity and the Monstrous in *Othello*', *Shakespeare Reproduced: The Text in History and Ideology*, edited by Jean E. Howard and Marion F. O'Connor (New York: Methuen 1987); Ania Loomba, *Gender, Race, Renaissance Drama* (Manchester: Manchester University Press, 1989); Patricia Parker, *Shakespeare from the Margins: Language, Culture, Context* (Chicago: University of Chicago Press, 1996); Robert Matz, 'Slander, Renaissance Discourses of Sodomy, and *Othello*', *ELH* 66 (1999): 261–276; Celia Daileader, *Racism, Misogyny, and the Othello-Myth: Inter-racial Couples from Shakespeare to Spike Lee* (Cambridge: Cambridge University Press, 2005); Lara Bovilsky, *Barbarous Play: Race on the English Renaissance Stage* (Minneapolis: University of Minnesota Press, 2008); and Jeffrey Masten, *Queer Philologies: Sex, Language, and Affect in Shakespeare's Time* (Philadelphia: University of Pennsylvania Press, 2016).

General Bibliography

Bach, Rebecca Ann. *Shakespeare and Renaissance Literature before Heterosexuality* (New York: Palgrave Macmillan, 2007).

Bromley, James M., and Will Stockton, eds. *Sex Before Sex: Figuring the Act in Early Modern England* (Minneapolis: University of Minnesota Press, 2013).

Chess, Simone. *Male-to-Female Crossdressing in Early Modern English Literature: Gender, Performance, and Queer Relations* (London: Routledge, 2016).

Chess, Simone, Colby Gordon, and William Fisher, eds. 'Early Modern Trans Studies', *Journal for Early Modern Cultural Studies* 19.4 (2019).

DiGangi, Mario. *Sexual Types: Embodiment, Agency, and Dramatic Character from Shakespeare to Shirley* (Philadelphia: University of Pennsylvania Press, 2011).

Drouin, Jennifer, ed. *Shakespeare/Sex: Contemporary Readings in Gender and Sexuality* (London: Arden Shakespeare-Bloomsbury, 2020).

Edelman, Lee. *No Future: Queer Theory and the Death Drive* (Durham: Duke University Press, 2004).

Friedlander, Ari. *Rogue Sexuality in Early Modern English Literature: Desire, Status, Biopolitics* (Oxford: Oxford University Press, 2022).

Garrison, John S. *Friendship and Queer Theory in the Renaissance: Gender and Sexuality in Early Modern England* (New York: Routledge, 2014).

Goldberg, Jonathan. *Sodometries: Renaissance Texts, Modern Sexualities* (Stanford: Stanford University Press, 1992).

Halberstam, J. Jack. *The Queer Art of Failure* (Durham: Duke University Press, 2011).

Halperin, David M. *How to Do the History of Sexuality* (Chicago: University of Chicago Press, 2004).

Jankowski, Theodora A. *Pure Resistance: Queer Virginity in Early Modern English Drama* (Philadelphia: University of Pennsylvania Press, 2000).

Katz, Jonathan Ned. *The Invention of Heterosexuality* (New York: Penguin-Plume, 1996).

Klosowska, Anna, Greta LaFleur, and Masha Raskolnikov, eds. *Trans Historical: Gender Plurality before the Modern* (Ithaca: Cornell University Press, 2021).

Lochrie, Karma. *Heterosyncrasies: Female Sexuality When Normal Wasn't* (Minneapolis: University of Minnesota Press, 2005).

Masten, Jeffrey. *Queer Philologies: Sex, Language, and Affect in Shakespeare's Time* (Philadelphia: University of Pennsylvania Press, 2016).

Menon, Madhavi, ed. *Shakesqueer: A Queer Companion to the Complete Works of Shakespeare* (Durham: Duke University Press, 2011).

Nardizzi, Vin, Stephen Guy-Bray, and Will Stockton, eds. *Queer Renaissance Historiography: Backward Gaze* (Farnham, Surrey: Ashgate, 2009).

Orgel, Stephen. *Impersonations: The Performance of Gender in Shakespeare's England* (Cambridge: Cambridge University Press, 1996).

Sanchez, Melissa E. *Shakespeare and Queer Theory* (London: Arden Shakespeare-Bloomsbury, 2019).

Schwarz, Kathryn. *Tough Love: Amazon Encounters in the English Renaissance* (Durham: Duke University Press, 2000).

Shannon, Laurie. *Sovereign Amity: Figures of Friendship in Shakespearean Contexts* (Chicago: University of Chicago Press, 2002).

Smith, Bruce R. *Homosexual Desire in Shakespeare's England: A Cultural Poetics* (Chicago: University of Chicago Press, 1991).

Somerville, Siobhan B., ed. *The Cambridge Companion to Queer Studies* (Cambridge: Cambridge University Press, 2020).

Stanivukovic, Goran, ed. *Queer Shakespeare: Desire and Sexuality* (London: Arden Shakespeare-Bloomsbury, 2017).

Stockton, Will. *Members of His Body: Shakespeare, Paul, and a Theology of Nonmonogamy* (New York: Fordham University Press, 2017.

Traub, Valerie. *The Renaissance of Lesbianism in Early Modern England* (Cambridge: Cambridge University Press, 2002).

Traub, Valerie, ed. *The Oxford Handbook of Shakespeare and Embodiment: Gender, Sexuality, and Race* (Oxford: Oxford University Press, 2016).

Index

For the benefit of digital users, indexed terms that span two pages (e.g., 52–53) may, on occasion, appear on only one of those pages.

activism 1
actors, rhetorical power of 99
Aeneid, The (Virgil) 68–9, 78–9
affect 138–9
Africa 55, 60, 78–9
African queen 68–9, 81
Alberti, Cherubino, 'Jupiter and
    Ganymede' (after Polidoro da
    Caravaggio) 91
alliteration 142–3
All's Well that Ends Well (Shakespeare)
    celibacy and 18, 116, 139–43
    heteroeroticism in 18–19
    intersectional identities in 170–1
    marriage in 139, 142
    masochism and 146–8, 152
Amin, Kadji 2
Amorum Emblemata (Veen) 27
anal eroticism 152–5, 172
    Henry V and 152–3
    Romeo and Juliet and 152–3
    The Taming of the Shrew and 152–4
    Troilus and Cressida and 152–3
anal sex 18–19, 28–30, 146–8, 156, 181 n.43
anatomy and gender 84–5, 89–90
androgyny 54–5
animals 134, 144–5, 148–9, 155–6
Anthony and Cleopatra (Shakespeare)
    Cleopatra's relationships 20
    interracial desire and 80–3
    political disorder and 17–18
    sexual transgression and 17–18, 82–3
anus, as term 153
Anzaldua, Gloria 175 n.4
Aristotle, *Nicomachean Ethics* 22
arousal 28
Arvas, Abdulhamit 102–3
As You Like It (Shakespeare)

female friendship in 48–53
friendship and 23–4
gender identity and 18
gender transformation in 86–93, 173–4
homonormativity and 17, 23–4, 88
image from First Folio, *93*
intersectional identities in 170–1
queer temporality in 91–2
same sex relationships in 20
asexuality
    overview 18, 115–16
    intellectual and ethical urgency of 169,
        173–4
    language and 137–8
    men and 140
    nature and 138
    queerness of 133
    as unthinkable 132
    women and 125–7
    See also celibacy
auto-eroticism 39

Bacon, Anthony 22
Barker, Roberta 87–8
beauty 87, 90, 98, 100, 130, 166–7, 170–1
Beccadelli, Antonio, *Hermaphroditus* 8–9
'Birth of Adonis' (Galle, after Anthonie
    Blocklandt) 120
blackmail, sexual 131
blackness 60, 79–80, 98–101, 164, 166–7,
    170–1
body, the
    the mind and 134–5
    race and 110–11
boy actors 87–114
Bray, Alan 54
Bredbeck, Gregory 6
Britton, Dennis Austin 193 n.30

Brome, Richard 161–2
Brown, Pamela 99
Bruster, Douglas 44–5
Butler, Judith 2–4, 7–8, 89
butt, as term 29

Capel, Richard 15
Castlehaven, Earl of (1631 trial) 59
celibacy
  All's Well that Ends Well and 18, 116,
    139–43
  intimacy and 128
  language and 137–8
  Love's Labors Lost and 18, 116, 137–9
  Measure for Measure and 18, 116, 130–7,
    139
  A Midsummer Night's Dream and 18,
    116, 125–8, 139
  Romeo and Juliet and 18, 108, 116, 128–30
  scholarship on 131–2
  Venus and Adonis and 18, 116–25, 141
  women and 133, 139, 141–2
  See also asexuality; chastity
Chacuer, Geoffrey, *Troilus and
    Creseyde* 117–18
Changeling, The (Middleton,
    Rowley) 161–2
chastity 94–5, 110–11, 125, 128
  See also celibacy
'Chastity Defeating Love' (Furnius) 129
Chess, Simone 88, 103, 117
children, deaths of 72–3
Christianity 13–14
  vs. Judaism 33–4, 56
  marriage and 41–2, 160
Cicero, *De Amicitia* 20–2
circumcision 33–4
clothing
  cross-dressing and 94–5, 190 n.65
  gender and 87–8, 104–5
  men and 89–90
codpieces 94–5
comedies
  cross-dressing and 86–7
  gender and 85
Comedy of Errors, The (Shakespeare) 147,
    170–1
  heteroeroticism in 18–19

intersectional identities in 170–1
  sexuality in 162–3
Confessio Amantis (Gower) 157
Cooper, Danielle 115–16
courage 89–90
cousins 48, 182 n.52
Coviello, Peter 10
coyness and women 120–1
Crawford, Julie 39–40, 52–3
Crawford, Katherine 102–3
Crenshaw, Kimberlé 170–1
cross-dressing 4, 96–7, 191 n.67
  in *As You Like It* 86–7
  clothing and 94–5, 190 n.65
  comedies and 86–7
  in *Henry VI* plays 86–7
  sexual transgression and 110–11
  transgender experience vs. 85, 93–4
  in *Twelfth Night* 86–7
  in *The Two Gentlemen of Verona* 86–7
  women 85, 90, 94–5, 104–5, 110
cuckolds/cuckolding 39–40, 62, 78–80,
    171–2, 196 n.28

David (biblical figure) 14
De Amicitia (Cicero) 20–2
de Lauretis, Teresa 175 n.4
death
  of children 72–3
  language and 36
  in *Macbeth* 72–5
  sexual activity and 137
Deleuze, Gilles 149
desire
  interracial 75–83
  See also sexual desire
devil 54, 60, 72–3, 82–3, 104–6, 110–14,
    164–5, 170–1
Diana (mythological figure) 79
Dick, Philip K. 137
disability 163
discourses of sexuality 9–10, 13
drag
  gender and 3
  in Butler's work 3
Drayton, Michael, *The Mooncalf* 54–6,
    60, 82–3
Drouin, Jennifer 89–92, 188 n.31

Dugan, Holly 196 n.32
Duggan, Lisa 22–3
dysphoria 186 n.8

early modernity, as term 6
Edelman, Lee 41–2, 119
Edward II (Marlowe) 59
Elyot, Thomas 20–1, 33
England 14–15, 162–3
  France and 154
  in *Henry VI* plays 65, 67
  monarchic rule 70–1
  sexual disorder and 17–18
epistemology 4
erections 28, 61–2
eunuchs 34, 101–5, 170–1
Europe 13, 55

'Fable of the Mermaid' (Sadeler) 78
failure, queer 115–16
fantasy, queer 40
Faunt, Nicholas 22
favourite, figure of 59
femininity, performance of 69–70
feminization of men 123
Findlay, Alison 125–6
fish 112, 122–3, 135, 189 n.52
Fisher, Will 94–5, 189 n.50
flowers 122–4, 126–7
food 34, 47, 94, 117–18, 122–3, 136
Forker, Charles 158, 195 n.26
Foucault, Michel 9–12, 15–16, 177 n.35
France 154
Freeman, Elizabeth 6–7
Friedlander, Ari 11–12
friendships
  in *As You Like It* 48–53
  evaluating 31–3
  homonormativity and 20–1, 23, 33
  intimacy and 22–4
  language and 35–6
  likeness and 35–6
  marriage and 38–40, 51, 53
  between men 17
  in *The Merchant of Venice* 17, 23–4, 30–40, 52–3
  mutual 49
  in *Romeo and Juliet* 17, 23–30

same-sex 20–2, 24
similitude and 20–2
spirituality and 33–4
theories of 35
in *Troilus and Cressida* 64
truth and 49
in *The Two Noble Kinsmen* 23–4, 40–8, 54
fruit 28, 47, 103–4, 122–3, 126
Furnius, Pieter Jalhea, 'Chastity Defeating Love,' 129
futurity. *See* queer futurity; reproductive futurism

Galle, Philips
  'Birth of Adonis' (after Anthonie Blocklandt) 120
  'Lot and His Family Leave the City Sodom' (after Maarten van Heemskerck) 57
Gallery of Heroick Women, The (Le Moyne) 109
Garrison, John 38
Garzoni, Tomaso, *The Hospital of Incurable Fools* 144–5
gender
  ambiguity (in *Macbeth*) 72–3
  anatomy and 84–5, 89–90
  androgyny 54–5
  binary 102–3
  clothing and 87–8, 104–5
  comedies and 85
  crossing in Shakespeare's plays 18
  difference 84–5
  drag and 3
  as experimental 7
  hermaphrodites 55
  hierarchy among 79–80
  instability of 3–4
  inversion of 82–3
  language and 6
  medicalization of 84–5
  normativity and 2–3, 8
  1 Henry VI and 18
  passing 85
  as performance 3–4
  power and 152–3
  as practice 2–3

gender (*cont.*)
  signification and 6–7
  temporality and 95–6
  transgender studies and 84, 113–14
  transition 106
  See also intersex people
gender identity
  As You Like It and 18
  Twelfth Night and 18
  The Two Gentlemen of Verona and 18,
    93–102
gender transformation
  in *As You Like It* 88–93
  in *1 Henry VI* 108–14
  in *Twelfth Night* 101–7
  in *The Two Gentlemen of Verona* 93–101
genderqueerness 103–5
genitalia 12–13
Gloucester, Duke of 67–8
Goldberg, Jonathan 6, 156
Golden Age, The (Heywood) 45–6
Gorman, Sara 186 n.5
Gosson, Stephen 87–8
Gouge, William 14, 144–7, 159–60
Gower, John, *Confessio Amantis* 157
Greek culture 12–13, 40–1, 56–8, 64, 77–8
Gupta, Kristina 116
Guy-Bray, Stephen 182 n.50
gypsy, as term 185 n.29

Halberstam, J. Jack 41–2, 115
Hall, Edward 68
Hall, Kim 87
Halperin, David 11
Hamlet (Shakespeare) 158–9, 162, 164–5
'Happy Marriage, the Unhappy
    Marriage, The,' 37
Heng, Geraldine 33
Henry V (Shakespeare)
  anal eroticism and 152–3
  heteroeroticism in 18–19, 172
  language and 170
  political disorder and 17–18
  sexual transgression and 17–18, 56–8,
    146–7
  sodomy in 59–60
Henry VI plays (Shakespeare) 64–71
  cross-dressing in 86–7
  gender transformation in 108–14

marriage and 75–7
politics and 77–8
sexual disorder and 17–18, 56–8,
    64–71
women in 81–2
hermaphrodites 55, 104, 106
Hermaphroditus (Beccadelli) 8–9
Herrup, Cynthia 61–2
heteroeroticism 12–15, 18–19, 146–7, 170
  in *All's Well that Ends Well* 18–19
  in *The Comedy of Errors* 18–19
  in *Henry V* 18–19
  in *Measure for Measure* 18–19
  in *A Midsummer Night's Dream* 18–19,
    146–7, 165–6
  in *Othello* 18–19, 147, 167
  in *Pericles* 18–19, 146–7
  queer temporality and 172
  in *Richard III* 18–19, 147
  in *The Taming of the Shrew* 18–19
  in *Venus and Adonis* 18–19
heteronormativity
  marriage and 92–3, 115
  queer failure vs. 115–16
  queer time and 41–2
heterosexuality
  as term 9, 146
  epistemology and 4
  modernity and 12, 15
  as natural 3–4, 13, 172
  as performance 3–4
  in Shakespeare studies 15–16
  temporality and 41–2
  as unstable 4
Heywood, Thomas, *The Golden Age*
    45–6
Hic Mulier (pamphlet, 1620) 84–5
homoeroticism
  female 44–5
  friendship and 22, 24–5
  women 44–5, 51
homonormativity
  defined 22–3
  art on 27
  in *As You Like It* 88
  between cousins 43–4
  friendships and 20–1, 23, 33
  kinship and 24
  language and 42–3

limits of 31–2
in *Merchant of Venice* 30–40
in *Two Noble Kinsmen* 42–3, 45
women and 50–1
homosexuality
as term 9, 177 n.30, 177 n.37
queerness vs. 6–7
homosociality 14–15
Hospital of Incurable Fools, The
(Garzoni) 144–5
household governance 144–5
Howard, Jean 67
Huffer, Lynne 177 n.35
humanness 141
humor, sexual 26–8
humoral theory 117–18

identitarian knowledge 2
identity and religion 11–12
identity politics 4
incest 157–9
intersex people and characteristics 5,
84–5, 111–12, 185 n.2
intimacy
celibacy and 128
conversation as term for 42–3
cross-species 155–6
friendship and 22–4
language for 32–3
performance of 31–2

James, Henry 4
Jankowski, Theodora 126, 131–2
Jewish people 33, 39
See also Judaism; *Merchant of Venice,*
The (Shakespeare)
jokes, sexual 18–19, 28–30, 40, 154, 162–3
Jonathan (biblical figure) 14
Judaism
vs. Christianity 33–4, 56
See also Jewish people
juggling, as term 112
'Jupiter and Ganymede' (Cherubino
Alberti after Polidoro da
Caravaggio) 91

Kahan, Benjamin 7–8, 131–2, 177 n.37,
194 n.54
Karras, Ruth Mazo 11–12

Keegan, Cáel M. 179 n.69
Kemp, Sawyer 85–6, 93–4, 107
kink practices 39–40, 148–9, 155–6
kinship 24, 49–53, 182 n.52
Kuzner, James 149–51

labour 158
language
alliteration 142–3
asexuality and 137–8
celibacy and 137–8
death and 36
friendships and 35–6
gender and 6
homonormativity and 42–3
interpretive possibilities 169–70
for intimacy 32–3
metaphors 103–4
Romeo and Juliet and 180 n.16
sex and 190 n.61
sexual disorder and 62–3
sexuality and 6
LaPerle, Carol Mejia 185 n.29
Laqueur, Thomas 178 n.49
laws 136–8
queerness and 8
sexuality and 10–11, 193 n.43
sodomy 10
transgender people and 8
Le Moyne, Peter, *The Gallery of Heroick*
Women 109
Levine, Laura 87–8, 156
LGBTQIA+ people, use of term 5
likeness
friendships and 35–6
male friendship and 35–6
Lochrie, Karma 7–8, 15–16
Long, Kathleen Perry 185 n.2
'Lot and His Family Leave the City
Sodom' (Galle after Maarten van
Heemskerck) 57
love
kinship and 49–51
modern notions of 51–2, 170
Love, Heather 71
Love's Labors Lost (Shakespeare), celibacy
and 18, 116, 137–9
Luther, Martin 123, 133–4, 136,
138–9

Macbeth (Shakespeare)
  death in 72–5
  queer heteroeroticism and 75, 172
  queer temporality in 71–4
  sexual transgression and 17–18, 56–8,
    71–5
Marcus, Sharon 176 n.12
Marlowe, Christopher, *Edward II* 59
marriage 13–15, 50–1
  in *All's Well that Ends Well* 139, 142
  chastity during 39
  Christianity and 41–2, 160
  divorce 69–70
  equality in 159–60
  fidelity 39
  friendships and 38–40, 51, 53
  gender normativity and 103
  Henry VI plays and 75–7
  heteroeroticism and 146
  heteronormativity and 92–3, 115
  politics and 164
  queer temporality and 41–2
  rejection by women 142
  sexual disorder and 69–70
  in *The Tempest* 164
  The Two Noble Kinsmen and 47–8, 142
  views on 66
Marston, John 191 n.67
Marvell, Andrew, 'Upon Appleton
    House,' 127–8
masculinity, performance of 69–70
masks 90
masochism 147–52, 167
  All's Well that Ends Well and 146–8, 152
  Measure for Measure and 146–8
  A Midsummer Night's Dream
    and 146–9, 151
Masten, Jeffrey 16–17, 22, 92–3, 182 n.50
master/servant relationships 96–8
masturbation 15
McLuskie, Kathleen 85
Measure for Measure (Shakespeare)
  celibacy and 18, 116, 130–7, 139, 173–4
  heteroeroticism in 18–19
  masochism and 146–8
  queer failure and 171–2
  sexuality in 139, 141

medicalization of gender 84–5
medieval culture 11–12
men
  asexuality and 140
  boys vs. 189 n.50
  clothing and 89–90
  effeminacy 55–6, 102–3
  feminization of 123
  friendship between 17
  gaze towards 35
  hermaphrodites and 55
  manhood 89, 107
  marital advice addressed to 14
  meat associated with 135
  in *Merchant of Venice* 42
  passing as (women) 85
  performance and 89
  in *Romeo and Juliet* 42
  sexual identity and 11–12
  statues (sensuality with) 144
Menon, Madhavi 6–7
Merchant of Venice, The (Shakespeare)
  cuckold fantasies and 39–40,
    171–2
  friendships in 17, 23–4, 30–40, 52–3
  non-inclusive queer relations in 23
  same sex relationships in 20
  Shylock's bond in 33–4
Metamorphoses (Ovid) 52, 119, 144
metaphors 103–4, 123, 126–7
Midsummer Night's Dream, A
    (Shakespeare)
  animalistic sex 155–6
  celibacy and 18, 116, 125–8, 139
  heteroeroticism in 18–19, 146–7,
    165–6, 172
  masochism and 146–9, 151, 171–2
Mock-Marriage, The (Brome) 161–2
modernity
  heterosexuality and 12, 15
  sexuality and 10–13, 15–16
monogamy 14
Monogrammist IQV, 'Venus on a
    Chariot Pulled by Two Swans'
    (after Giulio Romano) 50
Montaigne, Michel de 22, 24–5, 49
Mooncalf, The (Drayton) 54–6, 60, 82–3

morality 8–9, 13–14
Moulton, Ian 8–9
music 151–2

Nardizzi, Vin 195 n.14
nature 164–5
  in *1 Henry VI* 108
  asexuality and 138
  aspects contrary to 13, 29–30, 166
  like seeking out like 20–1
  queerness and 106–7
  race (comparisons to) 77
  women and 108, 136, 157, 160
Ndiaye, Noémie 189 n.57
New England 13
Newman, Karen 38–9
Nicomachean Ethics (Aristotle) 22
normativity
  gender and 2–3, 8
  marriage and 103
  queerness and 6–8
  scholarship and 7–8
  sexual norms and 8
  sexual practices 8–9
  See also heteronormativity;
    homonormativity
nuns 119, 125–8, 130–1

'Of Civil Friendship' (Thomas
  Travilian) 21
1 Henry VI (Shakespeare) 34–5
  gender identity and 18, 86–7, 108–14,
    190 n.65
  racism in 108, 172–3
  sexual disorder in 64–8, 70
orgasms 26, 28, 140
Orgel, Stephen 187 n.28
Othello (Shakespeare)
  heteroeroticism in 18–19, 147, 167, 172
  race and 18–19, 104–6, 147, 165–8, 172,
    189 n.57
otherness 102, 162–3
Ovid, *Metamorphoses* 52, 119, 144
owe, as term 150

Panek, Jennifer 11–12
Parker, Patricia 56, 104

Passe, Crispijn van de
  'Pygmalion Falling in Love with his
    Statue,' 145
  'Young Woman Cheats On Her Old
    Husband, A' (after Jacques
    Bellange) 161
patriarchy 156, 167–8
penises 12–13, 26, 29–30, 33–4, 56, 58–9,
  104, 107, 111–12, 121, 123–4, 155,
  190 n.62
performance
  of femininity 69–70
  gender as 3–4
  heterosexuality as 3–4
  of intimacy 31–2
  of masculinity 69–70
  men and 89
Pericles (Shakespeare)
  heteroeroticism in 18–19, 146–7, 172
  incest in 157–9
philology, queer (Masten) 16–17
Plutarch 64
political disorder
  Henry V and 17–18
  Macbeth and 17–18, 75
  Titus Andronicus and 17–18, 76
  Troilus and Cressida and 17–18
politics
  depoliticization 22–3
  non-inclusive queer relations and 169,
    172–3
  racial purity and 80
Porter, Joseph 180 n.14
power
  gender and 152–3
  through submission 149
pregnancy 43, 111–12
pride parades 1
primogeniture 69–71
prophecy 73–4
prostitution 136, 144–5
Proust, Marcel 4
Przybylo, Ela 115–16
pucelle, as term 190 n.62
purse, use of term 32–3
'Pygmalion falling in love with his statue'
  (Passe) 145

queer
  overview 1–9, 175 n.4
  activist origins 1–2
  failure 115–16
  as negativity 6–7
  rejection of term by gay men/
    lesbians 1–2
  in Shakespeare scholarship 5
  Queer Nation (activist group) 1
  queer Shakespeare studies 5
  See also Shakespeare studies
  queer studies and transgender studies 18,
    171–2, 179 n.69
  queer temporality 41–2
  in *As You Like It* 91–2
  heteroeroticism and 172
  in *Macbeth* 71–4, 171–2
  marriage and 41–2
  in *Measure for Measure* 171–2
  in *1 Henry VI* 67–8
  in *3 Henry VI* 69–70
  in *Richard III* 163
  in *Twelfth Night* 106
  in *The Two Gentlemen of Verona* 95–6
  in *The Two Noble Kinsmen* 41–2, 171–2
  in *Venus and Adonis* 122–3
  See also reproductive futurism (Edelman)
queer theory 1–2, 175 n.4, 176 n.12
queerness
  of asexuality 133
  derogatory perceptions of 1
  fantasy 40
  homosexuality contrasted with 6–7
  law and 8
  negative conceptions of 1
  normativity and 6–8
  positive conceptions of 1
  sexual 8–9

race
  beauty and 100
  blackness 60, 79–80, 98–101, 164,
    166–7, 170–1
  body and 110–11
  interracial desire 75–83
  nature (comparisons to) 77
  Othello and 18–19, 104–6, 147, 165–8, 172
  otherness 102
  skin 90, 98–9, 108
  stereotypes 60
  in *The Tempest* 164
  white supremacy 87
Rackin, Phyllis 67, 107
Rainolds, John 87–8
Rambuss, Rick 155–6
rape 13, 124–5, 157, 192 n.19
  in *Titus Andronicus* 60–1
  in *Troilus and Cressida* 61–2
Rape of Lucrece, The (Shakespeare) 124
religion and identity 11–12
reproductive futurism (Edelman) 41–2,
    73–4, 119, 130, 136
  See also queer temporality
resonance, asexual 115–16
Rich, B. Ruby 1
Richard II (Shakespeare), favorites in 59
Richard III (Shakespeare)
  heteroeroticism in 18–19, 147, 163–5
  queer temporality in 163
  self-representation in 163
Roman Empire 17–18
Romeo and Juliet (Shakespeare)
  anal eroticism and 152–3
  celibacy and 18, 108, 116, 128–30, 173–4
  homonormative friendships in 17,
    23–30
  language and 170, 180 n.16
  men in 42
  non-inclusive queer relations in 172–3
  sexual anatomy in 34
  sexual desire in 26
  single couples in 20
  sodomy and 30
Royster, Francesca 80

Sadeler, Aegidius, II, 'Fable of the
    Mermaid,' 78
Salih, Sarah 11–12
same-sex relationships
  in Bible 54
  in *The Merchant of Venice* 20
  as unnatural 55–6
  See also homoeroticism;
    homonormativity
Sanchez, Melissa 11–12, 131–4, 148–9
Schwarz, Kathryn 69–70

Scourge of Villainy, The (Marston)
191 n.67
Sedgwick, Eve Kosofsky 2, 4–7, 178 n.47
self, the 97–100, 102, 119
self-representation 163
senses 134–5
sex work 136, 144–5
sexual desire 2–4, 11–12, 14–19, 26, 43–4,
47, 55–8, 61–2, 66, 68–70, 76, 80–1, 84,
116–17, 131, 133–40, 146, 150–1, 155–6,
158–9, 167–8, 172–4
in *Romeo and Juliet* 26
as social disorder 56–8
sexual difference 12–13
sexual disorder
Henry VI plays and 17–18, 56–8, 64–71
language and 62–3
sexual identity 11–12
sexual jokes 18–19, 28–30, 40, 154, 162–3
sexual norms and normativity 8
sexual practices
abstinence 13
anal 18–19, 28–30, 146–8, 156
anilingus 155
cunnilingus 155
death and 137
debauchery 40–1, 54
heteroerotic relations 12–15
masturbation 15
metaphors for 123, 126–7
normativity and 8–9
outside marriage 11–12
shame and 131–2
youth and 122–3
sexual transgressions 56
civic consequences of 56
cross-dressing and 110–11
Henry V and 17–18, 56–8, 146–7
Macbeth and 17–18, 56–8, 71–5
The Taming of the Shrew and 146–7
Titus Andronicus and 17–18, 158–9
Troilus and Cressida and 17–18, 56–8,
60–4, 80–1
sexual violence 13, 93–4, 124–5, 157,
192 n.19
sexuality
use of term 15–16
acts vs. identities 11

as binary 170
compulsory 128–9
discourses of 9–10, 13
as experimental 7
language and 6
law and 10–11
in *Measure for Measure* 139, 141
modernity and 10–13, 15–16
non-sexual 116
signification and 6–7
status and 15
in *Venus and Adonis* 133, 135, 162
shadow 96, 99–100
Shakespeare studies
overview 5, 173–4
heterosexuality in 15–16
See also queer Shakespeare studies
shame 131–2
Shannon, Laurie 20–1, 23, 35, 44–5
similitude and friendships 20–2
sin 13
sirens 77–8
Smith, Bruce 87–8
Smith, Ian 34–5, 195 n.15
sociability 32
social discourses 11
Sodom (biblical city) 54
sodomy 15, 54, 183 n.2, 195 n.15
as term 29–30
in *Henry V* 59–60
Romeo and Juliet and 30
Sonnet 52 134–5
Sonnet 95 (Shakespeare) 58–9, 134–5
Sonnets (Shakespeare)
beauty in 130, 142–3
sexual imagery 134–5
sexual orientation of speaker 5
white supremacy and 87
spiritualism 33–4
spirituality and friendships 33–4
statues 144
Stewart, Alan 182 n.52
Stockton, Will 39
Stretter, Robert 43–4
Stryker, Susan 95–6, 106, 185 n.1
Stubbes, Philip 87–8
submission, power through 149
substance/shadow 96, 99–100

Taming of the Shrew, The (Shakespeare)
anal eroticism and 152–4
heteroeroticism in 18–19
sexual transgression and 146–7
taxonomic discourses 4
Tempest, The (Shakespeare), marriage
in 164
temporality
heterosexuality and 41–2
See also queer temporality;
reproductive futurism (Edelman)
Teramura, Misha 21–2, 180 n.6
Theobald, Lewis 135
Thomas Aquinas 13
3 Henry VI (Shakespeare)
queer temporality in 69–70
sexual disorder in 69–71
thruples 24, 171–2
Tiptoft, John 20–1
Titus Andronicus (Shakespeare)
interracial desire and 75–80
political disorder and 17–18, 76
rape in 60–1
sexual transgression and 17–18, 158–9
Tomlinson, Sophie 99
Tosh, Will 22
transgender people
cross-dressing vs. 85, 93–4
dysphoria and transitioning 186 n.8
embodiment and 106–7
inappropriate curiosity about 104
laws and 8
transgender studies
gender transformation and 84, 113–14
intellectual and ethical urgency of 169,
173–4
queer studies and 18, 179 n.69
transphobia 101–2, 110–12
Traub, Valerie 44–5, 51, 127
Travilian, Thomas, 'Of Civil Friendship,' 21
trees 24, 28–9
tribade, as term 190 n.59
Troilus and Creseyde (Chacuer) 117–18
Troilus and Cressida (Shakespeare)
anal eroticism and 152–3
effeminacy in 63
friendship in 64

non-inclusive queer relations in 172–3
political disorder and 17–18
rape in 61–2
sexual transgression and 17–18, 56–8,
60–4, 80–1
Trojan War 64–5, 68–9, 78–9
truth
friendship and 49
The Two Noble Kinsmen and 49
Tuscan wars (*All's Well that Ends Well*) 150
Twelfth Night (Shakespeare)
cross-dressing in 86–7, 173–4
gender identity and 18
gender transformations in 101–7, 113–14
intersectional identities in 170–1
queer temporality in 106
Two Gentlemen of Verona, The
(Shakespeare)
cross-dressing in 86–7
gender identity and 18
gender transformation and 93–102
queer temporality in 96
sexual conservativism of 172–3
single couples in 20
Two Noble Kinsmen, The (Shakespeare)
friendship in 23–4, 44, 54
homonormativity and 17, 40–8
marriage and 142
queer temporality in 41–2, 171–2
truth and 49

unapt, as term 117–18, 192 n.9
universalization 4
'Upon Appleton House' (Marvell) 127–8
urban living 40–1, 130–1

vaginas 12–13, 28–30, 38–9, 56, 104, 140,
153, 155, 162
Veen, Otto van, *Amorum Emblemata* 27
Venus and Adonis (Shakespeare)
celibacy and 18, 116–25, 141, 173–4
heteroeroticism in 18–19
intersectional identities in 170–1
sexuality in 133, 135, 162
'Venus on a Chariot Pulled by Two
Swans' (Monogrammist IQV after
Giulio Romano) 50

violence, sexual 13, 93–4, 124–5, 157,
      192 n.19
Virgil, *The Aeneid* 68–9, 78–9
Virgin Mary 108
virginity 108–10, 117–18, 126, 133, 141–2,
      152–3

wars
   Trojan War 64–5
   Tuscan wars (*All's Well that Ends
      Well*) 150
wax, as sexual metaphor 123
Whately, William 160–2
Wilde, Oscar 4
Windholz, Jordan 140
Winter's Tale, The (Shakespeare) 144
women
   agency 147
   asexuality and 125–7
   celibacy and 133, 139, 141–2
   coyness and 120–1
   cross-dressing 85, 90, 94–5, 104–6, 110
   fighting by 107

fish associated with 135
friendship between 17
gaze at men 35
genitalia 38–9
   in *Henry VI* plays 81–2
hermaphrodites and 55
homoeroticism 44–5, 51
homonormativity and 50–1
marriage rejected by 142
modern views on 14
nature and 108, 136, 157, 160
perceptions of 26–9, 66, 81–2, 132
representation (in *Macbeth*) 71
same-sex intimacy between 45–7
sexual identity and 11–12

yokefellows 35–7, 50–1
'Young Woman Cheats On Her Old
      Husband, A' (Passe after Jacques
      Bellange) 161
youth and sexual practices 122–3

Zacchia, Paolo 181 n.43